SQL Server System Administration

Other Titles by New Riders

SQL Server™ System Administration

Sean Baird
Denis Darveau
Michael Hotek
John Lynn
Chris Miller

New Riders

201 West 103rd Street,
Indianapolis, Indiana 46290

SQL Server™ System Administration

Sean Baird
Denis Darveau
Michael Hotek
John Lynn
Chris Miller

International Standard Book Number: 1-56205-955-6

Library of Congress Catalog Card Number: 98-87723

Printed in the United States of America

First Printing: *November, 1998*

00   99   98   4   3   2   1

Publisher
David Dwyer

Executive Editor
Al Valvano

Acquisitions Editors
Stacey Beheler
Stephanie Layton

Development Editor
Stacia Mellinger

Managing Editor
Sarah Kearns

Project Editor
Clint McCarty

Copy Editor
Audra McFarland

Indexer
Cheryl Jackson

Technical Reviewers
David Besch
Neil Pike

Book Designer
Ruth Lewis

Cover Designer
Brainstorm Technologies

Proofreader
Maribeth Echard

Production
Louis Porter, Jr.

About the Authors

Sean Baird works as a Technical Director for the Software Solutions group at Empower Trainers & Consultants, Inc. As one of Empower's senior consultants, Sean spends his time leading projects and performing analysis and design on client/server and Internet applications. He has worked on a wide variety of business solutions for Empower's clients and has technical experience with much of the Microsoft product line. Sean has worked with SQL Server for several years and continues to sing the praises of this product, "though no one would really want to hear me sing," he adds. In addition to this book, Sean has presented on SQL Server at *MCP Magazine's* TechMentor conference and coauthored the New Riders book *MCSE Training Guide: SQL Server 6.5 Design & Implementation*. He obtained a bachelor's degree in Computer Science from the University of Missouri-Rolla and holds MCSE, MCSD, and MCT certifications. Sean currently lives in Kansas City, where he enjoys piloting the Empower hot-air balloon in his spare time.

Denis Darveau is a Senior Network Operating System Consultant with Zen Systems, Inc. in Sausalito, California. Denis has been involved with computer science since the early 1980s during his Air Force days as a Programmer/Analyst/Designer for the North American Air Defense Command (NORAD). After four years of teaching various operating systems, such as UNIX (Programming, Networking, and System Administration) and Oracle DBA, in 1994 Denis became a Microsoft Certified Professional (MCP), and at the beginning of 1996, he became a Microsoft Certified Systems Engineer (MCSE). His specialty is SQL Server 6.*x* and TCP/IP. Denis is also a Microsoft Certified Trainer (MCT) and has taught more than 100 Microsoft curriculum courses to hundreds of students across the United States and Canada. Denis is also coauthor of *MCSE Training Guide: SQL Server 6.5 Design and Implementation*, published by Macmillan.

Michael Hotek, a Microsoft Certified Systems Engineer, is a technical consultant with Modern Business Technology, a consulting firm in Schaumburg, Illinois that specializes in enterprisewide Web solutions. Hotek specializes in backend technologies including MS SQL Server, NT, Exchange, IIS, Oracle, and Sybase. He was a contributing author for *Special Edition Using Microsoft SQL Server 7.0* and maintains many articles at www.swynk.com/friends/hotek.

John Lynn has 15 years of experience in data processing and system analysis, is certified as an MCSD (Microsoft Certified Solution Developer), and has written many magazine articles about Microsoft application development and BackOffice technology (such as Visual Basic and SQL Server). Specializing in data mart/data warehouse development using Microsoft SQL Server, Lynn lives in Philadelphia with his wife and three children. Lynn can be reached at xjl@compuserve.com.

Chris Miller is a Microsoft Certified Systems Engineer and Microsoft Certified Solution Developer who has worked with SQL Server as both a developer and an administrator for five years. He is currently a database administrator for a small company that provides information analysis and production facilities to managed care organizations. He is a graduate of the University of Missouri-Rolla, a school known for teaching great engineers, computer scientists, and mathematicians. When he's not writing, he's probably working around the house, out flying with Sean Baird, or pretending to write while actually playing Age of Empires (much to the dismay of both his wife and his editors).

About the Technical Reviewers

These reviewers contributed their considerable practical, hands-on expertise to the entire development process for *SQL Server System Administration*. As the book was being written, these individuals reviewed all the material for technical content, organization, and usability. Their feedback was critical in ensuring that *SQL Server System Administration* fits your need for the highest quality technical information.

David Besch is currently working as a consultant specializing in developing business applications in Visual Basic and SQL Server. He received his B.S. in Computer Science from the University of Missouri-Rolla in 1993. After graduating, David went to work at a major Midwestern printing company to develop an electronic business forms publishing application. David worked as a developer using Pascal, C, and Visual Basic before devoting himself to SQL Server database administration for the projects he supports. He is certified as an MCSD with product certifications in Implementing and Administrating SQL Server and Visual Basic. David lives in Olathe, Kansas with his wife Cheryl and their cat Blaise.

Neil Pike is the Technical Director of his own company, Protech Computing, based in the U.K. Pike, through his company, specializes in NT, SQL Server, LANs, WANs, mainframe connectivity, hardware, performance tuning, and so forth. Although originally a mainframe systems programmer in Cics, MVS, VTAM, Supra, Oracle, and DB/2, Pike has been working with client/server technology since 1992. He is most recently a proud father: His daughter Grace was born June 6, 1998.

Dedications

To the people of World Balloon, Inc. and Empower Air Promotions, Inc. for helping make my dream of flight a reality.
—Sean Baird

To my mom and dad who have always stood by me.
—Michael Hotek

To my family, for their support.
—John Lynn

I would like to dedicate this book to my wife. She had to put up with me being grouchy and irritable while I was writing.
—Chris Miller

Acknowledgments

Sean Baird

I want to thank my parents, Roger and Mary Baird, and the rest of my family for their patience and understanding during the many months I was often incommunicado while working on this project. And for their love and support through the years, I thank my friends, especially David and Tiffany Noel, Chris and Jennifer Miller, David and Cheryl Besch, Rich Warsnak, Bill Graziano, and Beth Greenwold. I also want to thank the people responsible for much of the rest of the work on this book—my co-authors and editors. Special thanks go to Stephanie Layton for her patience and motivation, Stacia Lynn Mellinger for her excellent development edits, and David Besch and Neil Pike for their technical contributions and corrections.

Michael Hotek

There are so many people that I'd like to thank, but a few stand out well above and beyond. I'd like to thank my mom and dad for their ongoing support and for always being there to help along the way. Thanks to the people at Beloit Corporation: Dennis, who started me on this path, and Dave and JD, who taught me so much. Thanks to everyone at Modern Business Technology, especially Tim, Jennifer, Paul, and Scott, who gave me the opportunity that led to where I am. Thanks to Denice for making some difficult times more bearable. Thank you to Stephanie, Stacey, Stacia, Neil, and David for their help in crafting my small part of this book and for the wonderful experience it has been. Thanks to Sharon, Drew, Neil, Bill, and all the members of the swynk.com mailing list who have taught me more than I could have ever learned on my own. A very special thanks to Stephen Wynkoop for the mailing lists, the Web site, and the opportunity to help with numerous books and projects that have really expanded my horizons.

John Lynn

I would like to thank Karen Watterson for getting me started and keeping me on track with her in-depth knowledge and unique insight of the database industry.

Chris Miller

I would like to thank my editors for their hard work and patience. They have lent significant support, skill, and patience toward taking this book from the outline to the printer.

Tell Us What You Think!

As the reader of this book, *you* are our most important critic and commentator. We value your opinion and want to know what we're doing right, what we could do better, what areas you'd like to see us publish in, and any other words of wisdom you're willing to pass our way.

As the Executive Editor for the Networking team at Macmillan Computer Publishing, I welcome your comments. You can fax, email, or write me directly to let me know what you did or didn't like about this book—as well as what we can do to make our books stronger.

Please note that I cannot help you with technical problems related to the topic of this book, and that due to the high volume of mail I receive, I might not be able to reply to every message.

When you write, please be sure to include this book's title and author, as well as your name and phone or fax number. I will carefully review your comments and share them with the author and editors who worked on the book.

Fax: 317-581-4663
Email: avalvano@mcp.com
Mail: Al Valvano
           Executive Editor
           Networking
           Macmillan Computer Publishing
           201 West 103rd Street
           Indianapolis, IN 46290 USA

Table of Contents

I

Setup and Configuration

1

Setup: Troubleshooting and Advanced Topics

Chris Miller

THIS BOOK IS WRITTEN WITH THE assumption that you already have SQL Server installed. Anyone who can read and move a mouse can perform the initial setup of SQL Server. This chapter gives you a look at what can go wrong during setup and at some of the parts of setup that aren't very intuitive (or in some cases not very obvious):

- Troubleshooting Setup Problems
- Automated Setup
- Character Sets and Sort Orders
- Sizing the Master Database
- Upgrading from a Previous Version of SQL Server
- All About Autoconfiguration
- Setting Up Client Utilities

Troubleshooting Setup Problems

SQL Server setup is a setup program like every other setup program that's ever been written, which means it's just like every other program written, which means it sometimes doesn't cover exactly every situation that can happen as gracefully as it could.

Some installations have problems. This section shows you these common problem areas and offers solutions:

- Disk Space Problems
- Inability to Start SQL Server

Following those two subsections is a third that discusses the topic of resuming setup after a problem.

Disk Space Problems

The most common problem that occurs during setup is usually associated with limitations on disk space. This usually happens when the person performing the installation accidentally chooses the incorrect partition to copy files over to. Remember that SQL Server has to initially place all the system files and system databases on the same partition, so make sure there's plenty of room. A full installation of SQL Server, with all of Books Online local, requires about 200MB. Also keep in mind that SQL Server setup will toss a few DLL files into your system directory (usually \winnt\system32). So make sure there's 5–10MB available just to be safe there. A good safety measure is to have twice that available.

Inability to Start SQL Server

SQL Server may refuse to start during installation due to any number of factors. Check the following:

- *Is the paging file large enough?* Check the size of the paging file by opening the Control Panel, choosing System, and clicking on the Performance tab. Make sure that the paging size for all drives combined is at least 100MB. In most cases, the paging file should be the amount of memory available on the machine plus at least 12MB.

- *Is there enough disk space available for the paging files to expand?* For example, if the paging files are set to start at 75MB and grow to 125MB and no free space is available on the drive, the pagefile won't be able to expand.

- *Are the supplied user accounts correct?* SQL Server will prompt during installation for two user accounts. If the local system account isn't chosen, a user account with administrator privileges on the local machine must be chosen. There's a slim chance that the setup program won't catch a password problem here. The easiest way to find a password problem is to look in the Windows NT Event Viewer's System Log and for services that are unable to start due to a logon failure.

- *Are there anomalous disk or network problems on the machine?* Problems like files becoming corrupted during the copy process or a system that cannot validate a user account because it cannot contact a domain controller can cause problems of a transient nature. Make sure the box is stable before the installation, and perform any routine maintenance prior to installation.

- *SQL Server has to have a network configured in order to install.* In other words, if there is no network card in the machine and RAS is not installed, you must install the MS Loopback adapter and some associated protocols. This will provide SQL Server with enough of a network to complete the setup process.

- *SQL Server communicates with itself over the network, even on the local machine.* The local machine has to have a valid network address. For TCP/IP, that means that if you assign yourself a broadcast address or a network address (such as 10.1.1.1 with a subnet mask of 255.255.255.0), SQL Server will not install correctly.

The two biggest issues are disk space and system maintenance. Make sure the system has plenty of disk space above and beyond the requirements for SQL Server. If you're performing a clean installation onto a new machine, this shouldn't be a problem. If you're performing an upgrade installation, the system will need a lot of disk space to upgrade the databases, so it shouldn't be a problem there, either.

From a maintenance perspective, make sure the machine is up, running, and stable prior to the installation. Check the Windows NT Event Log, and in the case of an upgrade, check the SQL Server error log file. Clear up any and all problems you find before proceeding with the installation.

MAKEPIPE and READPIPE

If you discover anomalous network problems, you can use the MAKEPIPE and READPIPE utilities provided with SQL Server to test network connections. See Chapter 2 for details on troubleshooting client-side network problems.

Don't Upgrade a System That Isn't Running Smoothly

When I was still consulting full-time, we had a slew of clients who would run upgrades on their systems for the express purpose of fixing stability problems or even server-down issues. In one case, the server went from being unstable before the upgrade to being completely down after the upgrade. This resulted in a call to my firm to have me come out and fix the server that the upgrade broke. After looking through all the error logs and discovering some fairly major corruption and configuration problems, I went to restore from backup because the existing data had all been upgraded. But, one of the instabilities in the system was the backup software, so there were no backups. By hook and crook—and with a lot of help from Microsoft Product Support—and after spending a lot of time and money, we managed to get their data back.

The moral of this story: Don't install upgrades to improve stability. The 6.0 and 6.5 releases of SQL Server are stable products, but if the software isn't running right, an upgrade is just going to complicate the problem. The same is true of operating system upgrades. If Windows NT isn't running correctly, don't install service packs or upgrade to the newest, latest, greatest version. In addition, don't install software until the system is in a stable running state.

Those are the more common problems that occur during setup. But there is always potential for other really weird problems, such as hardware failures, power failures, network failures, and so on that aren't really SQL Server's fault. The only real solution in such cases is to start setup over again.

Resuming Setup

So, suppose SQL Server setup runs into one of the described problems, and then the setup program crashes horribly, leaving the server's drive space looking like an abandoned construction site. Fortunately, SQL Server 7.0 setup is very robust. You should be able to fix the problem and then start setup again. Note the first part of that sentence: *fix the problem*. Don't hope that SQL Server will figure out that it's out of disk space and magically install itself. It just isn't quite that robust. Fix what's broken by clearing disk space, plugging back in the power cord that was tripped on, and so forth. Then run the setup program again.

SQL Server setup is very careful. Even an upgrade installation will install into a directory different from the SQL Server 6.5 default directory so the files won't be falling over one another. Theoretically, either the DLL files are all compatible between versions, or they're in separate directories with different names, so there won't be any version conflicts.

Automated Setup

Automated setup options provided as part of the Microsoft SQL Server product enable multiple servers to be set up identically very quickly. This is especially helpful if SQL Server is being deployed to the desktop, and even more helpful if you are using a tool such as Microsoft Systems Management Server to perform the setup. This section covers the SetupSQL program and how to call it for an automated setup, as well as how to modify the file used to determine how SQL Server will install.

Using SetupSQL

The best way to perform an automated setup is to install SQL Server onto a computer exactly how you want it installed on all of the client computers. Then look on the hard drive for a file called SETUP.ISS. That file will contain all the settings you chose during the setup. (The file should be located in the \MSSQL7\INSTALL directory.)

To perform an unattended setup, you'll need to call the SETUPSQL.EXE program. This program takes the following parameters:

- `-f1<initialization file>`. This option specifies where the setup initialization file (SETUP.ISS) is located. (Note that there should *not* be a space between the -f1 and the filename.)
- `-s`. This option performs a silent setup. That means no user interface is necessary for the installation.

- -SMS. This option is used in conjunction with the START command and the /wait switch to keep control from passing back to the command shell. This is used when the installation is performed from a login script and the rest of the login script needs to wait until the installation is complete.

For example, to perform an installation using the SETUP.ISS file located on the server called Intrepid, you would use the following command line:

```
start /wait \\intrepid\sql70\x86\setup\setupsql
➡-f1\\intrepid\sql70\setup.iss -SMS
```

At this point, SQL Server setup will begin installing the software according to the instructions specified in the SETUP.ISS file.

Modifying the SETUP.ISS File

The Setup.ISS file uses the same format as a normal Windows INI file. That means it can be edited with the text editor of your choice. The Setup.ISS file is totally undocumented in Books Online, so tread lightly here and make lots of backup copies when you get it working the way you want it to. Remember, the best way to customize this file is to install it right once and use the file from that setup. This section is intended only to provide some very minor adjustments to the installation.

The first section you may want to change is the Registered User section. Open the SETUP.ISS file and search for the string "szname," which is the name that will appear in the user registration dialog boxes, such as in Help/About.

Next, search for "szDir." This defines the top level directory that SQL Server will use to install itself.

The final section of interest is the DlgServerNetwork section. If you want to change any of the network settings, such as the listen-on port or the pipe to listen on, search for the string "dlgServerNetwork" and make your modifications there.

That's all that you should change by modifying the SETUP.ISS file. If you need to add or remove components, you should reinstall and build a new SETUP.ISS file.

Character Sets and Sort Orders

Choosing the character set and sort order of a SQL Server installation is critical. After SQL Server is installed, the only way to change the character set and/or sort order is to reinstall SQL Server and rebuild all the databases. And that would require you to export all the data to text files, reinstall SQL Server, and reimport all the data. Backup and restore techniques will not work. Because importing and exporting all the data in every database is not a trivial operation, pay close attention to the sort order and character set you choose during installation.

A *character set* is the group of 256 characters that can be stored in CHAR, VARCHAR, and TEXT data types. The 256 characters have to represent all the data that can be stored in these types, including the upper– and lowercase alphabet, all the numbers, and all the symbols.

A *sort order* tells SQL Server what order to sort a given character set in. A sort order answers questions like these:

- Which goes first, uppercase or lowercase letters?
- Which goes first, letters or numbers?
- Which goes first, accented letters or unaccented letters?

Consider this list, which further illustrates the concept of a sort order:
APPLE, apple, Apple, appLE

If SQL Server were sorting the list, the results would vary based on the sort order. You can choose from several different options for a sort order:

- **Binary Order.** Binary order means the characters will be sorted strictly by the value of the character in the installed character set. It is also a strictly case-sensitive character set. For the normal American English character set (code page 437), that means the list "Z, a, 3, %" would be sorted as "%, 3, Z, a." This is the fastest character set to use from a database perspective because it is the simplest. The sample list shown previously would be sorted as "APPLE, Apple, appLE, apple."

- **Dictionary Order, Case Insensitive.** Dictionary order means the characters will be sorted in an order different from binary order. In Dictionary Order, Case Insensitive, the sort order has no preference on case, so a lowercase letter may appear before or after an uppercase letter in a result set. Any characters with diacritical marks are sorted after their corresponding character without a diacritical mark. So "ñ" appears after "n." The sample list shown previously could be sorted in any order because the sort order compares them all as equal.

- **Dictionary Order, Case Sensitive.** In this instance, uppercase characters will be sorted before lowercase, and an uppercase character with a diacritical mark will be sorted before a lowercase character. The list result would be the same as the binary sort: APPLE, Apple, appLE, apple. The only differences between Dictionary Order, Case Sensitive and a binary sort order are in the handling of diacritical marks, symbols, and numbers, which will be handled differently in binary sort orders depending on the chosen character set.

- **Dictionary Order, Case Insensitive, Uppercase Preference.** Any sort order that's modified with the word "preference" means that the sorting will work one way all the time, but comparisons will work another way. In the case of an Uppercase Preference, the word Apple will be sorted before the word apple, but if the two are compared in a SQL statement, they will be equal. The list would read "APPLE, Apple, appLE, apple."

- **Dictionary Order, Case Insensitive, Accent Insensitive.** In this case, uppercase and lowercase characters and characters with diacritical marks will all be sorted the same, so their order will be random in an output set.

Picking a character set and sort order is a fairly easy operation. Here are some guidelines to follow:

1. Is there data being upgraded from a previous version of SQL Server? If so, use the same sort order and character set as the previous version. The upgrade cannot change the character set or sort order. (This is why choosing the character set and sort order is such an important decision.)

2. Pick a character set that covers all the characters in the languages that will be in the database.

3. If the first two criteria haven't already determined the character set and sort order, choose the defaults.

That last point deserves a little more analysis. The binary sort order uses the least amount of overhead for sorting and is the fastest for returning data in sorted order. However, users aren't accustomed to reading data stored in all capital letters. And if a user performs a search for the name "McDonald" in a database with a binary sort order, and the only thing in the database is "Mcdonald" or "MCDONALD," the search won't return any rows. There are exactly two ways around this bug. Force the application to put everything in the database into uppercase (which is ugly), or force the application to build "pretty names" by taking "MCDONALD," looking it up, and searching for "McDonald."

According to Microsoft, using a case-insensitive sort order increases the amount of time used to perform comparisons of strings by about 20 percent. But, by the time the program has gone through the extra logic involved in trying to match the case, SQL Server could have probably already sorted the data for the user using a non-case-sensitive sort order. There are much better ways to improve performance than to write difficult-to-maintain code like name-cleaning schemes or using a very ugly workaround like putting everything into uppercase.

The main point here is that the overhead for sorting the data and dealing with mixed case is going to fall either on the client or on the server. It's usually best from a management standpoint to make it fall on the server because there's only one of those to upgrade and maintain, as opposed to hundreds or thousands of clients.

As a result of these tradeoffs, the best choice is usually the default character set and sort order, which is code page 1252 (the ISO standard character set) and the Dictionary Order, Case Insensitive sort order. This provides the best sorting functionality with a minimal impact on performance.

Sizing the Master Database

One of the "big deals" in previous versions of SQL Server was making sure that the master database was sized appropriately so as to not waste disk space and not become full. The default master database in SQL Server 7.0 is 9MB, and it will automatically grow when it reaches 9MB. So what was once a big deal is now a non-issue.

Upgrading from Previous Versions of SQL Server

SQL Server 7.0 supports upgrades from SQL Server 6.0 and SQL Server 6.5. It isn't possible to upgrade directly from SQL Server 4.2x or SQL Server 1.x. So if you use one of those older versions, upgrade to SQL Server 6.5 first, and then upgrade to 7.0. If the server being upgraded is participating in replication, upgrade it with the latest service pack for SQL Server 6.5 first, make sure the server is stable, and then upgrade to 7.0.

In order to accomplish everything Microsoft wanted, the SQL Server team at Microsoft made some very major changes to the way devices and databases are laid out on disk between SQL Server 6.X and SQL Server 7.0. As a result, there is good news and bad news about upgrading. The good news is that the upgrade process will work very well. The bad news is that you'll need a huge amount of disk space to upgrade a server to SQL Server 7.0 without copying the data to tape or to another server.

The way the upgrade works is essentially to copy all the data out of the SQL Server 6.5 databases into the new 7.0 format, so there has to be enough space available to hold all the 6.5 databases and all the 7.0 databases simultaneously. Fortunately, Microsoft saw that this could be a problem and developed several options to make the installation a little less painful. SQL Server will upgrade databases by pushing the databases onto tape, wiping out the entire SQL Server 6.5 installation, and then upgrading the databases from tape, which won't take much disk space at all. (You'll learn more about that in the next section.)

Also, there is a good chance that the new databases will actually be significantly smaller. Because the data is all being copied, it will be defragmented during the copy, so it will take less space. Also, text fields are much more space-friendly now. A text field with 100 bytes in it won't take up a full page. In addition, SQL Server 7 has dynamically sized devices, so if there's a lot of empty space in the old database, it will not necessarily carry that empty space over into the new databases.

Unicode Collation

The Unicode Collation option presented in setup is used to determine how unicode data will be sorted. Unicode data is stored in the types *nchar, nvarchar,* and *ntext.* This means that a totally different sort order can be applied to unicode data than to the normal ASCII data.

In most cases, and in all cases involving an upgrade, the default sort order should be chosen. The default is based on the character set and sort order already chosen. If you choose something other than the default, unicode data may be sorted differently than non-unicode data, making for some inconsistent results.

The SQL Server 7.0 upgrade process differs slightly from the process used to upgrade from SQL Server 6.0 to 6.5. Although it can use the data copy process, SQL Server 7.0 also offers two new options. SQL Server 7.0 can leave the previous version on the hard drive so that it is possible to switch back and forth between versions 7.0 and 6.5. (However, it is not possible to run both simultaneously.) Optionally, if disk space is at a premium, SQL Server 7 setup can back up the data to tape, wipe out the SQL Server 6.5 installation, and start fresh.

One step of the upgrade process can never be stressed enough: Be sure to make sufficient backups. Back up the data, and then if possible, take SQL Server down and back up the whole machine—data files and all. The key here is to create quality back-ups on reliable media.

The next sections cover the details of planning the upgrade process and choosing which options are appropriate for you, choosing the data transfer method, and using the SQL Server Upgrade Wizard. After that, you'll learn about the client configuration changes that are necessary in order for all the clients to talk to SQL Server 7.0.

Planning the Upgrade: Choosing Upgrade Options

There are two ways to perform the upgrade:

- Side by Side method
- Computer to Computer method

The *Side by Side* method is used to upgrade to the new version of SQL Server on a single computer. This upgrade involves transferring all the data from the old database devices into the new database files on a single machine.

The second upgrade method, *Computer to Computer*, is used to transfer the data from a source computer running SQL Server 6.5 to a target computer running SQL Server 7.0. The Computer to Computer method cannot be used for servers participating in replication, so if replication is being used, either turn it off or use the Side by Side method.

There are two ways to transfer data during the upgrade process:

- Using Named Pipes
- Using tape backup

First, consider using Named Pipes to transfer data. When using the Side by Side method with Named Pipes, the data is essentially copied using Named Pipes from the old devices directly into the new devices. When using the Computer to Computer method with Named Pipes, the data is transferred over the network. Therefore, both machines must share a security context (NT logon account) that can be used to authenticate the network communications.

The second method for transferring data is to use a tape backup. This can also be used in either the Side by Side or Computer to Computer scenario, as you can see in Figure 1.1. Instead of using Named Pipes, the data is copied onto a tape, which can then be read in by SQL Server setup during the upgrade process. In the Side by Side scenario, this provides time to remove the old database devices and clean up the server to make room for the new data. In the Computer to Computer scenario, this reduces the amount of network bandwidth used, at the possible cost of time if the tape drive is slow. A fast server with a good tape drive will be able to perform adequately with the tape transfer method.

With either of these scenarios, SQL Server denotes an import server and an export server. The import server is the SQL Server 7 box that will house the data after the upgrade. The import server is also the server that will be running the SQL Server Upgrade Wizard. The export server is the server that contains the data being upgraded, and it is a SQL Server 6.0 or SQL Server 6.5 server. In a Side by Side upgrade, the import server and the export server are the same.

Choosing an Upgrade Scenario and Transfer Method

The safest upgrade scenario is Computer to Computer, using a network cable for small-to-medium databases or a tape drive for large databases. The Computer to Computer method is the safest because the export server is not changed during the upgrade, so the data integrity is maintained. Copying things is always safer than over-writing them. The reason a tape backup transfer method is best for large databases is speed. If a server is hosting a large database, it is more likely to have a good fast tape drive hooked up to it, and in the case of most large databases, transferring data over from one server to another is going to be faster by using the tape drive.

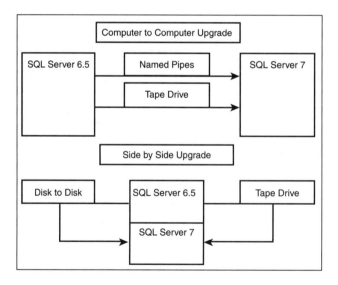

Figure 1.1   This diagram shows the two different transfer scenarios, and the two methods for transferring data that can be used with each scenario.

If you must do a Side by Side upgrade, be sure several backups of the server are available when you perform the upgrade. If a lot of disk space is available, use Named Pipes to perform the upgrade; otherwise, use the backup mechanism and delete the old data between the export and the import.

Using the SQL Server Upgrade Wizard

No matter how SQL Server is installed, the SQL Server Upgrade Wizard will be installed. Even if SQL Server 6.5 was not installed previously, the Upgrade Wizard will be installed in order to allow data to be pulled from another server in a Computer to Computer upgrade scenario.

If you are using the Side by Side scenario, make sure there is ample space to re-create the databases in SQL Server 7.0 format. If you are using the Computer to Computer scenario, the following conditions must be met:

- The sa password must be supplied for the export and the import servers.

- The import server must have SQL Server running, using an account other than LocalSystem in order for it to connect to other computers.

- Make sure no users are connected on either server during the upgrade process. Both servers will have their MSSQLServer services stopped and restarted, possibly several times.

- The database tempdb on the export server must be larger than 10MB.

- The currently logged on user must have Windows NT administrator rights on both the import and export servers.

The SQL Server Upgrade Wizard performs the tasks necessary to transfer data for the upgrade. The first page is the customary introduction page. On the second page, select which way the objects are to be transferred (export or import), how the objects will be transferred (via Named Pipes or tape), and how the verification process will be performed. See Figure 1.2 for details. The wizard supports two types of verification. The first type, Validate Successful Object Data Transfer, makes sure that all the objects transferred and their structures are correct. If that option is checked, the Exhaustive Data Integrity Verification option will be available. Check it to have the wizard perform a checksum on each object to ensure that it transferred in one piece.

The next page of the wizard is the code page selection page. The wizard connects to the export server and suggests a code page to use for the transfer. Use the default unless it is absolutely and without a doubt the wrong code page.

Next, the database selection page appears. Enter the server that's being imported from, along with valid login information for that server. If you're using the Side by Side scenario, don't change the server name; otherwise, do change the server name. The Optional Startup Arguments line can be used to start SQL Server with different flags than normal. If this line is left blank, SQL Server will be started with the same options it is normally started with. Next, choose the databases to be upgraded (see Figure 1.3). By default, all the databases on the export server except for master and msdb are selected. (Actually, the master and msdb databases cannot be upgraded, but certain settings can be imported, as you'll learn shortly.)

After choosing which databases are to be upgraded, you must decide how the new databases should be built in SQL Server 7. You have three options: Accept the default configuration, which is generated by the wizard; let the wizard use databases that have already been built on the SQL Server 7 server; or write scripts that will create the databases on-the-fly. If you choose the first option, the default configuration will check the import server and figure out where the devices need to go in order to have enough space. The default configuration is editable before it runs, so it is possible to accept the default and then modify the locations of the different files, as shown in Figure 1.4. If you choose the second option, build the devices in advance and make them larger than they absolutely need to be. If you choose the third option, you must script the creation of the database files and run the script from within the upgrade. The script should create the necessary databases with the correct layout.

So how do you know which option to use? If you are upgrading one SQL Server 6.5 server to one SQL Server 7.0 server, use the default configuration, but check to make sure the data is going onto the correct drives. If you are upgrading a bunch of servers that share a common database layout, write a script to create the new databases so they will all be created consistently. For maximum effect, it might be best to run the script manually instead of running it from within the upgrade. That way, if there are any problems in the script, they can be dealt with manually instead of through an aborted upgrade.

Figure 1.2   On the second page of the SQL Server Upgrade Wizard, choose between a tape transfer and a network transfer. If it is a tape transfer, indicate whether you are importing or exporting data on this step.

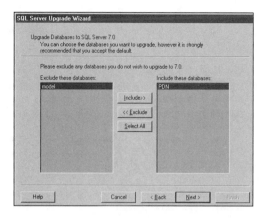

Figure 1.3   You must tell the Upgrade Wizard which databases you want to upgrade. Notice that the master and msdb databases don't even appear in the list.

After you set up the new databases, you have just a few more options. The next screen allows you to select which server options should be upgraded. The Upgrade Wizard can pick out all of the SQL Executive jobs, replication settings, and remote server setup information that is relevant to SQL Server 7, as shown in Figure 1.5. Essentially, this screen determines which elements will be imported from the master and msdb databases, alleviating the need to import these databases. Also on this screen, you must choose whether to use ANSI nulls or quoted identifiers.

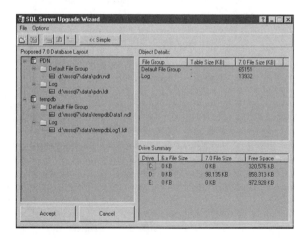

Figure 1.4   The Upgrade Wizard lets you select how devices will be built. This is the advanced version of the screen, which shows the space being allocated to each device as well as the devices' locations.

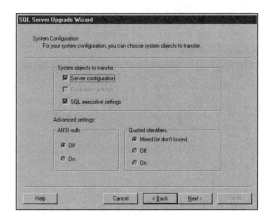

Figure 1.5   On this screen, you can specify which server settings are to be imported and whether to use ANSI nulls and quoted identifiers.

A few notes on housekeeping are appropriate here. First, if you've inserted objects into the model database so they will be propagated into all newly created databases, you'll need to reconstruct those objects by hand in order for them to exist in SQL Server 7.0. Also, remember that you can't upgrade the master database. So if you've placed stored procedures in the master database, you'll need to reconstruct them by hand, too. It's probably easier to simply let SQL Server 6.5's Enterprise Manager generate the SQL for these objects and then run it in SQL Server 7.0. Finally, if you aren't using SQL Server 6.5's replication or scheduled jobs, you don't need to worry about any of those options—just leave them turned off.

SQL Server 6.5 figured out whether or not ANSI null behavior was being used when a procedure was *started*. SQL Server 7.0 bases the behavior on the way the option was set when the object was *created*. Because objects are being created during the transfer, the option has to be set appropriately to guarantee good results.

In addition to the ANSI null option, you must decide what to do about the Quoted Identifiers option. This option is either turned on or turned off. The Quoted Identifiers option defines how SQL Server deals with double-quotation marks (""). If Quoted Identifiers is turned on, all object names can be enclosed in double quotation marks, allowing reserved words to be used as object names (which is not a good idea). The best example of a quoted identifier problem is this

SELECT "X" FROM T

where T is a valid object. If the Quoted Identifiers option is turned on, this will select all the values in the column named X in the table T. If the Quoted Identifiers option is off, this will return the character X once for each row in the table T.

If only single quotation marks are used to delimit character strings within the stored procedures, views, triggers, and rules that are being transferred, it is safe to use the Quoted Identifiers option. But if double quotation marks are being used around strings, turn off the Quoted Identifiers setting. Going forward, use only single quota-tion marks around data values, and reserve the use of double quotation marks for iden-tifiers.

After winding through all of these options, the upgrade process will kick off. Go grab some coffee and do some Web surfing. When the upgrade is complete, run through the logs and make sure that it worked as expected. The log files are kept on the machine running the Export Wizard in the directory \mssql7\upgrade in a folder named with the name of the server, followed by an underscore, the date, an under-score, and the time. For example, INTREPID_080998_132500 would be the upgrade run on the server called Intrepid on August 8, 1998 at 1:25 PM. That folder contains all the database-wide logs, such as those for creating the databases, importing tasks, and so on. There will also be a folder for each database that was transferred. Inside the folder is a set of files that describe all the objects that were transferred. If a file ends in ".ok," all the objects of that type transferred without error; if a file ends in ".err," the objects transferred had errors. All the files will be named using this format

<SQL Server 6 Server Name>.<Database Name>.<type>

where the <type> is the type of object being created, such as a stored procedure, rule, default, trigger, table, or constraint.

To scan these files, look for files that end in ".err." Each of these files contains a list of objects that were not imported, along with the error messages that were generated during the attempted import. Usually objects are not imported either because the database ran out of space or because of some scripting problem (such as syntax that is no longer valid).

Nulls: ANSI and Otherwise

SQL Server can handle comparisons involving NULL values in two different ways: through either the his-torical default SQL Server method or the ANSI standard method. Historically, the SQL Server standard has been that the statement "null = null" is true. The ANSI standard says that "null = null" is false, but that "null is null" is true. In other words, in the ANSI standard, arithmetic comparisons (equal to or not equal to) to null values always return false, but by using the special "is" operator, nulls can be compared. The SQL Server alternative is that the arithmetic operator " = " is equivalent to the "is" operator.

Why do you care? If the stored procedures, constraints, views, or triggers that are present in the database are not written to handle ANSI nulls, the behavior of the objects will change if the ANSI nulls setting is turned on during the transfer.

What happens if you pick the wrong one? SQL Server 7 decides whether or not ANSI nulls were on at object creation time. So you should set the ANSI_NULLS option using the SET ANSI_NULLS command, and then re-create the objects.

After the database has been upgraded, make sure that the client software being used can still connect to the server properly. If you used the Computer to Computer scenario, make sure that the old system is taken offline and the new system is accessible to the clients. The old system should be taken offline to prevent users from accessing it inadvertently.

Modifying the Clients

The existing clients should be able to access the data with no driver changes. Unfortunately, if you used the Computer to Computer scenario, you must tell the clients how to communicate with the new server. There are several ways to do this, and not all of them involve touching every single client machine.

The most direct route is to rename the new server with the old server's name. This little trick assumes the old server is truly offline. If it is, simply rename the server and reboot it, and the clients shouldn't even know anything changed.

If the clients are running only the TCP/IP sockets protocol, make changes in the DNS of the organization so that computers that request the IP address of the old server by name will get the new server. Or, if the clients all have the IP addresses on them, dual-home the server so it answers to both the old IP address and the new IP address.

Otherwise, change the driver settings on all the client machines so they point to the new server. This option probably involves the most legwork, but it is also probably the best long-term solution. There are a variety of ways to approach this task. Having a technician move from computer to computer is probably the low-tech version. If Microsoft's SMS product is deployed, packages can be built using the SMS Installer that will make the necessary changes to the drivers.

This concludes the discussion on upgrading. Key points to remember are the two different backup scenarios, the two different transfer methods, and the options available. Because the process itself is guided by the wizard, it is very straightforward. The one point that can't be emphasized enough is that you must have good, reliable backups available in the event of a mishap.

All About Autoconfiguration

In SQL Server 6 and all prior versions, after SQL Server was installed, the next automatic task was configuration. You had to specify the amount of memory used by SQL Server, as well as the number of simultaneous user connections, locks, open objects, and open databases in order to optimize the amount of memory in the system. In addition, you had to find the proper balance between SQL Server and Windows NT memory utilization to make sure that SQL Server had as much memory as possible for data cache but that Windows NT had enough memory that it wasn't paging and reducing overall system performance.

Most of those problems go away in SQL Server 7. The term autoconfiguration is used to encompass all the settings that SQL Server now sets dynamically as it runs.

SQL Server monitors the memory needs of the operating system and decreases its memory footprint accordingly, by reducing the amount of data in cache when the operating system needs more memory in order to fulfill certain functions.

This section addresses the Memory, Locks, Open Objects, and User Connections configuration objects, which are the options in SQL Server 6.5 most commonly reset by the administrator when setup is complete. These settings can be changed either in SQL Enterprise Manager (right-click on the server and choose Properties) or by using the `sp_configure` system stored procedure. Figure 1.6 shows the SQL Enterprise Manager window used to change minimum and maximum server memory settings. In this case, the minimum is set to 0, so it will be autoconfigured, and the maximum is set to the maximum amount of memory in the machine, so it will also be configured automatically.

Memory

The memory setting in SQL Server is now autoconfigured by default. SQL Server takes a certain amount of memory to hold itself and its basic data structures and then takes huge hunks of memory to use as data cache. SQL Server checks every few minutes to see whether the amount of free memory on the system has dropped below a threshold value of 5MB. If the amount of available memory is below 5MB, SQL Server releases some memory back to the operating system. If the amount of memory exceeds 5MB, SQL Server grabs the available memory for use as data cache.

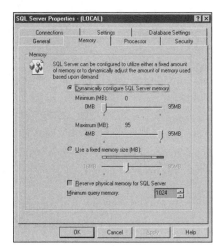

Figure 1.6　The SQL Enterprise Manager screen used for changing the minimum and maximum server memory settings.

There are now three memory settings that you need to worry about. The old "memory" setting has been replaced by two new configuration parameters: Minimum and Maximum. The first option, Minimum, defaults to 0 and is the minimum amount of memory that SQL Server will use, specified in MB. The Maximum setting defaults to 2,147,483,647, or 2GB. If you leave the settings at their defaults, SQL Server will vary the amount of memory between 0 and 2GB. This setting can be tuned either by increasing the Minimum to a higher number, which would cause SQL Server to take a certain amount of memory all the time, or by setting Minimum and Maximum to the same number, which would force SQL Server to use only the specified amount of memory.

The best approach is to leave these settings alone. SQL Server is pretty good at handling the amount of memory that it has, and any tinkering you do here will just be one more thing to document.

Locks

In SQL Server 6.5 and earlier, the locks setting controlled how many locks could be used in the database. If the number of locks in use got close to that specified by the Locks setting, bad things would start to happen, which caused the users to think SQL Server was crashing.

To alleviate this problem, SQL Server 7 dynamically allocates the memory to be used for locks. This memory is allocated directly from Windows NT, provided that the amount of memory currently in use by SQL Server is not equal to the amount specified in the maximum server memory configuration option. If memory for the new lock cannot be allocated, the lock attempt will fail, and users will start complaining that the server has crashed.

The best way to deal with the Locks setting is to leave it alone. If the memory setting is being manually configured, however, it's probably best to configure the Locks setting as well to prevent contention for memory.

Open Objects

The Open Objects parameter determines how many database objects can be open simultaneously. This is the total number of tables, views, stored procedures, defaults, rules, triggers, and constraints that are in use at any given time.

The Open Objects setting works the same as the Locks setting in its memory allocation scheme. Again, leave it alone unless the amount of memory is being configured manually, in which case, it is a good idea to configure it manually as well.

User Connections

The User Connections parameter controls the number of simultaneous user connections that SQL Server can accept at any given time. This isn't a licensing restriction, because a given client computer that has a valid license can connect to SQL Server several times. Rather, the User Connections parameter is used for allocating the amount of memory and number of handles to be used to track user connections. This parameter also defaults to 0 and behaves the same as the Open Objects and Locks settings. Once again, leave it alone unless you have an overwhelming need to change it.

Recommendations for Setting Options

For a large, dedicated SQL Server running Windows NT, the autoconfiguration will perform as advertised and allow the best performance. If other applications are running on the SQL Server, it may be desirable to increase the minimum server memory option so SQL Server won't deallocate itself into a performance abyss when the other application tries to allocate all the available memory on the machine. For smaller servers or workstations, however, don't touch anything; just let SQL Server manage itself.

If you decide to fix the amount of memory for use by SQL Server, go ahead and fix the settings for Locks, User Connections, and Open Objects also, or at least monitor the In Use statistics in Windows NT Performance Monitor to ensure that the memory used for locks, open objects, and user connections isn't causing a shortage of cache space.

Setting Up Client Utilities

SQL Server comes with a number of client utilities that are to be used both on the server and on the client workstations that need to manage the server. These utilities include the following:

- **BCP**. The Bulk Copy Program is used to import and export large amounts of data.

- **ISQL**. Interactive SQL is the command line utility used to connect to SQL Server and send SQL batches either from the console or from a file of saved commands.

- **OSQL**. ODBC Interactive SQL is the same as ISQL, but it runs through the ODBC interface.

- **ISQLW**. ISQL for Windows is a Windows-based utility that can be used to send queries to SQL Server. In the Start menu, the icon may be labeled "Query Analyzer."

- **CNU**. The Client Network Utility runs from the Control Panel (CLICONFIG.CPL), allowing the network protocols to be configured, as described in Chapter 2.

- **Profiler**. The SQL Server Profiler allows queries to be monitored and tracked to allow performance enhancements.

- **MMC**. The Microsoft Management Console program runs the SQL Server Enterprise Manager.

Installing these utilities is a piece of cake. Put in the CD, choose to install SQL Server 7, and choose a custom installation. Then deselect the Server Components option, leaving Management Tools, Client Connectivity, and Books Online checked. Then click Next and choose the destination disk.

For each of these tools (except for the SQL Enterprise Manager), the configuration is mostly complete when the installation is over. The only thing left to do (which all the tools have in common) is configuring the client network protocols, and for most installations the defaults are okay.

The SQL Server Enterprise Manager is an MMC Snap-In that allows SQL Servers to be managed in the enterprise. For this application, you must tell the application where the SQL Servers are by registering the servers. To do so, choose Action, Register SQL Server, and then follow the instructions in the wizard. The wizard prompts you to choose an authentication method (you can use either your Windows NT account or a standard SQL Server login). Then add the SQL Server to the appropriate group.

Conclusions

Microsoft did a very good job of making this setup program work correctly. Keep these simple rules in mind, and everything should work fine:

- Make sure there are clean network and security connections for upgrading databases.

- Pay attention and follow the onscreen instructions.

- Make sure adequate disk space is available for either an upgrade or a fresh install.

That's really all there is to it. Autoconfiguration takes about half the complexity out of figuring out how the server is going to run, so it's pretty hard to mess up.

2

Connectivity and Network Configuration

Chris Miller

ONE OF THE MOST IMPORTANT YET most often overlooked parts of SQL Server is network connectivity (and the configuration thereof). Networking is very important to SQL Server: It wouldn't be much of a Server product if it couldn't communicate. However, this chapter isn't devoted to explaining TCP/IP or any other network protocol. That's covered in other books. (Microsoft went to a lot of trouble to ensure that SQL Server uses the Windows NT provided protocols and libraries for communications, so anyone with a solid grasp of how Windows NT networking works will be right on top of this chapter.) This chapter shows you how SQL Server interacts with the network, from the server-side networking libraries to the client-side network components.

Why is there such in-depth coverage of networking? In short, the documentation on how SQL Server networking happens and how to configure it on both the client side and the server side tends to fall through the cracks. The server side is an installation issue, and the client side is a developer issue, and a reference that includes both perspectives for the database administrator has been sorely lacking.

Here's what we're going to cover:

- Server-Side Networking
- Client-Side Networking

■ Configuring ODBC

■ Examining OLE-DB

Server-Side Networking

When Microsoft created Windows NT, one of the design goals was to provide a robust development platform for applications. To achieve this goal, the designers created a very powerful set of services to be built into the operating system to handle many operations that a server would need, such as file access, print services, and networking. SQL Server is largely independent of the network, and only the lowest layers of SQL Server need to be network aware. The distinguishing capabilities of these lower layers are isolated into network libraries, as illustrated in Figure 2.1.

Server-side network libraries can be broken into two groups. The first group relies on the Windows operating systems network architecture to provide communications services. This group includes the following:

■ Named Pipes library

■ Multi-Protocol library

■ Local RPC library

■ Shared Memory library

The Named Pipes library uses a simple communications system based on the UNC structure of the network. A named pipe has a full UNC path, such as \\Server\Pipe\SQL\Query. For the local server, this can be abbreviated to \\.\Pipe\SQL\Query. From a programmer's perspective, programming named pipes is very similar to programming for file-based input and output. It shouldn't be surprising, then, to find out that using this library requires the client to be validated by

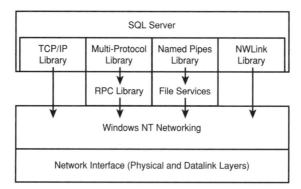

Figure 2.1   The relationship between some of the supported protocols in SQL Server and how they interact with the Windows NT networking services.

Windows NT. That means when a client connects, the user must be authenticated by the Windows NT security system.

The Multi-Protocol system uses Remote Procedure Calls, or RPCs, to communicate between clients and servers. RPC is a secure protocol, and as with Named Pipes, the user must be authenticated by Windows NT.

Another library that fits into this group is the Local RPC library. Despite the apparent contradiction in having a local remote procedure call, this is a real protocol. Local RPC is used by processes running on the Windows NT server to communicate with the SQL Server (such as the SQL Enterprise Manager tool running on the server or the SQL Agent).

The Shared Memory libraries are also used for communication between processes running on the same server. The Shared Memory library is automatically installed, cannot be removed, and has no configuration options, so it isn't discussed a lot.

Because both Named Pipes and Multi-Protocol libraries use the Windows network architecture, they are essentially protocol-independent. Named Pipes can be used on any protocol that file services are supported on, which means it can be used with IPX/SPX, TCP/IP, Banyan VINES, and NetBEUI. RPC can be used with any protocol that supports the remote procedure calls, which includes the same ones. The only protocol that really isn't supported is DLC.

The second set of server-side network libraries is the protocol-dependent libraries, which include the following:

- NWLink
- TCP/IP Sockets
- Banyan-VINES SPP libraries

Unlike Named Pipes or Multi-Protocol, these libraries don't use Windows-specific file services or RPC. The TCP/IP Sockets library, for example, uses TCP/IP sockets and works just like any other socket-based program such as Telnetd or an Oracle listener daemon. SQL Server includes libraries for IPX/SPX, TCP/IP Sockets, Banyan VINES, and even AppleTalk's ADSP protocol.

Each of these libraries requires the use of certain settings as a means of identifying itself. For example, to configure the TCP/IP library, the port number must be specified. With IPX/SPX, AppleTalk ADSP, or Banyan VINES SPP, a service name has to be provided, which usually but not always is the same as the server name. Also, if one of these libraries is going to be used, the appropriate protocols must be installed in the Windows NT Network Control Panel. In other words, if IPX/SPX must be supported, the NWLink IPX/SPX protocol must be installed.

On the server side, very few files and a low level of complexity are involved because the networking is handled by the operating system. SQL Server maintains the server-side libraries so it can interact with some networks in different ways. For example, the Multi-Protocol library, which uses RPC mechanisms to communicate, enables SQL Server to provide integrated security. The files used to implement the network libraries are located in the \MSSQL\BINN directory. Table 2.1 lists the files used.

Table 2.1   **SQL Server's Server-Side Network Library DLL Files**

File	Use
SSMSSH70.DLL	Local RPC (used only to connect back to the local server)
SSMSSO70.DLL	TCP/IP Sockets
SSNMPN70.DLL	Named Pipes
SSMSRP70.DLL	Multi-Protocol
SSMSAD70.DLL	ADSP (AppleTalk)
SSMSSP70.DLL	NWLink IPX/SPX
SSMSVI70.DLL	Banyan VINES SPP

It's also worth mentioning that the functions involved in these DLLs are documented as part of Open Data Services. That means new libraries can be written by third parties, although it's not very common.

Installing Server-Side Libraries

You install server-side network libraries by using the Network Libraries Configuration utility. By default, the Named Pipes, TCP/IP Sockets, and Multi-Protocol are installed on Windows NT. However, only TCP/IP Sockets and Multi-Protocol are installed on Windows 95; Windows 95 does not support Named Pipes.

The following steps walk you through how to install a new server-side protocol after SQL Server has been installed:

1. Start the Network Libraries Configuration utility by choosing Start, Programs, Microsoft SQL Server 7.0, Server Network Utility.

2. The General tab displays a list of the currently configured protocols and their settings, as shown in Figure 2.2. Click the Add button to add a new network protocol.

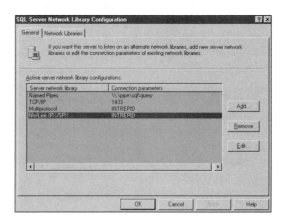

Figure 2.2   The currently configured network protocols and their settings.

3. In the Add New Network Library Configuration dialog box, shown in Figure 2.3, choose the network protocol to use and enter the appropriate settings. For example, if you choose TCP/IP, you must either enter the port number to listen on or accept the default.

4. Click OK to close this dialog box, and then click OK again to close the Network Libraries Configuration utility.

5. Stop and then restart SQL Server to put your changes into effect.

As you probably noticed, step 3 in the preceding list is a little vague. The following subsections cover each of the different network libraries in greater detail and explain the settings for each.

Named Pipes

This is one of the default protocols for SQL Server on Windows NT. It requires the client to be authenticated by Windows NT, so either the client must have a user account or the guest account must be turned on.

The only setting you have to configure for this protocol is the pipe that will be listened to for incoming connections. The default pipe is \\.\pipe\sql\query (the UNC path to the pipe, where \\. represents the local machine). This path can be changed, but if it is changed, all of the clients will have to be told where to find the SQL Server because they all default to the same path for the pipe.

TCP/IP

This protocol also is a default for SQL Server on Windows NT. In addition, it is a default protocol for SQL Server on Windows 95. This protocol does not require any Windows NT authentication.

The only setting necessary for this protocol is the port number that SQL Server

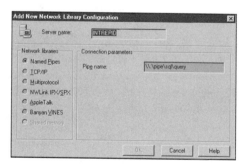

Figure 2.3   The Add New Network Library Configuration dialog box, where new protocols are configured for the server.

should listen on. The port number 1433 is the default port and is assigned and documented by the Internet committee that assigns numbers. If you must change this port number, be sure to check the file called SERVICES, which is found in either C:\WINDOWS\SERVICES on Windows 9X or C:\WINNT\SYSTEM32\DRIVERS\ETC\SERVICES on Windows NT. This file contains a list of all the known services, and any port number that is not in this list can be used by SQL Server.

TCP/IP must be installed on both the client and the server for this protocol to work.

Multi-Protocol

The Multi-Protocol library is a default library for both Windows 95 and Windows NT. The Multi-Protocol library uses remote procedure calls, or RPCs, to communicate with the server. Therefore, it will work with any RPC-compatible network protocol, including TCP/IP, NWLink IPX/SPX, and NetBEUI. The Multi-Protocol library requires Windows NT authentication, just as the Named Pipes protocol does.

The only setting you need to configure for Multi-Protocol is the encryption setting. If this setting is turned on, the RPC libraries on the client and the server will negotiate a level of encryption on their own, and all login and data messages between the client and the server will be encrypted. This does require a small amount of overhead on both the client and the server, however. So don't use it if it's not necessary.

NWLink IPX/SPX

This protocol uses the NetWare-compatible NWLink protocol set to communicate between clients and servers. In order for this protocol to work, an IPX/SPX-compatible protocol must be installed on both the server and the client. The only setting necessary for this protocol is the Novell Bindery Service Name, which is usually the same as the server name. This is the name that clients will use to connect to the server.

AppleTalk

This protocol uses the AppleTalk network protocol to communicate between clients and servers. The servers must be Windows NT Servers (which actually have to be running Windows NT Server), and they have to have File and Print Services for Macintosh running. The only setting for this protocol is the AppleTalk Service Object Name, which is usually just the name of the server.

Banyan VINES

The Banyan VINES SPP protocol can be used to communicate between clients and servers. The Banyan software for Windows NT must be loaded on the server. That includes the Banyan VINES protocols for Windows NT. Also, Banyan support is available only on the Intel platform; it is not available on the Alpha platform. To set up the Banyan VINES network library, you must enter the fully qualified StreetTalk Service

Name in the format *servicename@group@org*, where *servicename* is usually the server name.

After installing the network libraries with SQL Server setup, you must restart the SQL Server services. This will load all the network libraries. To ensure that all the drivers start successfully, check the Windows NT Event Log or the SQL Server Error Log for error messages. For example, if the AppleTalk ADSP library can't be loaded because of a duplicate service name, an error will be recorded in the log.

SQL Server Network Libraries Performance Hint

Here is an important performance hint for using SQL Server network libraries: Install as few as possible. The goal with network libraries is to cover the base of installed users. By installing only the necessary protocols, you avoid additional memory and processor overhead that comes with having multiple protocols installed. In addition, the fewer protocols that are loaded, the less complex the installation is. Less complexity means fewer things can break, and the system is easier to manage.

Client-Side Networking

The client side of the network looks very similar to the server side. Client-side network libraries handle communications between the programming interfaces and the network software installed on the client. Two major programming interfaces are in use today: ODBC and OLE-DB. Both of these interfaces use the same client-side network libraries.

The client libraries are the same as the server libraries as far as which protocols are supported. The difference is that the clients initiate connections, so they need a tool that configures which libraries to use with which servers. This tool is called the SQL Server Client Configuration utility.

The Client Configuration utility allows the user to choose a default network protocol to be used to connect to servers and then to specify particular servers that won't use the default library and configure their network libraries to work with the server.

A Convenient Workaround

When the Multi-Protocol library is being used to attach two Windows NT systems and the two systems are in different domains with no trust relationships, it can be difficult to establish a good connection through the NT security layer. Here's a good workaround. Basically, what is required is a validated connection to the server before SQL Server makes a connection. Then SQL Server can "piggyback" off the previous connection's security. To establish such a connection, use this command: NET USE \\<Server>\IPC$ /user:<DOMAIN>\<USER>. It doesn't really matter what share you're connected to; the IPC$ is just a convenient share with full access. In place of <DOMAIN> and <USER>, just enter a domain and a username that the SQL Server will accept. Then you can use SQL Server tools, and the connections should work just fine.

For example, suppose you have a network of five servers, of which four are running Named Pipes and the fifth is running TCP/IP Sockets. You would specify Named Pipes as the default protocol and then indicate that the fifth server won't use the default. You configure it to use TCP/IP Sockets by entering its server name and specifying the port number the server is listening on—usually 1433.

The following steps walk you through an example of how the SQL Server Client Configuration utility might be used:

1. Start the SQL Server Client Configuration utility by choosing Start, Programs, Microsoft SQL Server. This brings up a dialog box with three tabs: General, Network Libraries, and DB Library Options.

2. On the General tab (see Figure 2.4), notice that the default is set to Named Pipes. Named Pipes is always the default protocol until it's specifically changed.

3. To add an exception to the list, click the Add button. The Add New Network Protocol Configuration dialog box appears.

4. As an example, add a server called "Fred" with a TCP/IP Sockets connection. (The server name doesn't necessarily have to be the real name of the server; it is just the name that all calls will use to open this connection.) In the Computer Name box, enter the name or IP address of a server. Then click OK.

5. Start REGEDIT and go to HKEY_LOCAL_MACHINE\Software\ Microsoft\MSSQLServer\Client\ConnectTo. Notice that there are two values in this key. One of them will be named with the server name you entered in step 3 (Fred), and the value will be the name of the library (DBMSSOCN) followed by the parameters (the computer name you entered in step 3 and the default port number of 1433). The other value will be named DSQUERY. DSQUERY is the default value, and it is set to DBNMPNTW, which is the Named Pipes library.

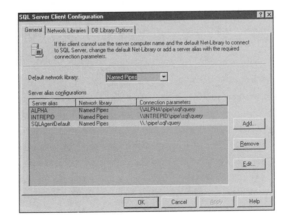

Figure 2.4   The General tab of the SQL Server Client Configuration utility.

6. Close everything up.

It's interesting to note that all the settings for the client libraries are stored in the Registry in the same place. Therefore, it's possible to install the client software by saving the settings in the Registry key mentioned in step 5 and then installing that Registry and the appropriate files on the new client workstation. That should make client configuration easier, but it probably isn't supported by Microsoft.

The client libraries are kept in separate DLL files and are very similar to the server-side libraries. Table 2.2 lists the client-side DLL files. The easy way to tell a server-side library from a client-side library is that the server-side libraries all start with SS (for "Server Side"), whereas the client-side libraries usually start with DB. These libraries are stored in \MSSQL7\BINN, except for the Named Pipes library, which is stored in either the WINDOWS\System or the WINNT\System32 directory.

Choosing Client-Side Protocols

If a server has multiple server-side libraries running and a particular client can access several of them, which library should the user choose? Such a decision should be based on the following criteria:

■ Does the application force the user to log in? If so, using integrated security won't help much, so any protocol can be used.

■ Does the client communicate over an open channel, such as the Internet? If so, the encryption offered by Multi-Protocol would be a nice added layer of security.

■ Is the client always logged on as a valid Windows NT domain user? If so, using the Named Pipes or Multi-Protocol library won't incur extra overhead.

The goal is to try to use Named Pipes or Multi-Protocol whenever possible. Both of these protocols use integrated security, validating the user without the user having to enter a separate password. If the client's application asks for a username and password anyway, it doesn't much matter what protocol is being used because the user still has to remember a separate password.

Table 2.2   **Client-Side Networking DLL Files**

DLL File	Network Library
DBNMPNTW.DLL	Named Pipes
DBMSSOCN.DLL	TCP/IP
DBMSRPCN.DLL	Multi-Protocol
DBMSSPXN.DLL	NWLink IPX/SPX
DBMSADSN.DLL	AppleTalk ADSP
DBMSVINN.DLL	Banyan VINES SPP

Definitely try to use Multi-Protocol for a connection over an open channel. The extra layer of encryption is very nice. If, however, Multi-Protocol and Named Pipes aren't options, you will have to use whatever protocol is available on the network.

Troubleshooting Client Connectivity Problems

Client/Server connectivity problems are diagnosed from the bottom up. In other words, check the physical layer of the network, and then the networking components, and so on until the application itself is called into question. In this section, we'll focus primarily on TCP/IP troubleshooting, but all troubleshooting will be similar.

If there is a connectivity problem between the client and the server, first determine whether there is a good network connection from the client to the server. Use the following process to test a TCP/IP connection:

1. Open a command shell. Ping the local machine at address 127.0.0.1. If this fails, there is a network configuration problem on the local machine.

2. Ping the local machine's external TCP/IP address. To find out what the local IP address is, use WINIPCFG in Windows 9X, or type **IPCONFIG** at a command prompt in Windows NT. If this fails, there is a network configuration problem on the local machine.

3. Ping the default gateway's address (which you can also find by using WINIPCFG or IPCONFIG). If this fails, check to make sure that your local IP address and the default gateway are in the same subnet. If the two addresses are in the same subnet, there is a problem with the cabling to the client or the default gateway itself. If the two machines are on different subnets, the local machine is not configured properly.

4. Ping the server by IP address. Then ping the server by name.

   Make sure that the address that was returned from the ping by name command is the same as the address that was returned from the ping by IP address. If it isn't, there's a DNS problem on the network.

   If the pings fail and you get the message Destination host unreachable, there is a router configuration problem.

   If the pings work, there is network connectivity between the client and the server.

After confirming network connectivity, look for other sources of problems. Start up the SQL Server Client Configuration utility and check to make sure that either the default network protocol is set correctly or that the exception protocol for the problem server is configured correctly. Then check the server-side network libraries and determine whether they are supporting the correct protocols.

As a last resort, install the client software from the SQL Server 7.0 CD onto the client, and then connect to SQL Server using ISQL/W. ISQL/W is the easiest connection to make; if it works, there is very likely a problem in the software that's preventing connectivity.

That covers how the base layers of network communication work between the client and the server. So far, you've learned about the client- and server-side network protocols. Now you need to delve into the topic of the API sets that applications use to communicate over these protocols: ODBC and OLE-DB.

Configuring ODBC

ODBC, or Open Database Connectivity, was Microsoft's first attempt at making a standard interface that allows programs to talk to databases. ODBC was ultimately successful in beating out the competition, but it isn't easy to use or administer.

ODBC uses a driver model to allow programmers to learn one API that will access multiple databases. ODBC itself consists of some core components that access drivers for each database back-end. The programmer writes his program to access ODBC, and ODBC handles talking to the database and returning responses.

In order for a program to use a database via ODBC, a data source must be created. The program can create the data source, but more commonly the data source is created by using the ODBC Administrator program. This program allows the user to create a named configuration that links the name, a particular database driver, and specific information for that driver. When the program runs, it looks for the specific name, called a Data Source Name, or DSN. When the program uses ODBC to access the DSN, the ODBC core brings up the drivers and establishes a database connection using the parameters specified. Usually the parameters specified include the server name and the database name.

The ODBC core consists of six files on Windows NT. Three of them are involved with running the administration program, and the other three actually do the work of talking to databases. The files are listed and defined in Table 2.3.

The first three files are involved with creating and maintaining data sources. The fourth file, ODBCCR32.DLL, manages database cursors, which provide data structures for programs to modify databases with. The ODBC32.DLL is the central part of the core driver set. This DLL file manages the connection between the application and the

Table 2.3 **ODBC Core Component DLL Files**

File	Definition
ODBCCP32.DLL	The administrator program
ODBCCP32.CPL	Starts the administrator program from Control Panel
ODBCAD32.EXE	Starts the administrator program from a command line
ODBCCR32.DLL	Manages cursors
ODBC32.DLL	The core driver manager
ODBCINT.DLL	Internationalization DLL

database-specific driver. ODBCINT.DLL contains the internationalization settings, such as the error messages that ODBC returns.

Because this is a SQL Server book, it would be nice to know about the SQL Server driver files for ODBC. The primary file is SQLSRV32.DLL, located in the WINDOWS\SYSTEM or \WINNT\SYSTEM32 directory. This is the primary driver for ODBC. In addition, there is a file called SQLWOA70.DLL, which implements a nifty wizard to help the user get through creating a DSN for a SQL Server.

Another great feature for SQL Server ODBC is the great backward compatibility that's built in. The SQL Server 7.0 ODBC driver can be used with SQL Server versions 4.21a and up. For any version of ODBC to work, however, a script called INSTCAT.SQL has to be run on the SQL Server. This script became a standard part of SQL Server installations starting with SQL Server 6.0.

Coming up is a look at ODBC from an administrator's perspective. First, in the "ODBC and OLE-DB Client Installation" section is a step-by-step overview of how to install the data access utilities. Then in the "ODBC Gotchas" section, a little bit more overview into the issues that are common in ODBC implementations. Then, a quick tutorial on how to install ODBC data sources, and then some troubleshooting hints.

ODBC and OLE-DB Client Installation

Microsoft has come to realize that installing the data components onto client computers is a very complex problem for network administrators, database administrators, and developers. As a result, they developed a new package called the Microsoft Data Access Components, or MDAC. MDAC is the answer to a lot of questions about how to install various components. This chapter will cover acquisition and installation of MDAC for clients.

MDAC is available on Microsoft's Web site at `www.microsoft.com/data`. There are different packages for each operating system, so be sure to download the correct one. The version on Microsoft's Web site will always be the most current version.

Installing MDAC is very straightforward. Run the executable and follow the instructions. When the installation is complete, ODBC and OLE-DB libraries will be installed and ready to use. All that's left is to understand what makes ODBC blow up (see the next section, "ODBC Gotchas") and how OLE-DB works.

Hang On to the Old...

Make a copy of all of your old versions of MDAC and archive them in case you need them later to troubleshoot or to ease the transition to newer versions. It's not unusual for a user to install new software only to find that it has bugs. Consider the old archived versions to be a sort of insurance policy.

ODBC "Gotchas"

The biggest problem with ODBC is version control. Currently the ODBC specification is at version 3.5, so the core files are version 3.5X or later. Keeping all the DLL files in sync and at the correct version is critical to reliable performance. The new ODBC administrator helps a lot by keeping track of versions on the About tab.

Fortunately, Microsoft is aware that this is a problem and has provided a solution of sorts. Microsoft is now packaging all of the client libraries, ODBC drivers, and OLE-DB updates in one package called the Microsoft Data Access Components, or MDAC. By downloading the version of MDAC specific to the operating system and architecture of the client computer, you can install the newest, latest, and greatest versions of ODBC and the client network libraries.

Unfortunately, that doesn't necessarily fix all the problems. Sometimes the unexpected happens, and the new drivers don't perform as advertised. For example, during the upgrade from SQL Server 6.0 to 6.5, if the ODBC drivers on the clients were updated, certain programs would quit working. Someone at Microsoft made a change to the default setting for how NULL values were handled to increase ANSI compliance. Many programs, including Microsoft Access, relied on the old setting and these programs crashed with the new ODBC drivers. The fix was to either change the setting or revert to the old drivers.

The best practice here is to maintain a library of driver sets for each operating system and architecture in your environment and to document which ones have been tested and are known to work, which ones have been tested and are known to have unresolved issues, and which ones just don't work. Don't always rely on the newest drivers to resolve a problem; always keep some older drivers that are known to work.

Using the ODBC Administrator

The ODBC administrator program is used to create data source names, or DSNs, so that programs can access databases. The ODBC administrator is installed whenever ODBC is installed, which means it's installed when SQL Server is installed or when any Microsoft product that works with databases is installed (such as Microsoft Access or Microsoft Excel). Also, the ODBC administrator is installed with the MDAC package.

The easiest way to start the ODBC administrator is from Control Panel. Selecting the ODBC object in Control Panel start the ODBCCP32.CPL applet, which starts programs in the ODBCCP32.DLL file.

Follow these steps to use the ODBC administrator to configure a data source:

1. Make sure that the client libraries are configured. If the server is running Named Pipes, everything is set. If it's not, use the steps in the section "Installing Server-Side Libraries" (earlier in this chapter) to configure the network library.

2. Start the ODBC applet in Control Panel. The ODBC Data Source Administrator dialog box (see Figure 2.5) contains seven tabs:

- User DSN. Data sources that are available only on the local computer to the current user.
- System DSN. Data sources that are available to any user on the local machine.
- File DSN. Data sources that are stored in files. These files can be saved on network shares and used by multiple users on multiple machines.
- Drivers. A list of the installed drivers with version numbers.
- Tracing. Options for logging of ODBC calls on the local machine. This feature is very useful for debugging, but it extracts a performance penalty for overhead and creates very large trace files if it is left on for too long.
- Connection Pooling. Settings that allow a connection to stay available after it has been closed in order to improve efficiency. You can configure how long the connection will remain available after it has closed.
- About. Names and version numbers of all the core components.

Keep in mind that not all these tabs will be available on all platforms or with all versions of ODBC.

3. On the User DSN tab, click Add. Then choose SQL Server and click Finish. This starts the SQL Server Data Source Wizard.

4. Enter the name for the data source, a brief description of the data source, and then the name of the server, which can be typed or chosen from the drop-down list. Click on Next.

5. Choose the appropriate authentication method for the server (see Figure 2.6). Click on Client Configuration to see how the server connection will be made. (Notice that the screen that appears is part of the SQL Server Client Configuration utility.) Make sure the Connect to SQL Server to Obtain Default

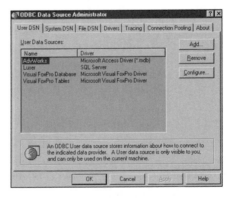

Figure 2.5   The ODBC Data Source Administrator dialog box, showing the User DSN tab.

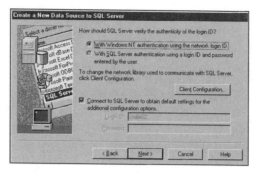

Figure 2.6 When creating a SQL Server data source, you can choose the authentication method for the server.

Settings option is checked. This allows ODBC to select the correct default codepage translation and language information for the client. Click on Next.

6. The wizard connects to the SQL Server and figures out what databases you have access to. On the next screen, choose to connect to the "pubs" database by default. The other options on this screen deal with how the connection will handle some very specific ODBC stuff. The Create Temporary Stored Procedures option is valid only when connecting to older versions of SQL Server; it tells ODBC to create stored procedures to handle running prepared statements. The Use ANSI Quoted Identifiers and Use ANSI Nulls, Paddings, and Warnings options have to do with specific behaviors for the ANSI standard. The final option, Use the Failover SQL Server, specifies that the server is part of a cluster, and that if it isn't available, another part of the cluster will be identified for use. Click on Next.

7. The next screen is dedicated to the topics of internationalization and logging performance data. The internationalization settings won't need to be changed here in the U.S., but elsewhere these will need to be modified to suit the local environment. The settings for logging performance data enable you to save queries that run for a long time so they can be optimized, as well as to log statistics. Click on Next.

8. The last screen allows you to test the data source. Run the test to ensure that the data source has been installed.

The important part of setting up an ODBC driver is entering the Data Source Name. Programs access ODBC data sources via DSNs, so if the DSN is incorrect, the program won't be able to find the database and will usually fail ungracefully. The DSN is not case sensitive, and leading and trailing spaces are trimmed, so as long as the right characters are there in the right order everything should work.

ODBC settings are saved in the Registry in two keys:

HKEY_LOCAL_MACHINE\Software\ODBC\ODBC.INI and HKEY_
CURRENT_USER\Software\ODBC\ODBC.INI. Remember that ODBC is sup-
posed to be a multivendor standard, so it isn't in the Microsoft key. All of the user
DSNs are stored in HKEY_CURRENT_USER, and the system DSNs are stored in
HKEY_LOCAL_MACHINE. In addition, HKEY_LOCAL_MACHINE contains
information about how ODBC is installed and which drivers are installed. That infor-
mation is located in HKEY_LOCAL_MACHINE\Software\ODBC\
ODBCINST.INI.

The ODBCINST.INI key is a good place to start looking at how ODBC fits into
the Registry. The ODBCINST.INI key has subkeys for each driver that is installed, as
well as subkeys for the ODBC core, ODBC drivers, and ODBC translators. The
ODBC core subkey contains the usage count for the ODBC core. The ODBC drivers
subkey contains a list of all the drivers installed on the local machine. The ODBC
translators subkey contains a list of all the codepage translation DLLs that are installed.

For each ODBC driver, there is a subkey that contains the critical information
about that driver, including the path and filename of the driver and its setup file. The
driver is the actual part that is used when accessing the database; the setup DLL is
what generates the screens shown in the ODBC administrator program. Each driver
may have specific settings that are stored in the subkey as well, such as timeout values
or other connection settings.

The ODBC.INI key links a data source with a driver and the settings used to make
the connection. In the case of a SQL Server data source, the database name, server
name, last user, and security type all fall into the data source. In addition, every data
source stores the data source name (DSN), the description of the DSN, and the driver
used by the DSN.

While ODBC provides a call-level interface to different databases, OLE-DB provides a more object-driven approach to database access. The official Microsoft answer
as to when to use which is that ODBC should be used for old stuff, but new stuff
should use OLE-DB.

Troubleshooting ODBC

To troubleshoot ODBC, first follow the guidelines for troubleshooting client connection problems (covered earlier in this chapter). Then try the following potential fixes:

1. Open the ODBC Data Source Administrator and select the About tab. Verify
   that the versions of the core components are all the same. Microsoft sometimes
   changes file contents without changing version numbers; if the version numbers

---

ODBC and Registry Editing: Don't Go There!

You should set up and configure ODBC drivers and data sources only through the ODBC administrator
program. These Registry entries are very complex and are touchy about being hand-modified. The official
Microsoft line is that "Unpredictable results" may occur if these entries are modified manually.

match but things still aren't working right, check the file sizes, dates, and times. If necessary, reinstall the core components by reinstalling MDAC (the Microsoft Data Access Components) from a common source.

2. Go to the Drivers tab in the ODBC Data Source Administrator. Ensure that the driver is installed for the database to which you're trying to connect.

3. Make sure that the data source is correctly built and the name is correct. Check the name first, and then go into the data source and make sure that the correct driver, database, and so on are chosen. For SQL Server, check to make sure that the correct authentication mode is selected. The network login ID method is for integrated security, and the SQL Server authentication method works for mixed security.

4. Use the SQL Server ODBC Connection Wizard's Test Data Source button (in the ODBC Microsoft SQL Server Setup dialog box) to verify database connectivity.

The key to making sure that ODBC is working is to make sure the client network is configured properly, to make sure the SQL Server client configuration is configured properly, and then to check the ODBC drivers.

Examining OLE-DB

OLE-DB is a long-awaited concept for many application developers because it gives them the ability to access a database the same way they access other objects, such as OLE Automation objects and ActiveX objects. OLE-DB provides access to databases by using the same programming models and calls used to access the Windows operating system services. While it is subject to many of the same version-conflict problems as ODBC, it does not require the user to set up data sources, making OLE-DB much easier to deploy. OLE-DB shifts the burden of knowing what kind of data source is being accessed from the driver to the calling program. When a program attempts to access a database through OLE-DB, it has to know the name of the server and the driver to use in order to establish the connection. For ODBC, this was all kept in the ODBC data source.

OLE-DB defines *information providers* and *information consumers*. A SQL Server database can be both a provider of information, sending out data to consumers, and a consumer of information, via replication or the Data Transformation Services. OLE-DB uses a driver model similar to that of ODBC. Certain drivers for OLE-DB are designed for SQL Server and Oracle, and drivers for VSAM and DB/2 on mainframes are forthcoming. This provides access to more data than ODBC because of the more generic interface provided by OLE-DB.

Although OLE-DB has specific drivers for given data providers, it is also able to access ODBC data sources. This provides a bridge between what is now available in the realm of OLE-DB (which is very limited) and the large variety of ODBC drivers.

ODBC has been around for several years now, so many drivers are available for different databases.

There really isn't anything to configure in OLE-DB. The applications that use OLE-DB are responsible for making sure the correct files exist. The only exception occurs when OLE-DB is used to access data via ODBC, in which case the ODBC data sources must be configured first.

Conclusions

One of the most overlooked parts of SQL Server configuration is the configuration of the network components. The server- and client-side components use an installable-driver model to handle which protocols they are going to use. On the client side, ODBC and OLE-DB use the same installable-driver model to provide a semblance of vendor-independent database access. Troubleshooting the client and the server starts at the bottom level: Make sure that a network connection exists and functions properly, and then move up the chain until you can isolate the problem and correct it.

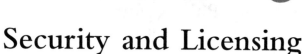

3

Security and Licensing

Denis Darveau

Companies install a Relational Database Management System (RDBMS) such as SQL Server 7.0 in order to store vital corporate information for day-to-day use by their personnel. For the same reason you secure the company premises, you need to protect your SQL Server database. This is sometimes referred to as *data security*.

The security architecture in SQL Server 7.0 addresses potential security problems. Along with security comes a related and somewhat unpopular topic: software licensing issues. Microsoft provides various licensing schemas to fit every company's needs. This chapter combines security and licensing issues in SQL Server 7.0, including the following topics:

- Security philosophy
- What to secure and why
- Cost justification
- The SQL Server 7 security model
- Implementing an effective security model
- Troubleshooting security problems
- Licensing issues

This chapter contains in-depth coverage of the security architecture, with extensive coverage of such security features as *authentication* (the authorized access to the system) and *permissions* (which allow access to the database).

These two basic parts form the essence of your data security. It is imperative that you, as a system administrator, thoroughly understand the Security Architecture of SQL Server 7.0 in order to ensure a maximum level of protection for the data that is your company's bread and butter.

Security Philosophy

In order for your company's RDBMS to be efficient, the following three principles must apply:

- **Accuracy.** The database must always be kept up-to-date, and the data must be modified only by the appropriate personnel (for example, a customer's address might be modified by Sales personnel only).

- **Consistency.** The objects in the database should go through a series of business integrity checks by using tools such as Triggers and DRI (Declarative Referential Integrity) constraints, and they should be accessed by the appropriate personnel (for example, employee salaries and bonuses should be accessed by Finance personnel only).

- **Availability.** The databases must be available at all times to prevent anyone from accidentally (or maliciously) dropping a table because the wrong rights were accidentally given.

A strong approach to security will contribute to a high level of accuracy and consistency and will help protect your databases from accidental or intrusive deletion. Depending on his or her past experience, a system administrator's views on security will fall somewhere between a lackadaisical attitude and an iron-fist approach. A good administrator will try to maintain a high level of security by following these principles:

- Keep the system physically secure to prevent accidental or intentional destruction.

- Allow only the proper personnel to access the server.

- Allow personnel to access only the database, object, or statement appropriate for their particular jobs.

- Regularly monitor access by using Windows NT auditing and Event Log features.

- Maintain a log of security incidents and look for trends.

What to Secure and Why

As a Database Administrator (DBA), one of your most important tasks is establishing and maintaining data security. Unfortunately, security in any company has always been considered an unwelcome necessity. Yes, the performance of your server is important, but it does not matter how well SQL Server performs if there is unauthorized access to the information or if the data is inaccurate or inconsistent. You must continuously keep up with security on your system because if you do not, hackers (in some cases, the competition) will.

Security on a server is separated into five hierarchical levels:

- *Level 1: Server Security.* Controls the physical access to the server. Most companies take pride in making sure that the server is in a secure physical environment (such as a locked room). This prevents anyone from logging on to the server directly and prevents theft of the server and its data. If someone with malicious intent has physical access to the hard-drive, both SQL Server and NT security are totally irrelevant.

- *Level 2: Operating System Security.* Controls the connectivity with the server, either locally or remotely on a network. For example, a legitimate user must be able to log on to the Windows NT network to access SQL Server. (This level is often called "authentication.")

- *Level 3: Application Security.* Controls the connectivity with the application by using a client-type software. In most cases, after the client has been granted access to the network, access to SQL Server is controlled through application security. (This is often considered part of authentication.)

- *Level 4: Database Security.* Allows SQL Server to control access to its databases. Even though a client is given access to SQL Server, access to the various databases is controlled via database security. (This is called "permissions.")

- *Level 5: Object Security.* Allows the administrator to provide a more granular and controlled access to the various components of a database such as tables, views, triggers, and stored procedures. (This is part of permissions.)

Figure 3.1 illustrates this hierarchy of security levels.

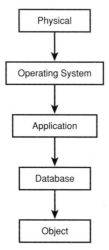

Figure 3.1   Security is separated into five basic hierarchical levels.

Although level 1 is important, this chapter concentrates on security levels 2 through 5.

Cost Justification

Again, security is the kind of thing no one likes to invest time in, but that must be given attention for the sake of the company. In the end, the company data is your bread and butter, and protecting that data is everyone's responsibility. Each user must protect the data he or she retrieves from the database. However, most of the responsibility falls on the system administrator's shoulders. The big questions are "How secure is secure?" and "How much time and effort should I invest as the system administrator?" Let me attempt to answer this question.

Keeping in mind the various security levels, you can see that relaxed physical security of the system might force you to replace a server. And it is obvious that the cost of replacing a server these days can become quite costly. Although replacing the server might not be as expensive for a small business as it is for a large enterprise, the cost is comparable considering that the expense is relative to the size of the budget. As I mentioned earlier, protecting data is the system administrator's most important task. I think a particular old saying truly applies to these circumstances: If you do not tighten up the security around your SQL Server, you might as well give out the "keys to the castle"!

But do you want to be somewhat conservative in your approach to security, or do you want to be zealous, maybe to the point of paranoia? Everyone has his own experiences and feelings about security, and obviously, in most cases the level of security needed is relative to the importance of the data being protected. Military information stolen from the government's computers can have more devastating effects on national security than a list of customers stolen from a small marketing firm. However, it is interesting to point out that the method used to protect the data is pretty much the same in both cases: firewalls, physical security of the servers, a secure operating system, and a secure application for authentication and user permissions.

You can create an account for each individual in the company, or each person can use a generic account. You can use roles to group users, or you can add all users to the same role. You can give all users full access to the tables or give selected users access to selected tables; or you might limit access with the use of views and stored procedures. You can even put triggers on *every* table just to audit who has done what (but that requires more CPU resources because of the overhead). How you establish your system security depends on the information you're protecting and on what the military affectionately calls establishing a "need-to-know" basis!

Bypassing the OS Security Level

It is possible for a client to access a database on a SQL Server without having first been validated by the operating system. In SQL Server 7, this is called "mixed mode" (as opposed to Windows NT "authentication mode" in Windows NT). An example of this occurs when SQL Server is installed on a Windows 95/98 system. You'll learn more about this later in the chapter in the section "The SQL Server 7.0 Security Model."

Whatever method you will use, adding security features to a SQL Server requires a great amount of effort on the administrator's part and can become quite expensive in terms of time and resources. You must determine whether the importance of the company data justifies the cost of the additional efforts needed to maintain a truly secure RDBMS such as SQL Server 7.

The SQL Server 7.0 Security Model

Usually, you must be authenticated on a system before you can access the data. In Windows NT, for example, just logging on to the server with your name and password does not give you permission to access the data on a SQL Server. In keeping with the five security levels described earlier, the SQL Server 7.0 security model can be divided into the following two areas:

- *Authentication,* which handles remote access to SQL Server (Security Levels 2 & 3).

- *Permissions,* which handles remote access to the various databases and the associated objects on SQL Server (Security Levels 4 & 5).

In the SQL Server 7.0 security model, authentication is validated by using *security modes*, and permissions are validated by using *security roles*.

Authentication Through Security Modes

The security mode encompasses the Operating System Security and Application Security levels and provides authentication validation. To authenticate a user accessing the server either locally or remotely, SQL Server 7.0 uses one of two methods: Windows NT Authentication or SQL Server Authentication. These two authentication methods (as opposed to three in previous versions) are referred to as security modes.

- *Windows NT authentication mode.* In this mode, SQL Server uses Windows NT authentication to let the user access SQL Server after the user has logged on to the server or the network. SQL Server assumes that the user has already been validated by the operating system, so no further check is performed.

- *Mixed mode.* In this mode, SQL Server uses either Windows NT authentication or SQL Server authentication. SQL Server first checks to see whether the user is using a SQL Server login account. If so, SQL Server authentication takes place, the password is verified, and the user is granted access to SQL Server. However, if the user is not authenticated with SQL Server authentication, a check is made by using Windows NT authentication to validate access to SQL Server.

It is important to remember that regardless of which security mode is used, any user accessing SQL Server must have an account on SQL Server. This account is called a *SQL Server login*. In Windows NT authentication, the NT user account is the SQL Server login; in SQL Server authentication, however, a specific SQL Server login must be created on SQL Server.

Permissions Through Security Roles

SQL Server 7.0 provides a new feature called security roles. The best way to explain roles is to say that security roles are to SQL Server what groups are to Windows NT. Microsoft realized that creating a single administrative account such as System Administrator (SA) was not granular enough. (You had to be an sa to perform any administrative task on the server. If you wanted to give one of your administrative assistants the right to dump and restore databases, you had to give him or her the SA account password.) By creating security roles such as db_backupoperator and allowing members of that role to back up and restore databases, the administrator can be more granular in assigning administrative tasks. Carrying on the analogy just offered, remember that groups contain Windows NT users; similarly, roles contain SQL Server logins.

SQL Server roles can be categorized into two types:

- *Server roles.* Used for administrative tasks on a SQL Server. They can contain NT users, NT groups, or SQL Server logins.

- *Database roles.* Used to assign database permissions. Database roles can contain NT users, NT groups, SQL Server logins, and other database roles.

Using SQL Server security modes for authentication and SQL Server security roles for permission provides a solid foundation onto which you can build an effective security model. The following section explains how you can achieve this task.

Implementing an Effective Security Model

Implementing an effective security model is obviously important for any administrator. You can implement an effective security model by following these steps:

1. Do some careful up-front planning.
2. Choose a security mode.
3. Configure security roles.
4. Assign statement and object permissions.

Planning

The importance of planning ahead can never be overemphasized. A contractor does not start building a house and then sit down and come up with a drawing. Careful planning goes into the details of the architect's drawing in which every room, window, and door is measured to the nearest tenth of an inch. Likewise, you must follow guidelines when planning your company security model:

1. You must first identify the authentication mode that best serves your administrative needs.

2. Having identified an authentication mode, you must add the necessary NT users to the SQL Server.

3. Next, you determine which users will be performing server administrative tasks, and you assign those users to the appropriate server roles.

4. Then, you must decide which users should have access to which databases, and you add those logins to the appropriate database roles.

5. Finally, grant the appropriate users or roles the proper rights to objects in the database.

The following sections provide a more detailed version of how to use the preceding steps to prepare a sound security model.

Choosing a Security Mode

Mixed mode is more flexible than NT authentication mode. Whereas NT authentication mode allows you to use only NT accounts, mixed mode gives you the flexibility of adding users who do not happen to have Windows NT accounts. In addition, if some system administrators do not have rights to create user accounts, they can overcome that problem by creating SQL Server logins. If your users already have Windows NT accounts, they should use those accounts. That saves you from having to create a SQL Server login for each and every user. This is even more important if the company has a large number of users.

Although mixed mode is usually the default mode chosen during installation and is used by most SQL Server administrators, NT authentication is by far the more secure mode of authentication.

The following procedure details how to set up NT authentication mode on SQL Server by using Enterprise Manager:

1. Expand a server group.

2. Right-click on the specific server.

3. From the context menu, select Properties.

4. In the Properties dialog box, select the Security tab (see Figure 3.2).

5. Under Authentication, select either SQL Server and Windows NT or Windows NT Only.

6. Click OK.

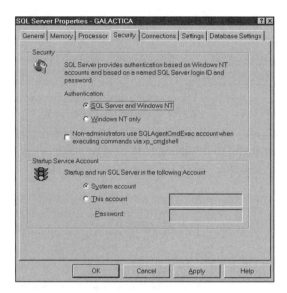

Figure 3.2 Use Enterprise Manager to set up authentication mode in SQL Server 7.0.

After you've chosen the appropriate authentication mode, any user accessing SQL Server must do so by using a SQL Server login or a linked server login. Let's take a closer look at these two types of logins and how they can be used.

SQL Server Logins

As mentioned earlier, you can grant a Windows NT user or group access to SQL Server, or you can add a SQL Server login.

A Windows NT user can be granted access to SQL Server either directly via the user account or through a Windows NT local or global group membership. Granting such access can be accomplished in two ways:

1. Using Enterprise Manager

2. Using Transact-SQL Statement

To use Enterprise Manager, perform the following steps:

1. Expand a server group and select a server.

2. Highlight Logins.

Windows95/98 Mixed Authentication Modes Only

Because Windows 95 and Windows 98 cannot authenticate Windows NT accounts, Windows NT authentication mode is not available when SQL Server 7.0 is installed on these operating systems. Only mixed mode is available.

3. From the drop-down menu, select Action, and then click New Login.

4. Select Windows NT Authentication (see Figure 3.3).

5. Enter the Windows NT account (user or group) to add.

6. Optionally, enter a default database and language.

To use Transact-SQL Statement, type the following command:

```
EXEC sp_grantlogin 'Galactica\JohnP'
```

You can replace `sp_grantlogin` with `sp_denylogin` to deny an NT user access to SQL Server, or you can replace it with `sp_revokelogin` to remove an NT user who has already been given login access.

If mixed security mode is used and the user does not have an NT user account, the administrator must create a SQL Server login. You can create a SQL Server login in two ways:

1. Using Enterprise Manager

2. Using Transact-SQL Statement

To use Enterprise Manager, perform the following steps:

1. Expand a server group and select a server.

2. Highlight Logins.

3. From the drop-down menu, select Action, and then click New Login. The screen shown in Figure 3.4 appears.

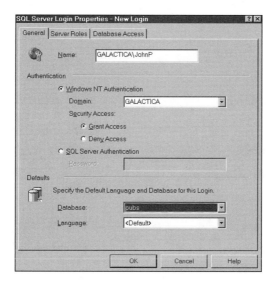

Figure 3.3   A Windows NT user account named JohnP from the domain called Galactica is granted access to SQL Server.

4. Enter a name for the SQL Server login.

5. Select SQL Server Authentication.

6. Enter a password.

7. Optionally, enter a default database and language.

8. Click OK. Then re-enter the password to confirm it.

To use Transact-SQL Statement, type the following command:

```
EXEC sp_addlogin 'MariaM'
```

To remove a SQL Server login, replace `sp_addlogin` with `sp_droplogin`.

Linked Server Logins

When SQL Servers need to communicate for either distributed processing or remote procedure calls, SQL Server uses a linked server login. This linking process is accomplished by mapping a SQL Server login on the current server to another login on the remote server.

It is important to note that if a user has been authenticated by using Windows NT authentication, SQL Server logins can be linked automatically by using security account delegation, whereby SQL Server uses Windows NT security credentials of the user sending the request to validate access to the linked server instead of mapping Server logins.

Figure 3.4 Add the SQL Server login MariaM for SQL Server authentication.

As you learned earlier in the chapter, Windows 95/98 SQL servers cannot make use of Windows NT authentication because they are not aware of NT Security account delegation. To that effect, a SQL Server login at a Windows 95/98 server will have to be mapped to a Windows NT account or SQL Server login on the remote server. For example, suppose you need to map the SQL Server login MariaM to the SQL Server login JoeB with no password on linked server Server98. You could accomplish this in two ways:

- Using Enterprise Manager
- Using Transact-SQL Statement

To perform the described task by using Enterprise Manager, follow these steps:

1. In a server group, expand a server.

2. Highlight Linked Servers.

3. Right-click the linked server (such as Server98) and click Properties.

4. Click on the Security tab and select the local user you want to add (MariaM).

5. If the local user is to connect to the linked server by using his or her security credentials, check Impersonate.

6. If the local user is to be mapped to a SQL Server login on the remote server (as it is in this case), do not check Impersonate. Instead, enter the remote user name (JoeB) and remote password (none in this case).

7. Click on the Apply button and close the window.

To perform the described task by using Transact-SQL Statement, enter the following command:

```
EXEC sp_addlinkedsrvlogin 'Server98', false, 'MariaM', 'JoeB', NULL
```

Configuring Security Roles

As was mentioned earlier, the SQL Server security model is based on authentication and permission. Authentication "modes" allow users to access SQL Server, and permission "roles" allow users to interact with the databases and their objects. There are two types of SQL Server roles: server roles and database roles. Configuring appropriate security roles for your users on SQL Server is paramount to data security. If a user other than the local administrator were given rights to the Sysadmin server role, that user could potentially do serious damage to the SQL Server. Likewise, a user given the db_owner database role could potentially damage any object in that database.

Authentication Using the Guest Account

When a Windows NT user has access to SQL Server but does not have access to a database by using his/her own account, access is allowed if a Guest user account has been created for that database. The Guest account is automatically added to each database upon creation, by default. It can be removed at any time except from the Master and Tempdb databases, in which it must exist at all times.

Server Roles

Server roles contain logins that enable users to access and administer SQL Server. Just as Windows NT has built-in local groups, SQL Server 7 has predefined server roles. New server roles cannot be created; only new database roles can be added.

Fixed Server Role	Is Permitted To...
sysadmin	Perform any activity in SQL Server.
serveradmin	Configure serverwide settings.
setupadmin	Install replication and manage extended procedures.
securityadmin	Manage server logins.
processadmin	Manage processes running on SQL Server.
dbcreator	Create and modify databases.
diskadmin	Manage disk files.

To add a user to a server role by using Enterprise Manager, perform the following steps:

1. Expand a server group and select a server.
2. Highlight Server Roles.
3. In the right pane, right-click a role (in this case Server Administrators) and select Properties.
4. In the Server Role Properties dialog box (see Figure 3.5), click on Add.
5. Select the login you want to add (in this case Galactica\JohnP). Click OK.

To add a user to a server role using Transact-SQL Statement, type the following command:

```
EXEC sp_addsrvrolemember 'Galactica\JohnP', 'serveradmin'
```

You can replace addsrvrolemember with sp_dropsrvrolemember to remove the member from the specified server role.

Database Roles

Database roles are created at the Database Security level for use by a specific database. SQL Server also has several predefined database security roles:

SYSADMIN Role

The rights of a member of the sysadmin role span all other server roles. In addition, any member of the Windows NT local Administrators group is automatically a member of the Sysadmin role.

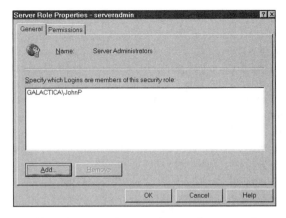

Figure 3.5   Adding the user Galactica\JohnP to the server role serveradmin.

Fixed Database Role	Is Permitted To...
db_owner	Perform any activity of all the other database roles and any database administrative tasks.
db_accessadmin	Add or remove any Windows NT accounts or SQL Server users from the database.
db_datareader	View data in any user table in the database.
db_datawriter	Add, change, or delete data from any user table in the database.
db_dlladmin	Add, modify, or drop any object in the database.
db_securityadmin	Manage SQL Server database roles, as well as statements and object permissions related to the database.
db_backupoperator	Back up the database.
db_denydatareader	Make schema changes to the database (but not see any data in the database).
db_denydatawriter	View the data in the database (but not change any data).

Membership in Several Roles

In SQL Server 6.x, a user could be a member of only one group in addition to Public. In SQL Server 7.0, a user can be a member of as many roles as necessary to perform his or her tasks on the server.

Tip on Database Security Role Membership

You can add any Windows NT user or group or SQL Server user or role to a SQL Server database role. However, keep in mind that only members known to the database can be added to the role. If a Windows NT user or group that is not a member of the database is added to a database role, SQL Server automatically adds the user or group to the database. A member of a database cannot be added to the role membership for another database. In addition, any member of a fixed database role can add other users to that particular role.

Again, as you can create new Windows NT groups, you can create new database roles. This is an excellent feature if a SQL Server System Administrator does not have any right to create or manage NT groups on the server or if the SA would like to create a more defined role for a select group of users and logins, For example, suppose a company department is involved in a new project "X" with a limited lifetime. The SA could create a new database role called ProjectX and add the names of all logins involved in the project.

When creating a new database role, you will be required to choose between a standard or application role. The standard role contains members; the application role has no membership but requires a password.

To create a new database role by using Enterprise Manager, perform the following steps:

1. In a server group, select a server.

2. Double-click Databases, and then double-click the specific database (in this case, Pubs).

3. Right-click Database Roles and select New Database Role. The screen shown in Figure 3.6 appears.

4. Select either Standard Role or Application Role (Standard Role in this case).

5. If you chose Standard Role, click on Add and select the logins you want to add (guest, in this case). Then click OK.

6. If you chose Application Role, enter a password in the Password text box.

7. Select OK to close the window.

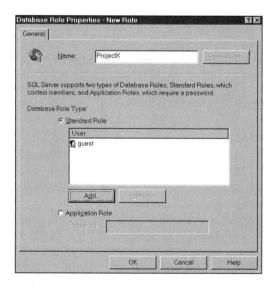

Figure 3.6   Create the new database role ProjectX and add the user guest to this role.

To create a new database role by using Transact-SQL Statement, type the following command:

```
EXEC sp_addrole 'ProjectX'
```

Note that you can replace `sp_addrole` with `sp_droprole` to remove a role from the database.

To add a member to an existing database role by using Enterprise Manager, follow these steps:

1. Expand a server group and select a server.

2. Expand Databases and expand a database.

3. In the right pane, right-click a role and select Properties.

4. Click on Add.

5. Select the login you want to add and click OK.

For example, to add the member DomainA\PeterM to the database role ProjectX by using Transact-SQL Statement. To do so, type the following command:

```
EXEC sp_addrolemember 'DomainA\PeterM', 'ProjectX'
```

As you might guess, you can replace `sp_addrolemember` with `sp_droprolemember` to delete a member of the specified database role.

The "public" role (called the Public group in previous versions of SQL) is added to every database upon creation. As in previous SQL versions, any user added to a database is automatically added to the public role.

Assigning Statement and Object Permissions

After you have determined which security mode to use on your SQL Server, identified security roles on both the server and the database, and created logins and assigned them to the appropriate server and database roles, you must start thinking about proper access permissions on the database objects and statements.

Granting Access to a Database

Before a user is granted access to objects or statements in a database, the user must be granted access to that database. Only SQL Server logins can be granted access to a database. If you remember, a SQL Server login can be a Windows NT user or a specifically created SQL Server login. You can, however, grant an entire Windows NT group access to a database, which would greatly simplify your work as an administrator.

Once again, you can grant a user access to a database by using either Enterprise Manager or Transact-SQL.

To use Enterprise Manager, perform the following tasks:

1. In a server group, select a server.

2. Double-click Databases and expand the selected database.

3. Right-click Database Users and select New Database User.

4. Select the appropriate login name or Windows NT group, and then type in a user name (optional). See Figure 3.7.

5. As you can see, the public role is already selected. Select any additional database role you want the user to be a member of. Then click OK.

To add Galactica\JoeB to the Pubs database using Transact-SQL Statement, execute the following statement:

```
EXEC sp_grantdbaccess 'Galactica\JoeB', 'Pubs'
```

You can replace sp_grantdbaccess with sp_revokedbaccess to deny a user access to the specified database.

Database Owner (DBO) and Guest

When a new database is created, two users are automatically created: Database Owner (DBO) and Guest. You already know that if a Guest account has been created on the database, a user who has logon access to SQL Server but has no account in the database will be given the rights equivalent to the Guest account. When the DBO account is created, all members of the Sysadmin server role are automatically mapped to that account.

Figure 3.7   Adding the user Galactica\JoeB to the Pubs database. By default, when you add a user to a database, the public database role is selected.

Restriction

Only members of the db_access and db_owner roles can grant users access to a database.

Some things to keep in mind about these two accounts:

■ The Guest account can be removed at any time from any database except the Master and Tempdb databases. The DBO cannot be removed from any database.

■ Any object created by a member of the sysadmin fixed server role is automatically owned by DBO.

■ Only members of the sysadmin fixed server role and the db_owner fixed database role can change the owner of a database. To make that change, you would use the following Transact-SQL command:

```
EXEC sp_changedbowner 'JohnP'
```

Creating databases and objects is covered in Chapter 4, "Storage Management."

Database Object Owner (DBOO)

Objects in a database include the following:

■ Tables

■ Indexes

■ Views

■ Triggers

■ Stored procedures

The DBO of a database or a sysadmin can grant a user permission to create an object. A user who creates an object becomes the owner—the *Database Object Owner* (DBOO). There is no specific account for this, but the creator has all rights over the object. However, before anyone else can access the object, the owner must grant users permission to use the object.

You can grant five types of object permissions on a database object. SELECT, UPDATE, INSERT, and DELETE statements can be used on tables, views, and stored procedures; the EXECUTE statement applies to stored procedures only. Specific definitions follow:

■ **UPDATE.** Allows the user to modify the contents of an object.

■ **INSERT.** Allows the user to add rows to an object.

■ **SELECT.** Allows the user to select rows and columns in an object.

■ **DELETE.** Allows the user to delete rows from an object.

■ **EXECUTE.** Allows the user to execute a specific stored procedure.

For example, to grant JoeB permission to SELECT on a table called Authors, the database owner can use either Enterprise Manager or Transact-SQL statement.

To use Enterprise Manager, follow these steps:

1. In a server group, select a server.

2. Double-click Databases and expand the selected database. In this case, Pubs.

3. Double-click Tables, right-click Authors in the right panel, and select Properties.

4. Click on Permissions to see the screen shown in Figure 3.8.

5. In the row corresponding to JoeB, check the appropriate statement column. Then click OK.

To use Transact-SQL Statement, type the following command:
```
GRANT SELECT
ON Authors
TO JoeB
GO
```

Both REVOKE and DENY statements deny a user access to the specified object.

Permission Conflicts (GRANT, DENY, REVOKE)

When a user is given access to an object in a database, the assigned access permission can be GRANT, DENY, or REVOKE.

DENY permission overrides every other type of permission, regardless of the level.

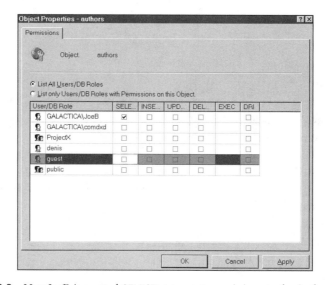

Figure 3.8 User JoeB is granted SELECT statement permissions to the Authors table.

Using the Full Path to Access an Object

When accessing an object using Transact-SQL, you need to remember that all users other than the owner must specify the name of the owner in the path. For instance, let's say that in the previous example, JoeB created the table called Authors. JohnP must specify JoeB.Authors to access the table. However, JoeB does not need to specify the owner. This is because SQL Server will first look for the object in the database owned by the current user and will then look in that owned by the DBO. If SQL Server does not find the object, it generates an error message.

For example, if JohnP is a member of the Marketing role and Marketing has DENY access to the Authors table, JohnP will be denied access to Authors even if he was explicitly granted access to that table individually (as in the earlier exercise).

REVOKE permission applies only to the level at which it is revoked. In the previous example, if Marketing has REVOKE access to Authors, JohnP will still be able to access the table by virtue of having been explicitly granted access to it. The reverse is true as well: If JohnP has REVOKE access but Marketing has GRANT, JohnP will still be able to access the table because he is a member of Marketing.

GRANT permission removes DENY or REVOKE at the current level. If the user has DENY at another level, however, that user will still be unable to access the object. If the user has REVOKE at another level, that user will be able to access the object by virtue of being granted access to the object regardless of the level.

A good rule of thumb is that if you really want to deny a user access to an object, explicitly DENY the user (or the group if necessary). REVOKE user access to an object may be necessary but is a little risky, especially if you are using groups and roles for object access.

Complexity of Ownership Chains

Views can be used as a very effective security mechanism. It may be necessary to prevent an employee from accessing all the columns in a table. For that purpose, the administrator could create a view that would retrieve only certain columns in a table and grant permission to the employee for the particular view. For example, JoeB could create a view called View1 for Table1 and grant PeterK access to the view. To do so, he would use the following commands:

```
USE dbase1
GO
CREATE VIEW View1 AS SELECT fname, lname FROM Table1
GO
GRANT SELECT ON View1 TO PeterK
```

Enabling Other Accounts to Grant Rights

Only object owners are allowed to GRANT rights on an object. However, it is possible for a DBOO to give someone else the ability to GRANT by specifying the WITH GRANT OPTION in the statement. You need to keep two things in mind regarding this issue:

1. It is important that you be extremely careful when using the WITH GRANT OPTION statement because you do not have any control over which accounts will be granted that permission (for example, GRANT ALL ON authors TO JoeB WITH GRANT OPTION).

2. When revoking that GRANT right from someone, you should always use the CASCADE option to revoke the permission from all other accounts that may have been granted the right (for example, REVOKE GRANT OPTION FOR ALL ON authors TO JoeB CASCADE).

In this example, common sense dictates that PeterK should not have SELECT right on Table1; otherwise, the VIEW permission is meaningless.

Stored procedures can also provide an effective security mechanism on a database. Stored procedures can control access and update databases by executing a series of statements in a logical order. This would save the administrator from dealing with complex table and view permissions, and would enable the administrator to prevent a user from accidentally modifying a table or accessing data erroneously. It is viewed as a highly restrictive security mechanism but one that is extremely effective.

As in the case of the views, common sense dictates that the user should not have access to Table1 directly; otherwise, the stored procedure permission is meaningless.

Views can be created from a table or another view; stored procedures can be created from views, tables, or other stored procedures. These types of dependencies make up the *ownership chain*. The view View1 in the previous example is dependent on the table Table1. If a stored procedure Procedure1 was created from View1, the procedure would be dependent on the view and the table.

Things get more complicated when you add permissions to all this:

- **Scenario 1.** In the previous example, JoeB owns Table1 and View1. JoeB grants permission to PeterK on View1. When PeterK tries to access View1, SQL Server checks only for PeterK permission on View1 because JoeB owns both the table and the view.

- **Scenario 2.** Let's say a new table Table2 is created (owned) by JohnP. JoeB creates a stored procedure Procedure1 using Table1 and Table2 and grants EXECUTE permission to PeterK. Because the procedure is created from two tables owned by two different owners, the ownership chain is *broken*. Thus, when PeterK tries to execute Procedure1, SQL Server checks permission on both Procedure1 and Table2 for access by PeterK.

When an ownership chain is said to be broken, SQL Server checks every broken link in the chain for access permission by the user executing the statement or query. If, for example, in Scenario 1, JohnP had created View1, the chain would have been broken because JoeB owns Table1 and JohnP owns View1. When PeterK would attempt to access View1, SQL Server would check for permissions on both the view and the table.

Although views and stored procedures are great security mechanisms, they can be an administrative burden when it comes to granting access to them. A good rule of thumb for a system administrator is to restrict object creation to only a minimum number of select people. Keep your DBOs to a minimum, and your life will be much happier (yes, there is such a thing as a happy system administrator).

Application Security

Before you conclude this section, you should know about a new security feature of SQL Server 7.0. Application roles are used less frequently than the other two roles, but nonetheless they can be extremely useful for programmers and system administrators. Let's say, for example, that a Human Resources employee requires SELECT, UPDATE, and INSERT permission to the Employee table using a particular application such as Access, but you do not want that employee to have access to the table via SQL Query Analyzer. An application role can be created in that database to allow the employee to access the table via only one specific application. As you can see, this can be a very useful tool for database administrators.

In the following scenario, user JohnP requires access to the Authors table in the Pubs database via MS Access. However, you do not want John to be able to access the table by using SQL Server Query Analyzer. You could use the following steps to establish an appropriate application role:

1. Create a user database role in Pubs that will deny SELECT, INSERT, and UPDATE permissions for the Authors table and add JohnP to the membership of this role.

2. Create an application role in the Pubs database and give it SELECT, INSERT, and UPDATE permissions on the Authors table.

When the application runs, it sets the application role by running the stored procedure sp_setapprole with the appropriate password. When JohnP accesses the table by using the application, everything is correct. But if JohnP attempts to access the table by using any other program, he will be denied.

Encryption

It is difficult to talk about security without talking about data encryption capabilities. Encryption is a method of protecting sensitive data by modifying it in an unreadable form. The following three rules apply to encryption in SQL Server 7.0:

- Logins and passwords stored in the SQL Server system tables are always encrypted. This prevents any user and even administrators from viewing the passwords.

- Network packets sent between the client and the server can be encrypted by configuring the client to use SQL Server Multiprotocol Net-Library. You can establish such a configuration by choosing Start, Settings, Control Panel and clicking the SQL Server Client Configuration icon.

- Stored procedures, views, and triggers have definitions stored in the *syscomments* system table. These can be encrypted to protect their definitions from being viewed. To do so, you would include the WITH ENCRYPTION option in the statement when creating the object.

Remember that a sound security model is based on authentication and permissions. In SQL Server, authentication is based on two modes (SQL Server authentication and Windows NT authentication), and permissions are based on two types of roles (server and database roles). If you follow these simple steps, everything should go well:

1. Configure the authentication mode you prefer.

2. Authorize the various user accounts to the SQL Server.

3. Authorize the various SQL server users to the appropriate databases.

4. Assign the users to the appropriate server role (such as sysadmin).

5. Assign the users to the appropriate database roles (such as DBO).

6. Create views and stored procedures, and then grant users access to the appropriate views and stored procedures.

Troubleshooting Security Problems

Troubleshooting an application such as SQL Server 7.0 can be a tedious task. You must approach it in the same methodical way you would if you were troubleshooting hardware or any other software. If you are careful, you will notice that most security-related problems are quite easy to solve.

Unfortunately, the messages returned by the application or the operating system are not always clear. And you will rarely see a suggested solution attached to the error message. Keep in mind, however, that SQL Server security messages are related to either authentication or permission.

If a user is denied access, the thinking process should be simple:

1. As mentioned earlier, SQL Server will first authenticate the user, depending on the authentication mode. If the user cannot connect to the server, he or she did not pass the authentication process. The user should be able to connect with \\server\IPC$ even before a connection can be made to SQL, but the user must have basic NT network access rights. To verify that the user has the proper access rights, use the command NET VIEW \\server. If this command returns the error message 5 Access Denied, the user isn't a valid NT user, and this should be fixed before looking at SQL permissions.

2. If the user is properly authenticated, SQL Server checks to see whether the SQL login used is in the applicable database and what rights, if any, were given to that login.

Because most people are visually inclined, Enterprise Manager is often the easiest way to troubleshoot security. You can also use Microsoft SQL Query Analyzer, one of the tools in Enterprise Manager.

The following are two stored procedures that can help: sp_helplogins and sp_helpuser.

sp_helplogins lists all the SQL logins on the connected server.

- **Command:**

      EXEC sp_helplogins

  Sample result:

LoginName	SID	DefDBName	DefLangName	AUser	ARemote
DomainA\JohnP	0x0105000..	Northwind	us_english	yes	no

```
DomainA\JoeB      0x0105000.. Northwind      us_english  yes  no
sa                0x01        master         us_english  yes  no
(3 row(s) affected)
LoginName         DBName      UserName          UserOrAlias
DomainA\JohnP     master      JohnP             User
DomainA\JohnP     model       JohnP             User
DomainA\JohnP     msdb        JohnP             User
DomainA\JohnP     Northwind   JohnP             User
DomainA\JohnP     pubs        db_accessadmin    MemberOf
DomainA\JohnP     pubs        db_backupoperator MemberOf
DomainA\JohnP     tempdb      JohnP             User
DomainA\JoeB      Northwind   JoeB              User
DomainA\JoeB      pubs        JoeB              User
sa                master      db_owner          MemberOf
sa                master      dbo               User
sa                model       db_owner          MemberOf
 .
 .
 .
(15 row(s) affected)
```

sp_helpuser lists the SQL Server users and Windows NT users in the specified database.

■ **Command:**

```
EXEC sp_helpuser
```

Sample result:

```
UserName         GroupName    LoginName       DefDBName UserID SUserID
-----------      ---------    ----------      --------  ------ -------
dbo              db_owner     sa              master    1      1
JoeB             public       DomainA\JoeB    pubs      6      7
DomainA\JohnP    db_owner     DomainA\JohnP   Northwind 5      6
DomainA\JohnP    db_ddladmin  DomainA\JohnP   Northwind 5      6
DomainA\JohnP    db_datareader DomainA\JohnP  Northwind 5      6
DomainA\JohnP    db_datawriter DomainA\JohnP  Northwind 5      6
guest            public       NULL            NULL      2      NULL
INFORMATION_SCHEMA  public    NULL            NULL      3      NULL
(8 row(s) affected)
```

In addition to logins and users memberships, you can find out more about roles and roles membership by using these two commands: sp_helprole and sp_helprolemember.

sp_helprole lists database roles for the selected database.

■ **Command:**

```
EXEC sp_helprole
```

Sample result:

```
RoleName                 RoleId IsAppRole
---------------------    ------ ---------
public                   0      0
db_owner                 16384  0
db_accessadmin           16385  0
db_securityadmin         16386  0
db_ddladmin              16387  0
db_backupoperator        16389  0
db_datareader            16390  0
db_datawriter            16391  0
db_denydatareader        16392  0
db_denydatawriter        16393  0
(10 row(s) affected)
```

sp_helprolemember lists role membership for each role in the specified database.

■ **Command:**

```
EXEC sp_helprolemember
```

Sample result:

```
DbRole                   MemberName          MemberSID
db_accessadmin           DomainA\JohnP       0x01050000000…
db_backupoperator        DomainA\JohnP       0x01050000000…
db_datareader            DomainA\JohnP       0x01050000000…
db_datawriter            DomainA\JohnP       0x01050000000…
db_ddladmin              DomainA\JohnP       0x01050000000…
db_owner                 dbo                 0x01
db_owner                 DomainA\JohnP       0x01050000000…
db_securityadmin         DomainA\JohnP       0x01050000000…
(8 row(s) affected)
```

Three additional role commands will complement the two preceding commands:

■ sp_helpdbfixedrole. Lists fixed database roles and their descriptions.

■ sp_helpsrvrole. Lists the server roles and their descriptions.

■ sp_helpsrvrolemember. Lists the membership of fixed server roles.

Diagnosing Object Permission Problems

The stored procedure sp_helpprotect returns information about user permissions for an object in the current database.

■ **Command:**

```
EXEC sp_helpprotect 'titles'
```

Sample result:

Owner	Object	Grantee	Grantor	ProtectType	Action	Column
dbo	titles	guest	dbo	Grant	Delete	.
dbo	titles	guest	dbo	Grant	Insert	.
dbo	titles	guest	dbo	Grant	References	(All+New)
dbo	titles	guest	dbo	Grant	Select	(All+New)
dbo	titles	guest	dbo	Grant	Update	(All+New)

(5 row(s) affected)

Diagnosing Statement Permission Problems

sp_helpprotect returns information about user permissions for statement permissions in the current database.

- **Command:**
  ```
  EXEC sp_helprotect NULL, NULL, NULL, 's'
  ```

Sample result:

Owner	Object	Grantee	Grantor	ProtectType	Action		Column
.	.	guest	dbo	Grant	Create	Default	
.	.	guest	dbo	Grant	Create	Procedure	.
.	.	guest	dbo	Grant	Create	Rule	.
.	.	guest	dbo	Grant	Create	Table	
.	.	guest	dbo	Grant	Create	View	.
.	.	public	dbo	Grant	Create	Procedure	.

Examining the System Tables

Another method for troubleshooting security accounts in SQL Server 7.0 is through the System tables. This is usually done by using SQL Server Query Analyzer with the SELECT statement. The following system tables are related to security:

- **sysmembers**: Lists the accounts that are members of each database role in the specific database.

- **syspermissions**: Lists the permissions associated with each user, group, or role in the specific database.

- **sysprotects**: Lists the permissions that have been applied to each security account in the specific database.

- **sysservers**: Lists all the servers registered in the current SQL Server list (only in the Master database).

- sysusers: Lists all Microsoft Windows NT users, Windows NT groups, Microsoft SQL Server users, and SQL Server roles associated with the specific database.

- sysobjects: Lists all objects created in the selected database.

- syslogins: Lists all SQL Server logins in the system (only in the Master database).

- sysoledbusers: Lists users and password mapping for the specific linked server (only in the Master database).

- sysremotelogins: Lists all remote users allowed to call remote stored procedures (only in the Master database).

Thorough familiarity with these tables will enhance your ability to troubleshoot security problems in SQL Server 7.0. Here is an example to illustrate the procedure you should follow to troubleshoot a security account problem.

Suppose you want to find out whether JoeB is able to use the SELECT statement in the Authors table of the Pubs database. You would use a procedure similar to the following:

1. First, you confirm that JoeB is on the list of SQL server users with this command:

   ```
   USE Master
   SELECT * FROM syslogins
   ```

2. If the name exists, type the following command to make sure JoeB is listed in the Pubs database.

   ```
   USE Pubs
   SELECT * FROM sysusers
   ```

   If JoeB is listed in the database, find the corresponding UID number in the first column:

   ```
   uid     status name
   0       0      public ...
   7       14     JoeB
   ```

3. Then, with the following command, look for the UID number 7 in the second column of the sysprotects table of Pubs:

   ```
   USE Pubs
   SELECT * FROM sysprotects
   id          uid     action protecttype columns
   117575457   7       193    205         0x01
   ```

The result indicates that UID 7 was GRANTed (205) SELECT (193) permission on all columns (0x01) in table 117575457 (Authors). This last number can be found by running the following query:

```
USE Pubs
SELECT * FROM sysobjects

name                              id
authors                           117575457
```

Numerous additional system tables can help a system administrator troubleshoot security in SQL Server 7.0. Many of them are discussed elsewhere in this book. It is obvious that SQL Server Enterprise Manager has a much friendlier interface, but that is not always available to the local administrator, in which case the Query Analyzer or the command prompt might be the only tool available.

Licensing Issues

Licensing fits well in a chapter on security. While a user must have the correct permissions to access the resources on a server, the appropriate licenses must be in place for users to *legally* access the server. This section covers not only the basics of SQL Server Licensing, but some commonly misunderstood licensing concepts. This section does *not* mention software prices, however, because Microsoft's pricing programs tend to be more volatile than their licensing. For the most up-to-date information on licensing and pricing, you can check out Microsoft's Web site at `http://www.microsoft.com/enterprise/licensing`.

Licensing Basics

You need to be familiar with a couple of fundamental concepts before you get into a full discussion of SQL Server licensing issues. The next few sections introduce you to the basics of BackOffice licensing and the differences between the per-server and per-seat licensing modes. If you are already familiar with BackOffice licensing, you may want to skip to the next major section, "Common Licensing Misconceptions."

BackOffice Licensing

Microsoft's licensing architecture for the BackOffice product line is designed to be quite flexible, ensuring that you purchase only the licenses you need. It's also fairly simple to understand. You need to know about two types of licenses:

- **Server license.** A server license authorizes you to install a BackOffice product on a *single machine*. That is, if you plan to build three NT Servers, you will need three NT Server licenses—one for each server. If you plan to install SQL Server on two of those machines, you will need two SQL Server server licenses—one for each of those machines.
- **Client Access License (CAL).** A CAL authorizes a single-client workstation to use the services provided by a particular BackOffice product. That is, if a client uses services provided by NT, SQL Server, and Exchange on one server, that client will need a separate CAL for each product to legally use all three of the services provided by that server.

As with most licensing architectures, you will need to upgrade licenses when you upgrade a product. For instance, if you upgrade an existing SQL Server from version 6.5 to 7.0, you will also need to upgrade your SQL Server server license and the SQL Server CALs. Now that you've been introduced to the two types of licenses, take a look at the two licensing modes you can use when installing a BackOffice product.

Per-Seat Versus Per-Server Licensing

Microsoft lets you choose a client licensing scheme that best fits your business needs. You can choose between two types of configurations: per-seat and per-server. See Figure 3.9 for an example of each.

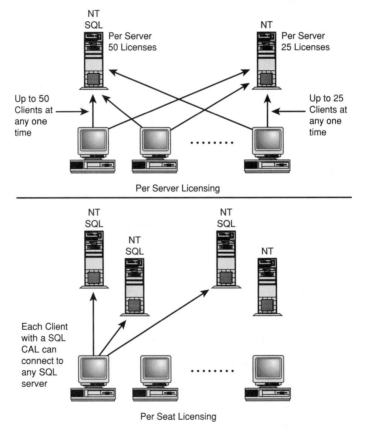

Figure 3.9 This diagram illustrates the difference between per-seat and per-server client licensing.

In per-server mode, a client access license is associated with a particular server. That is, at any one time, only a limited number of clients may be connected to the server. For example, if a SQL Server is licensed in per-server mode for 25 concurrent licenses, only 25 client workstations can use SQL Server on that machine at any given point in time. Per-server licensing is not available for all BackOffice products, only for NT, SQL Server, Site Server, and SNA Server. If you set up NT or a BackOffice application in per-server mode, you can switch to per-seat mode once.

In per-seat mode, a client access license is associated with a particular client. That client can use the services of any product for which it holds a CAL on any server in the organization. For instance, if a client workstation holds a SQL Server CAL, it can legally access any SQL Server in the organization. (Of course, the client must also have the appropriate SQL Server permissions to access the server, but the rest of this chapter deals with those issues.) If you set up NT or a BackOffice application in per-seat mode, you cannot switch to per-server mode without reinstalling the application.

Licensing clients in per-server mode is useful when you have a server intended for limited access or preproduction work, or if you have only one server providing a particular type of resource. On the other hand, if you have many servers in your organization and clients typically use multiple servers in a day (especially multiple servers providing the same services), per-seat licensing is often more economical.

Common Licensing Misconceptions

Now that you know about licensing in general, you're ready to learn about some common "gotchas" you may run into when considering SQL Server licensing.

NT Versus SQL Server Licensing

As was mentioned in the discussion of Client Access Licenses, you need a separate product CAL for each product a client uses on a server. This means that for an NT server that hosts only a SQL Server, clients connecting to that server may or may not need both an NT CAL and a SQL Server CAL. According to Microsoft, the only time a client needs an NT CAL is when the client is using one or more of the following services of the NT machine:

- File Sharing
- Print Sharing
- Remote Access Service
- Macintosh Services

In the past, we have seen administrators who felt they needed both NT and SQL Server CALs for clients connecting to a dedicated SQL Server machine. This is not the case.

Internet and Intranet Licensing

If you plan to publish any data from a SQL Server on the Internet, you will need to purchase an additional license called a "SQL Server Internet Connector." Basically, this is a software license that allows an unlimited number of Internet users to access data on a SQL Server. You will need one of these Internet Connectors for each server running SQL Server that provides data to Internet users.

If your SQL Server provides information to your organization through a browser-based *intra*net application, you will need a SQL Server CAL for each workstation that accesses the SQL Server.

Even though both Internet and intranet users access the SQL Server through a Web server, note the different licensing requirements, as shown in Figure 3.10.

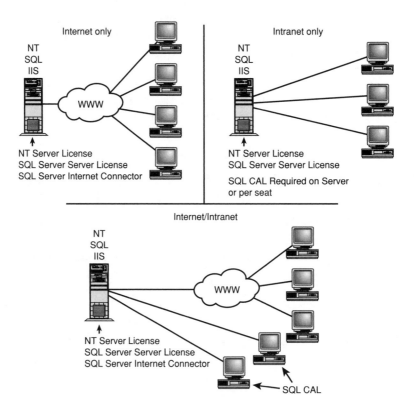

Figure 3.10   Here are some examples of SQL Servers providing data to Internet and intranet users; the diagram shows the required SQL Server licenses for each scenario.

Connections Versus Licenses

Another aspect of SQL Server licensing that is occasionally confusing for some administrators is the number of connections allowed per license. Some administrators become concerned because they think they need 200 CALs if their SQL Server was configured for a maximum of 200 connections. Thankfully, this is not the case; you need only one SQL Server CAL per *unique workstation* that accesses the SQL Server. Each workstation can use as many connections as it needs.

This rule applies even if client workstations are not directly connected to the SQL Server. For instance, if each SQL Server client connects to a transaction monitor or middleware layer, which then manages SQL Server connections, you still need a separate SQL Server CAL for each workstation.

Conclusions

SQL Server 7.0 offers numerous new features that enhance its security architecture. While the authentication model has been simplified to only two modes (Windows NT and mixed), the permission model has been enhanced to include roles, which will allow an administrator to be more efficient. These roles can be specific to the server so the administrator can assign various administrative tasks, or they can be specific to a database, enabling the SA to assign object permissions in a more granular fashion.

With security features come security concerns. An example of this is the use of the extended procedure xp_cmdshell, which is a well-known security hole that will be explained in greater detail in Chapter 5.

As you have learned, security requires a lot of work, and administrators are sometimes tempted to use shortcuts to simplify their consistently heavy schedule. There are many places where shortcuts are acceptable in a business; however, security should not be one of them. Just remember that you are the "guardian of the castle."

II

Day-to-Day Maintenance

4

Storage Management

Chris Miller

SQL SERVER IS ALL ABOUT STORING data. This chapter covers how SQL Server stores and keeps track of data. It is important for an administrator to understand how data is stored. It provides the foundation for understanding how SQL Server works, which is necessary for any type of performance-tuning operations. This chapter provides a lot of the terminology used in error messages; understanding the terminology helps you understand the error messages.

The chapter is structured in a bottom-up fashion. The basic element of SQL Server is the page, so it is covered first. Pages reside in extents, and the structure of extents is important because space is allocated in extents. So when more space is needed, SQL Server grabs an extent and divides it into pages. Extents have to be stored on disk somewhere, and SQL Server 7 introduces the concept of files and file groups, replacing the earlier UNIX-based model of devices.

After the discussion of how things fit together, you'll learn about performance tuning, which in this case includes a discussion of how to place data on disk drives and disk arrays to maximize throughput.

Here's a brief outline of the structure of this chapter:

- Storage Structures
  - Internal Structures (Pages, Extents, Tables, and Indexes)
  - External Structures (Files and File Groups)

■ Optimizing Storage
  • Multiple-Drive Systems
  • Single-Drive Systems

Internal Structures

To examine how SQL Server stores data, it's necessary to start at the bottom and work toward the top. In prior versions of SQL Server, the elementary element of storage was the *page*, which was defined as a 2KB block of disk storage. In SQL Server 7.0, the page is an 8KB block of disk storage. Pages, in turn, make up *extents*, which are eight pages, or 64KB. Extents are placed into *files*, which are sized by the administrator and can be up to 32TB (that's terabytes, or "REALLY BIG"). Files can then be placed in *file groups*, which can contain up to 32 files per database, for a maximum database size of 1,048,516TB.

Knowing that, take a detailed look at the different types of pages and how they all fit together into extents, followed by an examination of how extents fit into files and files fit into file groups.

A Quick Lesson in SQL Server Datatypes

SQL Server can store data in several different ways, depending on the type of data. There are three main types of data storage: character, numeric, and text/image. Data can be stored differently depending on what datatype it is, so understanding datatypes is critical to understanding how data is stored.

Character datatypes are strings of one or more characters—up to 4,000 or 8,000 characters, depending on the type of character data being stored. There are two types of character data. *Unicode data* uses two bytes to store each character and can store all international characters and symbols. Normal, or *ASCII data*, uses one byte for each character. Unicode strings can store a wider variety of symbols (64,000 different symbols, to be exact) but can be only 4,000 characters long. ASCII data can be 8,000 characters long but can store only 256 different characters.

Numeric datatypes encompass many different shapes and sizes, from the bit type (which can store only a one or a zero) to real and float types (which store 7 or 15 digits of precision with wide ranges).

Text and image datatypes are used to store large objects, ranging in size from zero bytes to 2GB. Usually, these are used to store binary objects, such as graphics. Text and image datatypes are always treated differently from character or numeric types because they aren't stored with the rest of the table. Instead, text and image data is stored out in the rest of the database, and the row actually contains just a pointer to the first page of the text or image data. Because of this, many database commands are specified to not work with text and image data.

Pages and Extents

A page is the fundamental element of SQL Server storage. Most data pages store rows of data, or records. All the storage in SQL Server is broken into 8KB pages. Each page contains a 96-byte header, and 8,096 bytes of data space. In addition, the maximum size for a row in SQL Server is 8,096 bytes. Coincidence? No. A row cannot be larger than one page, not counting any text or image data.

Because SQL Server uses pages to store everything, the type of page varies depending on what type of data—system data, user data, or index data—is being stored. SQL Server uses seven types of pages:

- *Data pages.* Store rows of data. This will be the most common type of page in any database. Rows are stored on the page, and an offset to the beginning of each row is stored at the end of the page. As rows are written to a page, the offset of the row is written at the end of the page.

- *Index pages.* Store the structures involved in indexing.

- *Log pages.* Store log information. These will be found only in log devices. These pages track all the changes to other data pages.

- *Text/image pages.* Store text and image data.

- *Global Allocation Map pages.* Keep track of which pages are in use, so that when data needs to be stored, an unused page can be tracked down quickly.

- *Page Free Space pages.* Track which parts of pages are in use.

- *Index Allocation Map pages.* Map which extents are used and by which tables or indexes.

The first four types of pages are fairly self-explanatory; the rest will be covered in sections later in this chapter.

While the page is the fundamental element of data storage for databases, the extent is the fundamental element of space allocation for databases. When SQL Server doesn't have any available pages that it wants to write data on but it needs to write more data, it allocates an extent for usage by finding an extent that isn't in use and creating links to it. Extents are 64KB, which is enough space to hold eight pages.

Before SQL Server 7 came along, an extent was dedicated to an object. An extent also consisted of eight 2KB pages, or 16KB. Because the size of a page has quadrupled, the size of an extent has also quadrupled, going up to 64KB. For small databases or large databases with lots of small objects, it makes sense to have an extent hold data from multiple objects. SQL Server 7 implements this feature. SQL Server 7 provides two types of extents:

- Uniform extents hold data from one object only

- Mixed extents hold data from as many as eight objects

A page is still dedicated to an object, but an extent is not.

Extents have no internal overhead. Remember that a page has a 96-byte header used to store information about what's on the page and where the page fits in the database. Extents have no such data inside themselves; instead they rely on the Global Allocation Map pages to hold the meta-data.

So how does all this fit together? Examine how SQL Server manages storage allocation.

Storage Allocation

Now that all the pieces are in place, how do they fit together? As you learned, there are seven types of pages. The question of how these types work together to make a complete database is answered by the SQL Server storage allocation strategy.

SQL Server tracks which extents are used via a type of page called a Global Allocation Map, or GAM. A Global Allocation Map is a bitmask of the allocated extents in the database. A bitmask means that the entire page is divided into bits; if the bit is on, the extent is used, and if the bit is off, the extent is not used. Each GAM page can track about 64,000 extents (8,096 bytes at 8 bits per byte is 64,768 bits), or 4GB of data space. The first page in a database, page 0, is a GAM. When the entire GAM is used, another GAM is allocated 64,000 pages later.

In addition to the GAM, to optimize the use of space, SQL Server uses a Secondary GAM, or SGAM, page to track how an extent is used. Because an extent can be used by different objects, SQL Server has to keep track of which extents are being used by multiple objects and whether or not any space is available on those extents. By combining the GAM and the SGAM, three values are possible (see Table 4.1).

A zero on a GAM means that the extent is not allocated. When SQL Server needs to find a new extent, it searches for a GAM of zero, sets it to one, and uses the extent. When SQL Server needs a mixed extent with some free pages, it searches for a 1 bit in the SGAM. When SQL Server needs to allocate a mixed extent, it finds an unallocated extent in the GAM, sets the bit to 1, and then sets the corresponding bit in the SGAM to 1. Extents that can be used have a GAM bit of 0. So if a database has less than an even multiple of 4GB, the GAM bits for all the extents that don't exist are set to 1 as well. For example, the last 25% of a GAM page for a 3GB database is set to all 1s.

When searching for new space, SQL Server uses a complex algorithm to determine where that free space is. To increase efficiency, SQL Server spreads data throughout the space allocated. Devices are never filled in from the beginning to the end; instead, they are populated in a semi-random pattern to speed access.

Table 4.1 **GAM and SGAM Values**

Value	GAM	SGAM
Unallocated extent	0	0
Uniform extent, or full mixed extent	1	0
Mixed extent with available space	1	1

To find space within a page, SQL Server uses the Page Free Space page type. A Page Free Space page has a byte allotted for each page and can track 8,000 pages. The byte contains a value representing the amount of data on the page, given these choices:

- Empty
- Up to 25 percent full
- Up to 50 percent full
- Up to 75 percent full
- More than 75 percent full

By recording this data, SQL Server can determine where to put a page and whether a data page needs to be split up to maintain order for a clustered index.

So why is this all so important? There are two reasons. First, many error messages reference GAM and PFS pages, and this background provides some information on how to interpret those messages. Second, this is a drastically different methodology than was used in prior versions of SQL Server, and this shows some of the internals that must be understood in order to fully appreciate how the product has advanced. In prior versions, data pages were stored in doubly linked lists, and to find an empty data page, the list had to be traversed. By changing the allocation strategy, the efficiency of operations that require space to be allocated has increased dramatically.

Table Storage

All that talk leads to the topic of table storage. Tables fall into two categories:

- Clustered
- Heap

If a table has a clustered index, it is called a clustered table, and the data pages are stored in a doubly linked list. If a table does not have a clustered index, the table is called a heap, and the pages are just "out there somewhere," with no particular linkage or order between them.

Now that you've learned some fundamental data structure information, it's time to see how SQL Server uses those data structures to contain and find data within tables. First, you'll take a look at an unstructured, or heap, table. Then you'll see tables with clustered indexes, which are stored in structures, as well as how nonclustered indexes are stored. If you understand how indexes—especially clustered indexes—work, you'll find it much easier to optimize the use of indexes for various performance situations.

Heap Storage

Heaps are not stored in any particular order. One of the biggest predicted problems with the upgrade to SQL Server 7.0 is that some programs rely on data being in chronological order even if there is no clustered index to keep the data in that order. In prior versions of SQL Server, that actually worked because SQL Server kept the rows and pages in chronological order. In SQL Server 7, there's no guarantee that data will be returned in any order at all because of the way SQL Server 7 handles heaps.

A Brief Introduction to Data Structures

In case you fell asleep during your data structures class—as many folks (including the author) tended to—here's a refresher on the primary types of data structures used in SQL Server:

■ *Doubly linked list.* A doubly linked list is a sorted group of items, in which each item holds pointers to the next item in the list and the previous item in the list. It's a lot like one of those ball chains, where the ball is the item, and the little connector is the pointer to the next and previous items. As in a ball chain, there must be an anchor point at one end and some type of termination at the other. The anchor point provides a pointer to the start of the list, and the termination indicates the end of the chain.

■ *Binary trees.* Binary trees aren't actually used by SQL Server, but in order to understand how the next tree, a b-tree, works, it's important that you understand the binary tree. A binary tree is a data structure that consists of nodes and pointers. The top of the tree, or the root node, contains two pointers (hence the "binary" part of binary tree). The first pointer points to a node preceding the root in order, and the second pointer points to a node after the root in order. Each node then has two pointers that point to elements before it and after it. The bottom level of nodes is called the leaf level. In Figure 4.1, the root node contains the value E, and all the values less than E—such as A, C, and D—are on the left of E and are pointed to directly or indirectly by the left pointer of the root node. All values on the right side of E are greater than E. That rule is applied for all non-leaf nodes. The power of the binary tree is in searching. To find the value X, it's only necessary to read nodes E, R, and X. Also, the number of objects in a level grows very quickly. The next level in the tree pictured in Figure 4.1 would have eight more nodes, but it would add only one more hop to the maximum number of hops necessary to find a given item. In other words, every item that is added to the list doesn't add a huge amount of time to the search, and the tree gets more efficient as it grows.

■ *B-trees.* A b-tree is a structure based on a binary tree, but it has more than two pointers coming from each node. A b-tree node has several items in sorted order and will have $N + 1$ pointers coming out of it, where N is the number of values in the node. So if a b-tree had three items in it, it would have four pointers coming out of it. The first pointer would point to the items before the first item in the node. The second pointer would point to the items with values between the first and second items in the node. The third pointer would point to the items with values between the second and third items in the node. The fourth pointer would point to all the items with values higher than the last node. Figure 4.2 illustrates this concept. B-trees are used to store all of the indexes in SQL Server.

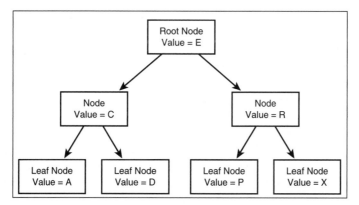

Figure 4.1   A binary tree is a data structure that consists of nodes and pointers. Understanding the binary tree is important for the administration of SQL Server.

Every table, whether it's clustered or a heap, has at least one row in *sysindexes*. That row will have an index id, stored in the field *indid* of either 0 or 1. If the id is 0, the table is a heap, and if the id is 1 the table is clustered. Also in the *sysindexes* table is a field called *FirstIAM*. This is the page number of the first page of the IAM, or Index Allocation Map, for the table. The IAM is a linked list of IAM type pages, which are used to determine what pages go with which tables. By following the linked list of IAM pages, SQL Server locates all the pages that go with a heap. The individual pages

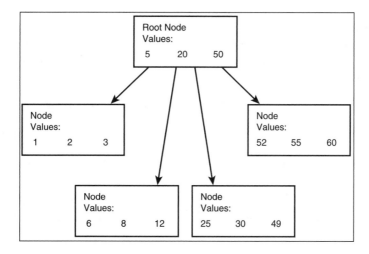

Figure 4.2   The b-tree structure is based on a binary tree, but it has more than two pointers coming from each node.

in a heap are not linked together, so the only way to find them all is to follow the chain of the IAM.

In general, a heap is not the best way to store data, just as a heap is not the best way to store laundry. Sure the laundry will all be there in the heap when it's needed, but how long might it take to find two matching socks? Most nontrivial tables will have clustered indexes on them, so they won't be heaps.

Clustered Table Storage

Clustered tables are stored in sorted order by the index key. In other words, if a table consists of names and addresses and the clustered index is on last name and then first name, the table is physically sorted in that order. If a query is written to select all of the names in a specific zip code area, the result set will come back sorted in name order at no additional cost. There can be only one clustered index per table.

A clustered index has a row in *sysindexes* with the *indid* set to 1. The *FirstIAM* field in that row points to the top of the binary tree that stores the index. The leaf nodes of the binary tree are the data pages themselves, and the leaf nodes are linked to each other in a doubly linked list. So if the entire table is scanned, the data pages can be read in sequential order without searching the entire tree but by following the doubly linked list to the next data page in order.

Figure 4.3 shows an example b-tree with leaf nodes for a table clustered by last name. Notice that the data pages are linked not only by the index, but also by their doubly linked list. To search for the value Smith, SQL Server would visit the root node and then be directed to the Miller-York page. Clustered indexes on large data sets will have multiple index levels, but Figure 4.3 shows only one index level before reaching the leaf nodes because a drawing gets very complex with multiple nodes. For a b-tree with four items and five pointers (called a 4,5 b-tree), a two-level tree will have a root node and five leaf nodes. A three-level tree will have a root node, five nodes on the middle level, and 25 leaf nodes.

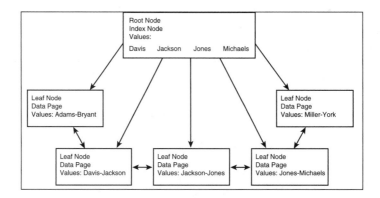

Figure 4.3 An example b-tree for a clustered index; notice that it isn't a true b-tree; it has links between all the leaf nodes.

SQL Server stores index data on the index pages. For example, if the index is on last name and then first name, the index pages will contain the actual last name and first name and then the necessary pointers. Because SQL Server uses 8KB pages and the index holds the names and pointers, each index node will have hundreds of values, so the b-tree structures tend to stay fairly flat. That means SQL Server doesn't need to read through a lot of index pages to find the data that is being searched for; instead, it needs to read only one page for each level of the b-tree.

Another key thing to remember about clustered indexes is that the leaf page is the actual data page. There is no real separation between the data and the index. When the index is rebuilt, the table is rebuilt. If a clustered index is rebuilt onto a file group, the whole table moves with the index because the file group is really just one object.

A simple analogy for the leaf nodes in a clustered index would be a traditional "white pages" telephone book. Each page has a guide that tells where the page begins and where the page ends. Each entry is kept in sequential order on the page, and each page is attached to the pages before and after it.

Any good database implementation book should offer a full set of guidelines for using clustered indexes, but here are a few pointers:

- Use clustered indexes for things that need to be returned in sorted order, such as names.

- Use indexes in general for items that are distinct. Last name is a good one, unless the item being indexed is a family tree, in which case a lot of entries will have the same last name. Don't index fields with a very limited set of values. An index on gender is nearly totally useless, as any query that uses it will return half the rows in the table on average.

- Clustered indexes on identity columns are a bad idea, because they concentrate all the new rows going into the table on the same page, which can cause contention even with row-level locking.

Secondary (Nonclustered) Index Storage

Nonclustered indexes are stored in b-trees in much the same way clustered indexes are stored. However, a nonclustered index does not have data pages as leaf nodes. Instead, the leaf nodes of a nonclustered index are pointers. If the nonclustered index is on a heap, the index actually points to the file, page, and row that matches the search criteria.

If the nonclustered index is on a table that has a clustered index, the pointer is the key to the clustered index. For example, if a table contained names and addresses, it would likely have a clustered index on name and a nonclustered index on address. A search for the address would return the name associated with the address. Then SQL Server checks the clustered index to find the actual data.

While this may seem wildly inefficient, it's actually a great improvement in efficiency. One of the major problems with clustered indexes is handling full pages. When a data page fills up, SQL Server has to split the page, putting half the data on one page and half the data on another. Then SQL Server gets all the pointers in the clustered index b-tree straightened out. If the nonclustered index had a pointer to the exact page the data was on instead of the value, SQL Server would have to go repair all the nonclustered indexes on the table every time a page split occurred. By using the clustered index, the page split operation is much faster because it has to repair only the pointers in the clustered index, resulting in improved efficiency. In Figure 4.4, a nonclustered index is used to track down the value of the correct record, and then the search continues into the clustered index.

Text and Image Datatype Storage

Text and image datatypes are special datatypes that are stored differently than conventional datatypes. Text and image data is treated by the user as a string of bytes up to 2GB in length. SQL Server stores the data on linked pages in the database.

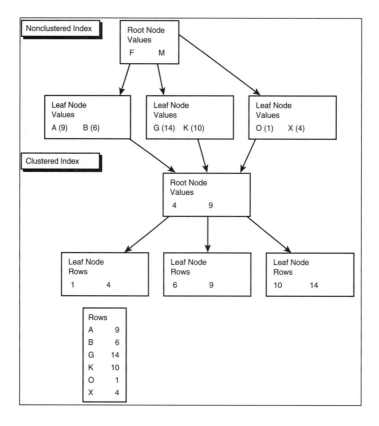

Figure 4.4   Here a nonclustered index is used to access the data in a clustered index. The nonclustered index is searched, and the key used in the clustered index is returned. Then the clustered index is searched for the new key.

A row that contains a text/image datatype actually holds a pointer to a structure on another page. This structure contains the information needed to access all the different pages the data could be stored on. If there are fewer than 64 bytes of data, the data is actually stored in the structure. If there are more than 64 bytes but fewer than 32KB of data, the structure points to the data pages that hold the data. If there are more than 32KB of data, the structure becomes the root node of a b-tree, with intermediate nodes that hold more pointers to the data.

This structured storage provides two benefits. First, it's possible to store data from different rows on the same page if the combined data does not exceed the 8KB page limit. Second, using a b-tree design access into the middle of the data is dramatically faster than having to access each page in sequence to find the particular bytes being searched for.

That covers how pages are used, as well as how indexes and text and image data are stored within the database. You might still have a lot of unanswered questions about how SQL Server stores data. For example, "Where does all this storage actually happen?" and "How can it be optimized for particular types of hardware?" Now that the base for that information has been established, the next topic is how data is stored on disk.

External Storage: Files and File Groups

All those pages and extents have to exist on disk somewhere, and in SQL Server, that somewhere is in files on disk. Previous versions of SQL Server used the notion of devices, which was derived from the old days on UNIX in which a device was an actual physical (or logical) device. Now, however, a file is a file, and the "device" terminology is gone. Because a database can contain multiple files, the construct of *file group* was created to enable users to manage groups of files together.

This section offers in-depth discussion of the following topics:

- Databases and files
- Growing and shrinking files
- File groups
- Removing files and file groups

A lot of the material in this section is groundwork; some of it demonstrates the use of particular features. It's all new to SQL Server 7, however, so the groundwork here is important—even to the advanced administrator.

Databases and Files

SQL Server databases exist in two or more files. One file is the default file for data storage, and the other is the default file for log storage. The only page type that hasn't been covered yet, the Log page, is stored only in log files. By default and convention, the first two files that make up a database are given the extensions .ldf and .mdf. The .ldf (Log Data File) files are log files, and the .mdf (Master Data File) extension desig-nates the primary data file. These are not enforced conventions, but it's a good idea to use them so that other database administrators will intuitively know what's going on. Either of these files can grow or shrink.

Every file on disk has a *logical name* and a *physical name*. The logical name is that by which the file will be referred to internally by SQL Server. The physical name is the name of the file on disk, complete with the path and extension. For example, a logical name could be MYDB_Primary, and a physical name could be C:\MSSQL7\DATA\ MYDB1.MDF.

Files in SQL Server 7 can grow and shrink. When creating the file, you can set the growth increments. A file can grow by either a certain percentage or a certain number of megabytes each time it needs to grow. In addition, a maximum file size can be set to keep the database from growing totally out of control.

Because a database will automatically grow, it can also automatically shrink. A back-ground process in SQL Server, running with very low priority, manages the shrinkage process by monitoring the unused space in the database. When certain thresholds are met, the background process compacts the data in the database and then removes the unused space from the end of the device. This is a very low priority process, so it won't run if there is much activity on the database, and it will be interrupted by the startup of activity.

If necessary, a database can hold multiple data or log files. For multiple data files, the rest of the data files will be given an .ndf extension. (Why .ndf? The best explanation is that it's one letter past .mdf.) Whenever an index refers to a data page, it refers to a file number and the data page, so there is a complete address of where a page exists within a database.

In prior versions of SQL Server, a single device could hold data from multiple data-bases. Files do not work that way. A file in SQL Server 7 can hold data from only one database. Databases and files have a 1-to-many relationship: A given file belongs to one database, but a database is made up of two or more files. Figure 4.5 shows the relation-ship between the different types of files and databases.

There are two ways to build a database. SQL Server Enterprise Manager provides a nice graphical interface for building databases. On the other hand, Transact-SQL offers a command for building databases.

Building Databases

The following steps outline the process of building a database with SQL Enterprise Manager:

1. Open SQL Enterprise Manager and make sure the server you want to work with is registered.

2. Open the Microsoft SQL Servers group, and then the SQL Server group, and then the server you want to work on.

3. Right-click on Databases and choose New Database. The Database Properties dialog box appears, as shown in Figure 4.6.

4. In the Name field, type in the name of the new database. The title bar then changes to reflect the name of the database you're creating. Notice how the auto-grow options are set, as mentioned in step 6.

5. In the Database Files grid, type in a filename and a location for the file. Then put in a starting size for the file.

6. Use the Automatically Grow File check box to indicate whether the file will be allowed to automatically grow. If it will grow, use the File Growth options to specify how big a file can get.

7. On the Transaction Log tab, enter the same type of data that was entered for the data files, including the name and location of the files.

8. Click OK to create the database. SQL Server will build the database. This may take some time; on a Pentium II workstation with a single hard drive, it can take up to a minute to build a 600MB database.

To perform the same operation in Transact-SQL, use this syntax

```
CREATE DATABASE <database name>
ON [PRIMARY] <filespec>, <filespec>...
LOG ON <filespec>, <filespec>...
```

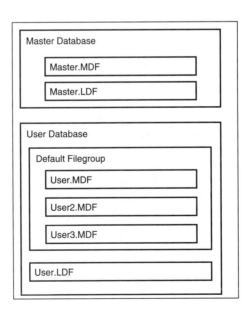

Figure 4.5   The relationship between a file, a file group, and a database.

where `<database name>` is the name of the database to be created. The `PRIMARY` keyword is used to denote the primary data file. Only one data file can be marked as primary, and if none is marked as primary, the first one will become the primary data file.

The `<filespec>` indicates the name, properties, and location of the file:

```
(    NAME=<logical file name>,
         FILENAME=<'Path, name, and extension for file'>,
         SIZE=<Initial Size >,
         MAXSIZE=<Maximum Size or the keyword UNLIMITED>,
         FILEGROWTH=<File Growth Increment>
)
```

Anywhere a size is specified, such as the Initial Size, the amount is specified as either KB or MB (the default). For example, a 2-megabyte database would be written as SIZE=2MB. Similarly, file growth can be specified as KB, MB, or %. Files must be made of whole extents, so all sizes will be rounded to the nearest 64KB barrier. The following example will build a database with a 200MB primary device, a 20MB secondary device, and a 100MB log device:

```
CREATE DATABASE Contacts
        ON      (Name=SecondaryDev,
FILENAME='D:\MSSQL\DATA\CONTACTS_SECONDARY.NDF',
SIZE=20MB
        ),
                PRIMARY (Name=PrimaryDev,

FILENAME='D:\MSSQL\DATA\CONTACTS_PRIMARY.MDF',
                        SIZE=200MB,
```

Figure 4.6   The Database Properties dialog box.

```
                    MAXSIZE=500MB,
                    FILEGROWTH=10%
       )
  LOG ON (Name=LogDev,
                  FILENAME='C:\MSSQL\DATA\CONTACTS_LOG.LDF'
                  SIZE=100MB,
       )
```

This creates the primary device so it will grow to 200MB and can reach a maximum size of 500MB by growing 10% at a time.

After creating a database, you might want to change some characteristics of the underlying files, such as the filename, file size, or maximum size. To do so, you use the ALTER DATABASE command as shown here:

```
  ALTER DATABASE Contacts
      MODIFY FILE (Name = PrimaryDev,
                            MAXSIZE=700
      )
```

This command changes the maximum size of the data file PrimaryDev to 700MB, returning "The command completed successfully."

Growing and Shrinking Files: An Example

The following example shows how databases and files grow. In the first step, the database is created with a 4MB data size and a 10MB log. The auto-grow increment for the data side is 1MB, and the maximum size is 15MB.

```
  create database mydb
      on (   Name=MyDB_Dev1,
             FileName="D:\MSSQL7\DATA\MYDB1_DEV.MDF",
             Size = 4MB,
             MaxSize = 15MB,
             FileGrowth=1MB
      )
      log on (Name = MyDB_Log1,
             FileName="D:\MSSQL7\DATA\MYDB_LOG.LDF",
             Size = 10 MB
      )
  go
```

This command returns the following:

```
  CREATE DATABASE: allocating 4 Mbytes on disk 'MyDB_Dev1'
  CREATE DATABASE: allocating 10 Mbytes on disk 'MyDB_Log1'
```

Next, execute sp_helpdb to have SQL Server return the specifications on the database and the individual file sizes:

```
  sp_helpdb mydb
  go
```

Running sp_helpdb provides the following result set:

```
name            db_size        owner             dbid    created      status
--------------------------------------------------------------------------
mydb            14.00 MB       sa                6       Jun 27 1998 no
➥options set

(1 row affected)


device_fragments                              size           usage
----------------------------------------------------------------
MyDB_Dev1                                     4.00 MB        data only
MyDB_Log1                                     10.00 MB       log only
 (2 row(s) affected)
```

Next, switch to the MyDB database with this command

```
use MyDB
go
```

which returns the following:

```
--The command completed successfully.
```

Then create a table with a line number i (an integer that is an identity) so it will start at 1 and count up by 1 each row. Specify a char field length of 8,000. That means there will be only one row on each page. Because the type is char, all 8,000 characters are stored. If the type was the more commonly used varchar, only the characters used would be stored. However, because wasting space is the whole point for this example, use char:

```
Create table MyTable(
    i int Identity(1,1),
    MyChars char(8000)
)
go
```

This returns the following ever-so-helpful line:

```
The command(s) completed successfully.
```

Now for the fun part. In order for the database to grow, it has to be populated. This script will loop through 8,000 iterations and insert a record into the table for each loop. Using the table MyTable, each row takes one page, so 8,000 rows at 8,192 bytes each should take just over 62MB to store. However, because the data file was created to grow to a maximum of 15MB, this is way over the limit.

```
declare @Ctr int

select @Ctr = 1

While @Ctr <= 8000
begin
```

```
        insert into MyTable (MyChars) values ("Foo")
        select @Ctr = @Ctr + 1
    end
    go
```

Running the batch will return the statement "1 row(s) affected" 1,624 times. When it runs out of space, it finally gives up and displays the following error message:

```
Server: Msg 1105, Level 17, State 42000
Unable to allocate space for object 'MyTable' in database 'mydb' because
➥the 'PRIMARY' filegroup is full.
```

This is a true statement: The default file group is full. You can deduce that because the command issued executed only 1,624 times instead of 8,000.

Similarly, this command

```
sp_helpdb mydb
go
```

returns:

```
name         db_size        owner            dbid    created      status
- - - - - - - - - - - - - - - - - - - - - - - - - - - - - - - - - - - - - - - - -
mydb         25.00 MB       sa               6       Jun 27 1998 no
options set

(1 row(s) affected)


=
device_fragments                          size         usage
- - - - - - - - - - - - - - - - - - - - - - - - - - - - - - - - - - - -
MyDB_Dev1                                 15.00 MB     data only
MyDB_Log1                                 10.00 MB     log only
```

(2 row(s) affected)

This shows that the data device has grown to its maximum of 15MB. All that really remains is to clean up the mess, which you can do with this command:

```
drop table MyTable
go
```

That little demonstration shows how files can grow. What about shrinking files? That takes patience. SQL Server will come along eventually and shrink the files. For the impatient, however, SQL Server provides the DBCC SHRINKFILE command:

```
DBCC SHRINKFILE ("<FileName">[, <Target Size>[, Options]])
```

The <FileName> argument is the name of the file to shrink, the optional <Target Size> is the size DBCC should try to shrink the files to, and the <Options> include EMPTYFILE, NOTRUNCATE, and TRUNCATEONLY. The <FileName> is the logical filename to be used. In the earlier example, it would be MYDB_DEV1, not D:\MSSQL\DATA\MYDB_DEV1.MDF. The <Target Size> is specified in megabytes and is the size that DBCC will try to shrink the file to. If the file contains more data than what's specified as the target size, the database will shrink to the size of the data. The options EMPTYFILE, NOTRUNCATE, and TRUNCATEONLY control what happens to the data in the file.

The EMPTYFILE command specifies that all the data in the file should be moved to other files to prepare for the shrinking file to be removed from the database. The NOTRUNCATE option specifies that the data should be compressed into the beginning of the file, but the space recovered should not be returned to the operating system, which means the file will not be truncated to the size it could be. The TRUNCATEONLY option specifies that the data should not be moved around at all, but the file will be trimmed down to the last allocated extent.

Therefore, to go back to the earlier example, run the following command:

```
Dbcc shrinkfile ("MYDB_DEV1", 4)
```

The result set will be:

```
DbId   FileId CurrentSize MinimumSize UsedPages   EstimatedPages
----------------------------------------------------------------
8      1      512         512         96          96

(1 row(s) affected)

DBCC execution completed. If DBCC printed error messages, contact your
➥system administrator.
```

The file has now been shrunk down to 512 pages, or 4MB. Only 96 pages in the file are used, so the file could theoretically be reduced even more. Databases cannot be shrunk smaller than the Model system database, which starts out at 1.5MB.

Growing and Shrinking Files: Best Practices

For a server implementation of SQL Server that is going to be used exclusively for hosting one or two databases, there are two philosophies of creating devices. If the SQL Server will be stopped nightly for a file-type backup, use the smallest possible devices that will still allow for moderate growth. In other words, if the data is currently 300MB and grows at 1MB per day, make the database 350MB and set it to grow in 50MB increments to a maximum of 600MB. Put a maximum on it just in case something bad begins happening to an application and it begins throwing data into the database causing it to grow very quickly. By limiting the maximum size, this type of problem can be at least reined in quickly, if not cleaned up more easily. If you follow this recommendation, it will be easy to back up the files without backing up a lot of empty space in the middle, reducing both the backup capacity and the restore time.

If the database is being backed up via traditional dump and load methods or by third-party products that essentially implement dump and load mechanisms, the size of the files doesn't impact the database size. In this case, establish the database size by figuring out how much data is in the database (for example, 300MB) and then the growth rate per day or per year (say, 1MB per day). In this case, the initial size of the database should be at 600MB to allow for about a year of production given 250 production days during the year. The available space should be checked monthly, if not as part of the daily maintenance routine. This process eliminates the overhead involved in growing and shrinking databases, while still providing some protection against rogue applications that fill up the database.

As far as log devices are concerned, it's important to monitor the log utilization and size the log appropriately. Avoid using auto-grow on transaction logs because it's easy for a transaction log to grow uncontrollably from a bad application. On a database in production, the log should start at 30–35 percent of the data volume and be adjusted upward from there.

On workstation implementations of SQL Server, auto-grow functionality significantly reduces the administrative overhead. Use auto-grow on those databases for the data and the transaction logs, but make sure that an unknowing user can't take himself out of commission by setting maximum size limits on both types of devices. Workstation implementations are designed to be used in situations such as field sales. If the database completely fills up the individual's drive, the laptop becomes a doorstop because every Windows application assumes there is a certain amount of free space that can be used for temporary files. Mail reading programs are very bad about this. So to avoid taking the entire laptop out of commission, make sure the files can grow to only a certain size and that the specified size is small enough to leave 50–100MB of free space on the drive so other applications can run.

File Groups

For performance reasons that will be covered a bit later in this chapter, you might want to create multiple files and place specific types of data into specific files on specific disk devices. Usually, this is done to spread the input and output to files across several different drives. Prior versions of SQL Server provided the concept of a segment to perform this operation; however, segments were very difficult to manage, were complex, and caused issues with backups. Replacing the concept of the segment in SQL Server 7.0 is the concept of a *file group*. (Most installations will not need to use file groups. They are specifically built for some specialized circumstances.)

When a database is created, the first data file that is built is placed into the default file group. All of the system tables reside in the default file group, along with any other tables that have been created but that weren't explicitly placed into a file group when they were created. If the default file group, or any other file group, runs out of space, problems will occur even if another file group is mostly empty. A table is placed in a file group and does not grow into any other file groups.

A file can be a member of only one file group. Log files are not considered to be part of any file group because they are managed separately.

You can place a table in a specific file group when you create it by specifying the file group in the CREATE TABLE statement. You can place indexes in specific file groups by using the CREATE INDEX statement. To place text or image data in a given file group, use the TEXTIMAGE_ON option in the CREATE TABLE statement.

After a table is created, you cannot move it to a different file group without rebuilding the table. There is no automatic process for copying; basically, the table has to be scripted, the data is copied out, the table is deleted and then rebuilt in the new file group, and the data is brought back in. You can move an index in SQL Server Enterprise Manager, but it's not really moving; it follows the same process that would be used to rebuild the index, but a different file group is chosen. For the TEXTIMAGE_ON option, if it isn't specified in the CREATE TABLE statement, the image data can't be moved without rebuilding the table. It's critical to understand where tables are and where they should be when creating databases.

One feature of file groups that makes them work from an administrative point of view is how they behave with the backup and restore process. In prior versions of SQL Server, it was necessary to track where devices and segments were created because after a device failure all the devices and segments had to be re-created by hand in the same order in which they were created in the first place. SQL Server 7 eliminates that foolishness because all the information about the file groups and files in a database is stored in the backup. So a backup will automatically rebuild files and file groups as necessary to become operational.

You can create file groups at the same time as the database using SQL Server Enterprise Manager. However, from Transact-SQL, you must build the database first and then add file groups to it. When using the ALTER DATABASE command, for example, you can use either of two commands. The first creates the file group, and the second builds a file that is added to the file group. Both of these commands must be executed before the file group can be used.

To build a file group in SQL Server Enterprise Manager, perform the following steps:

1. Start SQL Server Enterprise Manager and connect to the server you want to manage.

2. Open the Databases container and right-click on the database to which you want to add a file group.

3. In the FileGroup Properties dialog box, on the General tab, look through the listed files. Add a new file by entering the filename, logical name, and size. In the

File Group column, type in the name of the new file group. As shown in Figure 4.7, the new file group name is "Secondary."

4. Click OK to create the database with the new file group and the new file.

To perform a similar task using Transact-SQL, first execute this command

```
ALTER DATABASE mydb
     CREATE FILEGROUP FG1
```

which will return:

```
-- The command(s) completed successfully.
```

Then execute the following command

```
ALTER DATABASE mydb
     ADD FILE (
            NAME=FG1_DATA1,
            FILENAME='D:\MSSQL7\DATA\FG1_DATA1.NDF',
            SIZE = 3MB,
            MAXSIZE=3MB
     ) TO FILEGROUP FG1
```

which will return:

```
-- Extending database by 3 Mbytes on disk FG1_DATA1
```

Figure 4.7   The FileGroup Properties box. A new file is being added into a new file group called "Secondary."

Then enter this command to add a table to the new file group

```
use mydb
go

create table foo (
     i int
) on FG1
```

which will return:

```
-- The command(s) completed successfully.
```

The preceding commands will create the file group, create a new file in the file group, and then create a table in the new file group.

Removing Files and File Groups

In addition to adding files and file groups to a database, you can remove a file from a database with SQL Server 7.0. There are all kinds of uses for this capability. The life cycle of a database usually starts with a bulk import of data from some source. This tends to leave a lot of junk in the database that needs to be cleaned out after the data is imported, which will usually free up a lot of space. Also, when the database is created, the administrator usually has to make an educated guess at how big to make the database, and sometimes the guess is much too high. This provides a way to resize databases that are too large. In some cases, it might be desirable to move data from one physical location to another, which would involve creating a new file, copying the data to the new file, and then removing the old file.

To remove a file, first move all the data from the file to a new file using the DBCC SHRINKFILE command with the EMPTYFILE option. This safely moves all the data from the file into other files in the same file group and marks the file so it will not be used anymore. Then use the ALTER DATABASE command's REMOVE FILE option to remove the file. Once again, the file absolutely must be empty, so use the DBCC SHRINKDB command with the EMPTYFILE option to ensure that none of those pesky users dumped a bunch of data in there between commands. Here's an example.

First, add a file to the MyDB database you created earlier:

```
alter database MyDB
     add file(Name = "NewFile",
                    FileName = "D:\MSSQL7\DATA\NEWFILE.DAT",
                    SIZE = 2MB
               )
go
```

That command will return the following:

```
Extending database by 2.00 MB on disk 'NewFile'.
```

Having created the new data file, you can now remove it. First, shrink the file down to no size and mark it as unusable:

```
dbcc shrinkfile("NewFile", EMPTYFILE)
```

DBCC SHRINKFILE will return:

```
DbId   FileId CurrentSize MinimumSize UsedPages   EstimatedPages
-----------------------------------------------------------------
8      3      256         256         0           0


(1 row(s) affected)


DBCC execution completed. If DBCC printed error messages, contact your
➥system administrator.
```

Then remove the file with this command

```
Alter Database Mydb Remove File "NewFile"
```

which results in this nice confirmation message:

```
The file 'NewFile' has been removed.
```

You can accomplish the same thing in Enterprise Manager by opening database properties, highlighting the file to remove, and pressing the Delete key on the keyboard.

To remove a file group, first remove all of the files in the file group, and then remove the file group by using the ALTER DATABASE command's REMOVE FILEGROUP option, which has the same syntax as REMOVE FILE. There is no documented method for removing a file group from within Enterprise Manager.

Optimizing Storage

Now that the tools are in place and the foundation has been built, the topic of how to store data on different types of hardware can be covered. Two optimization methodologies need to be discussed, one for optimization of systems that have multiple logical drives and one for optimization of systems that have a single logical drive (usually a RAID array).

Which is better, to RAID or not to RAID? RAID and other disk array technologies offer two key benefits. The first, and the primary selling point, is redundancy. Striping with parity protects against single (and, in some implementations, multiple) drive failures by spreading redundant information across several drives. This results in a less-efficient use of the available disk space, but it also means that if a drive fails to power up, the other drives have enough information to rebuild the information on the lost drive. While a drive is missing from the array, the whole array runs 20–40% slower in most cases. Depending on the system manufacturer, the capability may be built in to swap a new drive in while the server is running, resulting in a lowered capacity until the new drive is caught up and online.

The other main advantage to using RAID is that a five-drive system can seek for and send out five times as much data as a single drive can. Throughput is increased because more drives are sending the data. This is a big win for SQL Server, which is very I/O intensive.

The advantage that non-RAID systems have is the ability to specifically place a table, index, or text/image column on a particular disk spindle. By breaking up the table data from the indexes, for example, the system can search for indexes and read data in parallel. Optimally, a very large database will have multiple RAID systems with multiple controllers, along with the advantage of being able to distribute data and specifically separate indexes and data to optimize data flow.

The upcoming subsections focus on the following:

- Optimizing data storage for multiple-drive systems

- Optimizing data storage for single-drive systems

- Building servers

RAID Systems

RAID, or Redundant Array of Inexpensive Disks, is a set of technologies that allow multiple less-expensive disks to take the place of larger more-expensive fault-tolerant drives, while maintaining low cost and high availability.

Three RAID levels are in common use. The first RAID level, called Level 0, is *disk striping*. This level stripes data across multiple drives, but it doesn't provide for any redundancy. Although this is a high-performance solution, it doesn't have the high availability that is usually associated with RAID.

The second common RAID level, Level 1, is *disk mirroring*. In this case, two drives are mirrored, making them exact duplicates of each other. If one drive fails, the other drive is still available. To take this a step further, Windows NT implements a technology called disk duplexing for systems with two drives and two controllers, so that if a disk or controller fails, the system can still run. Disk mirroring is usually used for system partitions or transaction logs, but not for data. Disk mirroring allows only half the available storage space to be used for data because the other half is completely redundant, which makes this a very expensive solution for large quantities of data.

The third common RAID level—and the most popular—is RAID 5. RAID 5, called *disk striping with parity*, combines RAID 0 and parity so that if any given drive is lost, the information on that drive can be reconstructed with the parity information stored on the other drives. This provides most of the speed that RAID 0 does because the system has to build and place parity information, but it also provides high reliability.

There are two ways to make RAID arrays. Windows NT Server can use RAID 0, 1, or 5 in software using Disk Administrator. All the processing for the RAID system is done by the CPU, and all the data travels across the bus on the system. Many server hardware vendors and some controller card vendors have built RAID systems in hardware. This provides a faster solution than the software RAID because it offloads much of the processing onto the controller card. In addition, most of these systems implement elaborate data caching schemes, which improve performance.

Optimizing Data Storage for Multiple-Drive Systems

The key to optimizing data storage is understanding how SQL Server treats data and then understanding how the data is going to be used. The first part has been covered throughout this chapter in relating how data pages and index pages work. The second part is a bit more of an art form.

An OLTP system will benefit greatly from having the transaction log and data space on separate drives. A transaction log is constantly being written to, and if you keep it separated from the data space, the data drives will be free to perform their combination of read and write operations while the transaction log hums along writing down every transaction. OLTP systems tend to have a few critical, high-volume tables that take a lot of write activity. Place the indexes for these tables on a separate disk to prevent the page splits that will occur from impacting the data disk performance.

Decision Support Systems can receive performance benefits from creating the non-clustered indexes on a separate drive from the data. Remember that the clustered index is the table, so a clustered index should be left on the data drive. By separating indexes and data, you can keep the parallel operations of reading indexes and finding the data for another connection separate and independent so they will run optimally. In addition, most DSS applications are updated nightly, and part of that update usually involves reindexing the data. Having the indexes on a separate disk will speed this process significantly.

OLTP Versus DSS

There are two primary types of database applications and, therefore, two primary types of databases. OLTP, or On-Line Transaction Processing, involves systems that perform a lot of writes but not a lot of reads. These are systems like reservation systems, ordering systems, and other systems in which users must insert and update a lot of data. DSS, or Decision Support Systems, is generally used for reporting. These are mostly read-only databases, which usually are updated on a nightly or weekly basis to support things like executive information systems, inventory control, and so on.

OLTP systems tend to be very write-intensive, so the optimizations that are done in OLTP systems are usually geared toward performing faster writes. DSS tend to be very read-intensive, with large nightly or weekly batch imports. These systems are optimized to perform faster reads.

Most large systems tend to specialize one way or another, but small to medium databases tend to take a lot of abuse from both directions. As a medium database grows, it has to evolve into one type of system or the other (or split into both) in order to handle the transaction and data volumes being placed upon it.

Determining which of the categories a particular system falls into is the first step in optimizing storage.

Optimizing Data Storage for Single-Drive Systems

On a single-drive system, the options are somewhat limited. If the single drive is a RAID array or just one disk drive in a workstation, certain things can be done to improve throughput. On a RAID system, make sure the controller is fast enough to handle the data being thrown at it. Add more cache memory to the RAID controller as necessary to ensure good performance. On a non-RAID system, make sure that a fast, high-quality drive and controller are installed and that the system has a lot of memory for caching.

The key advantage to a single-drive system is low maintenance. There shouldn't be any file groups to monitor. There's just one large file group for each database that handles everything. Don't break databases up into file groups unless there is some performance gain to be realized, which is not likely on a system with a single drive. On a single-drive system, a file group can become more of an administrative headache than a benefit.

Building Servers: Best Practices

One of the most challenging jobs of a database administrator is correctly specifying servers for different tasks. This section offers some guidelines to consider when purchasing servers for particular tasks.

If a system is being used for OLTP applications and requires high availability, use a hardware-based RAID 5 system for holding the data and a mirrored disk set for holding the transaction logs. This provides a high degree of recoverability for both the data and the log files, but it also separates logs and data onto separate volumes, which is a performance boost.

For Decision Support Systems, which are largely read-only by users and batch updated, use dual RAID arrays and maintain the data and the indexes separately. Usually during the batch update process, the indexes will be updated or even rebuilt. So holding them on a separate array provides a performance increase because the index array can be writing data while the data array is reading the data to be indexed.

If a large quantity of text/image data is used, use another RAID array to hold that data. This prevents space contention and bandwidth contention between the "normal" data being used and the text/image data.

Most of the server building process comes down to understanding the system that will be on the server. Is it primarily used to receive data, as in an OLTP system, or is it used as a data repository? Answering that question resolves a lot of the issues related to optimization in general.

For systems that perform a mix of OLTP and decision support, follow the guidelines for OLTP. If space and budget are available, separate the indexes onto their own array, but it's imperative that the OLTP transactions complete because they will be creating locks that will prevent the DSS transactions from completing at all.

Conclusions

A lot of this chapter has been foundational material regarding how SQL Server stores and finds data. For now, this is new to all of you, but the following list outlines the key topics from this chapter:

- Index structures
- Clustered indexes
- OLTP versus DSS
- Building servers

The entire chapter, however, was built to give you an understanding and appreciation of how SQL Server works and where your data is. By understanding the structures SQL Server uses, you can more easily visualize how SQL Server will perform operations, and you can hopefully draw some conclusions on how to make SQL Server more efficient.

5

The SQL Agent

Michael Hotek

T HE SQL AGENT IS YOUR AUTOMATED attendant. It performs all the automated processing that needs to be run on a SQL Server in order to meet the needs of your environment. It also provides the capability, through alerts, for SQL Server to react to adverse conditions and fix them or inform an operator.

In version 6.5 of SQL Server, the SQL Executive managed all the tasks on a server. The SQL Executive provided adequate support for most applications. However, it suffered from the necessity of defining multiple tasks and having no way of gracefully making them interact. SQL Server 7.0 has made great strides in this area. The SQL Executive has been replaced by the SQL Agent, which offers much greater functionality.

One of the greatest strides in the SQL Agent is its ability to create *multistep jobs*. This allows you to encapsulate all the actions that are performed in a single process within one job. Before, it was necessary to create a separate task for each step in the process.

In addition to multistep jobs, *dependencies* have been added as well. This brings the SQL Agent's job-processing capabilities up to the level of the industrial-strength applications that are being designed and deployed with SQL Server. Dependencies allow you to interrupt or redirect the job flow based upon the results of the current job step.

This chapter first offers a quick introduction to the SQL Agent and its features and uses. Then, because of the strong connection between SQL Mail and many other environments (including the SQL Agent), the chapter outlines the requirements and configuration of SQL Mail. Following that, you'll learn about the configuration of SQL Agent, as well as how to use the SQL Agent to create operators, jobs, and alerts. You'll also find information on setting up a master server (MSX) before the chapter ends with a series of case studies that outline the capabilities of the SQL Agent in real-world scenarios.

Introducing the SQL Agent

The SQL Agent consists of four features:

- *Operators.* An operator is a person within your organization who can be notified by SQL Server when an event occurs.

- *Jobs.* A "job" replaces the familiar "task" in previous versions of SQL Server. The job engine is now of industrial strength and can support the most complex requirements. Each job step can be executed by using a variety of methods. TSQL and CmdExec steps are still supported. The biggest advance is the ability to create step commands by using Active Scripting. Active Scripting consists of VBScript, JavaScript, or any ActiveX scripting agent, such as PerlScript.

  In addition to the different languages that can be used to create step commands, control of flow is also built into each step. You have the ability to define success and failure actions for each job step, to branch to alternative job steps, or to terminate a job at any time. Jobs will generally be configured for periodic processing, such as batch loads from external systems and backup routines.

- *Alerts.* Alerts are usually configured for your system based on Performance Monitor counters. In essence, this gives you the ability to configure SQL Server to notify you when it is having a problem. You'll learn more about alerts in a case study toward the end of this chapter. Properly configuring alerts can be one of the most important things you can do to streamline your administration.

- *Master server.* A master server, or MSX, is a server that you configure as a central control point. The master server gives you the ability to create a common job on a single server and have it run on multiple servers. The most common use for something like this is a backup. A backup script is normally created to be generic to the server, minimizing the impact of added and dropped databases. Without a master server, you would have to create a job on each server to run the backup. With a master server, you simply define the backup job on the master server. Periodically, all target servers will connect to the master, download any jobs that need to be run, execute them, and return status information to the master server.

Configuring SQL Mail

Although SQL Mail is not a component of the SQL Agent, it is a great enabler of communications. Having SQL Mail configured on your server gives the SQL Agent the ability to send email and pager messages to operators. In the case studies presented later in this chapter, SQL Mail is used as the primary notification mechanism. One of the case studies also investigates a method for tying the SQL Agent into SQL Mail to create a relatively powerful business system. Because SQL Mail has such a large impact on many environments, this chapter outlines the requirements and configuration of SQL Mail as well.

SQL Mail comprises many different components and settings that must all be configured in a certain order for the mail capabilities of SQL Server to be utilized. The required components include the following:

- Mailbox on the Exchange Server for use by SQL Server
- Microsoft Outlook or Microsoft Exchange mail client installed on the machine running SQL Server
- A profile setup for Outlook that accesses the mailbox on Exchange
- The services that SQL Server runs under, configured with actual logins instead of the system account
- The SQL Mail service

In order to configure all the components of SQL Mail, you will need to find both a Windows NT and an Exchange administrator or have those privileges.

When configuring SQL Mail, you will need to make quite a few far-reaching decisions.

In order to ensure proper operation of SQL Mail, you will need to have Outlook or the Exchange mail client running on the system. This means that you cannot log off the machine because doing so will shut down any open programs. You must lock the workstation instead.

Because you need to install and have the client software running on your SQL Server machine, you will need to set up a mail profile to access Exchange. Keep in mind that all profile information is stored by the user in the Registry. The profile that

---

Email Compatibility

Supposedly, it is possible to get SQL Mail to run with any MAPI-compliant mail system. However, in my experience, the only system that has been completely reliable is Microsoft Exchange. It also has the added requirement that you install an Exchange mail client on your SQL Server machine and have it running. Most administrators install Outlook and leave it minimized on the SQL Server machine. At the time of this writing, Outlook 98 was not working very well with SQL Server. Outlook 97 worked without any problems, however, so it is recommended that you use this version.

In some installations, SQL Mail will run properly without having the mail client running on the server. However, I have not gotten this to work reliably on every installation.

you configure for one user is not available or visible for another user. Because the mail client must be running on the machine with access to this profile, you will need to decide with which NT account everyone will log on to the SQL Server machine.

The use of the mail profile goes far beyond simply logging on to the machine. You need to use the same login for the SQL Server service as well. This means that you will have to select a particular NT account with administrator privileges that the SQL Server service will run under instead of using the local system account.

When you have made the required configuration decisions, you are ready to configure SQL Mail.

The following list of steps is rather long. Most people will be tempted to find a shortcut for this procedure. Every time I have done this, it required completely removing all components and starting over. The best lesson here is that if you follow this procedure step by step, SQL Mail will start up and run the first time through.

1. Locate the CD that contains the Outlook client.

2. Log off NT.

3. Log on to NT using the account that you have chosen to be the NT account to be used from now on.

4. Open the Services applet and change the account for the SQL Server service to use the account with which you are logged on to NT.

5. Stop and start SQL Server.

   You will be prompted to shut down the SQL Agent as well. Go ahead and shut it down and leave it that way. You will have to reboot later, so the SQL Agent will come back up.

6. Install Outlook by using the custom option, and select only the minimum components required. Make sure you select Exchange support.

7. Reboot the machine and log on to NT.

8. Make sure all services started back up properly.

9. Log on to the machine running Exchange.

10. Create a new mailbox that will be used by SQL Mail. The Windows NT account that you select will be the same account with which you are logging on to the SQL Server machine.

11. Go back to the SQL Server machine and start the Mail and Fax applet.

12. Create a new profile, selecting only the Exchange service.

13. Work through the wizard. When you are returned to the Profiles screen, highlight the profile you just created and click the Properties button.

14. If the name of the Exchange Server and mailbox are not underlined, click the Check Name button.

15. If you get a failure at this point, go back and verify all the settings for the profile. If you still have problems, uninstall Outlook and start over.

16. Before closing that dialog box, check the Connect to Network box and clear the Choose Connection Type box.

17. Start Outlook.

18. Send a mail message to the mailbox you just configured.

19. If the message does not appear in your inbox, contact your Exchange administrator to troubleshoot the mail delivery.

20. Start Enterprise Manager.

21. Right click on the SQL Mail icon, select Properties, and enter the profile name you just created.

22. Test the profile.

23. If you experience any errors at this point, check to see whether you've misspelled the profile name or if you are logged on to NT by using a different account.

24. Select the Auto Start check box and close the dialog box.

25. Right-click the SQL Mail item and select Start. You should see a dialog box that reports the successful start of SQL Mail, and the icon should change to a green arrow. SQL Mail is now running.

26. Open the Query Analyzer.

27. Using the xp_sendmail command, send a test message to the mailbox you created for SQL Mail:
    ```
    EXEC xp_sendmail @recipients = 'Michael Hotek',
    @subject = 'SQL Mail Test', @message = 'This is a Test.'
    ```

28. If you maximize Outlook, you should see the test message in the inbox.

That is all there is to configuring SQL Mail; it is now available for use.

Now that SQL Mail is configured and running, you can use the notification mechanisms in the SQL Agent. Email and pager notifications can be established for jobs and alerts.

Configuring the SQL Agent

The configuration of the SQL Agent is a fairly self-explanatory process. In most cases, the default values will be sufficient for just about any environment. However, there are a few things about the configuration of the SQL Agent that you'll want to consider.

The General tab contains an option for configuring an errorlog with captured trace information. This log can be invaluable when troubleshooting problems with the SQL Agent. This file will contain any error messages generated during job processing. It will also contain any print statements that have been placed in stored procedures run by the SQL Agent. This can help you pinpoint the exact location of an error.

Offline Folders

Outlook has the ability to be configured with offline folders. Do not set this up. If you set up offline folders, messages will accumulate in the outbox until someone physically initiates a mail upload.

The Advanced tab is where you will want to do most of your configuration. If SQL Server or the SQL Agent stops unexpectedly, you will want to have it automatically start back up. Because the SQL Agent runs all of the periodic processing, the last thing you want is the SQL Agent to shut down and not restart. This can cause a lot of work, and it has a big impact on the recoverability of your databases because all backups are normally handled by the SQL Agent.

Alerts are something you will want to take full advantage of within your environment. Alerts will be covered in detail later in this chapter. One important thing to note, however, is that just like jobs, alerts can be handled by a central machine. When setting up event forwarding, be very careful in choosing the SQL Server that will handle the events. This is called "event forwarding," but it is really "alert forwarding." Any event that occurs that does not have an alert defined locally is forwarded to the server designated for event forwarding. If an alert is not defined for that event on the forwarded server, the event is ignored. Events can generate quite a bit of traffic and will drain the resources on the server that handles them. Take care not to designate the server(s) that do your heaviest processing as servers to which events will be forwarded.

The final option on this tab enables you to define what constitutes an idle processor. Jobs can be configured to take advantage of idle time on the processor. This will allow you to gain the maximum benefit from your existing hardware while not impacting your performance with low-priority jobs. The default idle time should be sufficient in most installations. But properly setting this value can help you smooth the "peaks and valleys" of your processor utilization.

The Alert System tab has one item you should always configure. A fail-safe operator will receive any messages that cannot be sent to any operator. This is your safety net in case communication goes down between SQL Server and the operators. It is recommended that you set up the fail-safe operator with the `net send` option. Most of the communications problems you will encounter will be with the email or pager systems. If email or pager services fail, you will not be able to utilize them, so it does not make any sense to have your fail-safe operator set up with either of those options. `net send` will work in all cases unless the network goes down. Detecting that a network is down is much easier than detecting that messages are being hung in a mailbox. However, this does add the restriction that the machine you are sending the message to must remain up and running at all times.

The Job System tab contains two options that cause confusion in just about every installation. Every job that is executed places an entry in a history file. The history file is actually a table in the msdb database. You can specify that the history grows without bounds, but doing so is not recommended. Rather, it's recommended that you place a limit upon the size of the history that's kept. After this limit is reached, the oldest history entries are supposed to be purged from the table automatically. While this is nice in theory, in real life it doesn't work that way. You'll want to manually monitor the size of the history and purge it as necessary.

The other option in this tab allows you to restrict the accounts that can run CmdExec and Active Scripting job steps. The presence of these types of job steps provides a level of functionality that is unmatched in any other RDBMSs. With this functionality comes an inherent security risk that must be appropriately managed. These types of job steps are potentially as damaging as `xp_cmdshell` can be. You will want to limit the ability to run these types of job steps to users with sys-admin permissions.

Security Risks of `xp_cmdshell`

`xp_cmdshell` as well as CmdExec and Active Scripting job steps run at an OS level with the full authority and permissions of the account SQL Server is running under. SQL Server requires an account with local administrator permissions at a minimum. Most installations use a domain administrator account.

It's my experience that few organizations fully appreciate the power the `sa` account has over an NT network. This is the dangerous side of a double-edged sword because SQL Server is bound so tightly into Windows NT. If you allow `xp_cmdshell` or CmdExec and Active Scripting job steps to be run by any account, any user with a SQL Server login has the ability to execute any OS command (including things like `format c:`).

In a real-world demonstration of this, I was at a company that would not accept my recommendations concerning limitations on `xp_cmdshell`. They also did not believe the `sa` account could have that much authority within NT. This was a company that had a very high regard for electronic as well as physical security but did not have very much SQL Server knowledge. Every resource on the network was closely monitored, and, in many cases, access was severely limited.

The company was running under a master domain model, and SQL Server was running under a domain admin account in the master domain. Because all other domains trusted the master domain, this left them vulnerable to any command issued from the master domain.

An NT login was created with permissions to only a home directory. Every other resource on the network was specified as No Access. And it was verified that after logging on to the network, I would not be able to access any resources on the network.

I then logged in to SQL Server using the `sa` account and locked out the accounts of both NT administrators. After accomplishing that, a file was copied from a high-security area on the network to the administrator's home directory.

That was all it took to finally convince them of the importance of restricting things like `xp_cmdshell`. Even though the NT logon account did not have the authority to perform those actions, the authority was implicitly granted by virtue of having the `sa` logon to SQL Server.

Although this example was fairly innocuous and simple to reverse, I could just as easily have reformatted the hard drives on all servers, which would have been much more difficult to reverse than a locked-out user account was.

Make sure you restrict the ability to execute `xp_cmdshell` and run CmdExec or Active Scripting jobs; if you don't, you are leaving yourself open to attacks such as these. The other thing to keep in mind is that most security breaches occur behind the firewall by employees and not through external access.

Adding Operators

The first step toward deriving the full benefit of the SQL Agent is to define an operator or set of operators to be notified. This allows the SQL Agent to send messages to an operator informing her of particular events.

Follow these steps to create an operator:

1. In Enterprise Manager, select Action, New, Operator.

2. Define the types of notification systems that will be used and the account to which the message will be sent.

3. Define the on-duty hours.

Configuring Jobs

A job consists of one or more steps. Each job step can also have one or more schedules. The entire job engine has been completely rewritten in SQL Server 7.0. Hopefully, in the next few pages, you will gain a better appreciation for the dramatic advances this has brought to your environment.

Follow these steps to create a job:

1. Define a name and category for the job.

2. Select the Steps tab.

3. Define each step in your job with the appropriate execution type, user, database, and command.

4. For each job step, specify the output file, success actions, and failure actions.

5. Define a schedule for the job.

6. Define any notifications.

Following the previous steps is all there is to creating a job. However, there are many considerations when defining a job.

Each job can be defined in a category. This is simply a mechanism that allows you to easily group similar jobs. You can create new categories by right-clicking on the job's item and selecting the Categories menu. You are encouraged to take advantage of this because it will simplify some of the administration. Defining job steps is where you will spend most of your time.

As was noted in the SQL Agent configuration section and the earlier sidebar, two types of job steps pose a security concern. Be careful when defining job steps using either CmdExec or Active Scripting, and make sure you take into account any security options that have been set up. Failure to do so will cause the job step to fail.

You will not be using the replication types for job steps. If you configure replication on your system, these types of job steps will automatically be added to any replication jobs that are created to manage the process.

The majority of the job steps you create will be of the type TSQL. To maximize the performance and minimize the impact changes have on your environment, you should use stored procedures for any job steps. This enables you to modify the contents of the stored procedure without having to redefine one or more job steps.

Failure to use stored procedures could result in some unwanted side effects. When making modifications to the schema, most administrators remember to modify all the dependent objects. Job steps will not show up as part of any dependencies. If you forget to modify the job step as well, you run the risk of having a job fail, or worse, corrupting your data. This is also important when dealing with a master server environment. It is possible that one administrator would have the ability to modify objects on one of the target servers but would not have access to the master server. This makes modifying job steps even more difficult. If steps are all run from stored procedures, you can localize and minimize the impact of any business rule or schema changes that are required.

You have the option of specifying an output file for each job step. This is an invaluable aid when you need to troubleshoot the failure of a step. Any messages that are generated in the process of running the job step will be redirected to this file. Because all your scripts and procedures should be liberally sprinkled with constructs to report on the progress, you will be able to precisely pinpoint where the process is failing.

The success and failure actions are two of the most powerful additions to the SQL Agent. This gives you complete control over job flow, and it even allows you to possibly reset the entire environment to reprocess the job. This can be desirable if you're dealing with batch loads of data that fail. Be very careful when setting this up, however, as it is possible to create a closed loop. In some cases, a circular reference among your job steps might be desirable, but you should always have a way to break the loop.

The last extremely useful addition is a number of retries and a retry interval. This is especially useful when a job step relies on the presence of a file or some other external condition.

The Schedules tab poses a very interesting situation. In previous versions, running a task on multiple schedules required the duplication of that task. SQL Server 7 now enables you to define multiple schedules for each job. This can be very useful if you need to run lower-priority jobs that could execute frequently. For example, you could set one of these jobs to run when the CPU is idle, but also set up a specific time each day for it to execute to ensure that the job runs at least once per day during those times when the machine is very heavily used. Using multiple schedules is demonstrated in the report engine case study later in chapter.

The final thing to set up is the notification. Although every job you run in your environment is mission critical and must be completed, you should at least prioritize them. Obviously, if a job fails, an operator should be notified. But if the job is such that the business cannot function without it being complete, a notification should also be sent upon successful completion.

Configuring Alerts

Alerts in SQL Server consist of several components. Most alerts you will define are based on counters in Performance Monitor. Some additional alerts will be defined based on internal SQL Server events that are normally based on severity-level or error-message content.

The SQL Agent has been defined with much tighter integration into the Windows NT Performance Monitor. This integration has greatly streamlined the process of creating alerts based on Performance Monitor counters. In previous versions of SQL Server, it was necessary to have Performance Monitor running in order for alerts based on its counters to work. This is no longer necessary; alerts will be raised even when the Performance Monitor is shut down.

Notifications Gone Awry

It may sound flippant, but you should use common sense when defining what type of notification to send. Paging an operator at 3:00 a.m. to notify him or her that a noncritical job is complete is not a good idea. Notifications of this nature would best be handled by sending an email. Also, if you know a particular operator powers off his or her machine every night, it makes no sense to use a net send notification after working hours because there is no machine to send the message to. You might laugh about these types of scenarios, but people set up such notification methods quite often.

One case had very tragic consequences to a company. One of the operators was required to carry a pager at all times. The lead DBA had set up a notification to page the operator every time a job ran successfully or failed. Tired of being awakened at all hours of the night, the operator simply left the pager in her car. One day a large number of very important transactions had been processed in the system in preparation for a government audit the next day. That evening, backups failed, and the server chose that night to corrupt the databases and have hardware fail. No one knew this had occurred until they arrived in the morning to find a server offline, a failed backup, and corrupted databases.

The company went through a very intense day trying to explain to the auditors why the system wasn't running, why none of their books balanced, what had happened to all of the transactions from the previous day, and why those transactions could not be restored. Already fed up with the constant intrusions of the pager, the DBA (who was one of the best the company had ever had) decided the audit was the final straw and quit to find a new job. The person who had set up the notification schedule and who was responsible for overseeing the environment got fired. The company made it through the follow-up audit but spent the next year on probation. Approximately $3 million in transactions were never located, and quite a few angry customers who had worked with the company switched to one of their competitors. Within six months of coming off probation, the company closed its doors.

While it might be a stretch to say the company went out of business due to an extremely intrusive notification method, it was definitely a contributing factor to a whole series of events that rapidly snowballed.

The lesson to be taken from this is you must be very careful with everything that is configured in your environment. Even small details can rapidly grow into major problems if all of the ramifications are not taken into account.

One additional thing that can be used with alerts are SNMP traps. SNMP, or Simple Network Management Protocol, is widely used in network management suites such as Tivoli to monitor TCP/IP traffic. SNMP traps enable you to integrate the alerting mechanism into your overall network management systems. The fail-safe operator (discussed earlier) can be an effective fallback in an environment that does not have a management suite running. For those sites that do use SNMP and network management suites, an SNMP trap is a much more powerful and reliable alternative to a fail-safe operator.

Follow these steps to configure an alert:

1. Define a name for the alert.
2. Specify whether it will be based on a counter or a message.
3. If you are using an error-message–based alert, specify the database for which this particular alert will be active.
4. If using a Performance Monitor counter, select the counter and instance, and then specify the thresholds for the alert.
5. Specify whether you want to raise an SNMP trap.
6. Define any notifications.
7. Define a job to be automatically executed for this alert, if necessary.
8. Specify a delay between notifications.

You should consider creating alerts for the following Performance Monitor counters:

■ **Access Methods**

   ■ *Full Scans.* This statistic gives you the number of unrestricted full scans on either the base table or the indexes. A high rate of full scans can indicate the need for additional indexes.

   ■ *Page Splits.* This statistic gives you the number of page splits that occur as the result of overflowing index or data pages. A high rate of page splits usually indicates the need to reorganize the table to reestablish a fill factor. This can be accomplished by dropping and re-creating the clustered index.

■ **Buffer Manager**

   ■ *Cache Hit Ratio.* This statistic gives you the percentage of pages that were found in the cache without having to read from disk. You want to maximize this number in all systems. A low cache hit ratio indicates that you need to add more RAM to the server.

   ■ *Stolen Page Count.* This statistic gives you the number of buffer cache pages that have been stolen to satisfy other server memory requests. A high number of stolen pages indicates that you either need to add more RAM or are running too many applications on the server that are conflicting with SQL Server.

■ **Database Manager**

■ *Active Transactions.* This statistic gives you the number of active transactions for the database. When performance on the server markedly declines, you should monitor this statistic. A high number of active transactions does not necessarily indicate a problem. If you consistently have a high number of transactions and slow performance, you should add more RAM to the machine because the current transaction volume on the server has exceeded its current capacity. The other thing this could indicate is a poorly constructed application that holds transactions open for an extended period of time.

■ *Percent Log Used.* This statistic gives you the percentage of space in the log that is in use. If your transaction logs do not automatically grow, you will need to monitor this counter to prevent a transaction log from filling up.

■ *Repl. Pending Xacts.* This statistic gives you the number of pending replication transactions in the database. A high number of pending replication transactions normally indicates that you have a problem in your replication system. Either replication has "gone down," or the network connection has become a bottleneck.

■ **General Statistics**

■ *Total Memory (KB).* This statistic gives you the total amount of dynamic memory SQL Server is currently using. This number should always be a significant portion of the total server memory available. If your counters do not reflect this, consider adding additional RAM or relocating some applications to other servers. You can check the memory usage of the other processes using Performance Monitor or the Task Manager.

■ **Lock Manager**

■ *Table Lock Escalations.* This statistic gives you the number of times locks on a table are escalated. If you experience excessive blocking, you should consider monitoring this counter. A table lock is the most restrictive lock possible and should be minimized. A large number of table lock escalations can indicate an improperly coded application or that a large number of unrestricted queries are being run in the SQL Server.

■ **Locks**

■ *Lock Waits.* This statistic gives you the number of lock requests that could not be satisfied immediately and required the caller to wait. This indicates the number of locks that had to wait for system resources to be freed up to service a request. A large number of lock waits can indicate that you need to add more RAM to the server.

■ *Number of Deadlocks.* This statistic gives you the number of lock requests that resulted in a deadlock. A deadlock is a very serious situation and can cause a big performance problem as well as create unpredictable results in a client application. You should set up an alert for this counter that will trigger notification anytime a deadlock occurs. These should be immediately investigated to prevent any future occurrences. By using the SQL Profiler, it is possible to trap the SQL statements that lead to a deadlock.

■ **Log Manager**

■ *Log Flush Wait Time.* This statistic gives you the total wait time (milliseconds). A large wait time indicates that the checkpoint process had to wait for resources to be freed on the server. A large wait time can indicate the need to add more RAM to the server. You want to minimize the wait time so that transactions are flushed from the transaction log to disk in a timely manner.

■ *Log Flush Waits.* This statistic gives you the number of commits that are waiting on log flush. If you suddenly see your transaction log steadily increasing in size, you should monitor this statistic. A large and continually increasing value normally means that a transaction has been left open, which will prevent subsequent transactions from being flushed to disk.

■ **Replication Dist**

■ *Delivery Latency.* This statistic gives you the amount of time the commands were in the distribution database before being applied to the subscriber. Tracking this counter will reveal bottlenecks. A high delivery latency usually indicates a network bottleneck. A large and increasing latency usually indicates that the subscriber is no longer able to receive replicated transactions.

■ **Replication Logreader**

■ *Delivery Latency.* This statistic gives you the amount of time in seconds that it took the LogReader to deliver transactions to the distributor. A large number indicates a network bottleneck. A large and increasing number usually indicates that the distributor or distribution database is offline.

■ **Replication Merge**

■ *Conflicts.* This statistic gives you the number of conflicts that occurred in the Publisher/Subscriber upload and download changes. This value should always be zero. A non-zero value demands immediate attention. The subscriber must be notified that the merged transaction conflicted with data on the publisher, and the transaction conflict must be resolved before proceeding.

In addition to Performance Monitor counters, a few error-severity levels should be monitored. SQL Server comes with these alerts already defined. All you need to do is enable them and define an operator(s) to be notified. These are severity levels 19 through 25, each of which indicates a fatal error of some kind. These must be handled immediately, or you risk corrupting your data or damaging hardware. They can also indicate that your data is already corrupt and your hardware is already damaged.

When setting up notifications for alerts, it is very important that you define a delay interval. This tells the SQL Agent to ignore any additional messages of the same type for the interval you specify. Some alert conditions, such as most fatal errors, can persist for an extended period of time. You will notice this immediately if one of the alerts is ever triggered and you have not configured an appropriate interval. In such cases, one of the following things will happen: Your pager will light up like a Christmas tree; your mailbox will fill up; or you will receive a few hundred message boxes at your terminal, all within the space of a few seconds. This is because without an interval set, the alert is triggered every time the error occurs, and a notification is sent each time. As you know if you've worked on any system for very long, a few thousand errors of the same type can be generated within a few seconds. In some cases, an error can be triggered for every CPU cycle!

Setting Up a Master Server (MSX)

So far in this chapter, you have learned how to create operators, jobs, and alerts on a single SQL Server. This approach will generally suffice for most implementations. However, in environments with many SQL Servers, this can become very tedious. In addition to that, many tasks and alerts that you will configure should be run on multiple machines.

To streamline administration of multiple servers, you can configure the SQL Agent as a master server. The master server contains all jobs and alerts for your entire environment. Target servers connect to the master server and process scheduled jobs, and alerts are forwarded from the target server(s) to the master to be handled.

Two conditions are required for setting up a master server and one or more target servers:

- The master server must be running Windows NT.
- Each target server must be running the MSSQLServer and SQLAgent services under a domain account that has login privileges to the master servers.

The domain accounts under which SQL Server and the SQL Agent are running for a target server should be members of the domain admins group. This allows the target server to log in to the master server as sa by using integrated security. Although this poses a security risk, it is the easiest way to configure the target servers.

After you have set up all the prerequisites, designating the master is a simple matter of working through a wizard. Start Enterprise Manager, highlight the SQL Agent on the server you want to designate as the master, and select Actions, Multi Server Administration, Make This a Master to launch the Make MSX Wizard.

After completing the wizard, you will notice that the SQL Agent has an MSX designation after it. This denotes a master server. The operators will show a new entry named MSXOperator on the master and each target server. When you open the Jobs item, you will now have entries for local jobs and multiserver jobs.

Creating a job is almost the same as usual. The difference at this point is that you now have the capability of designating a job for multiple servers within the job definition.

Target servers periodically connect to the master server and check for jobs designated to be run. If any jobs are found, they are downloaded to the target server and executed. When a job is completed, a notification is sent to the MSXOperator at the location specified for the operator.

Case Studies

The remainder of this chapter is a series of case studies that demonstrate the real-world use of the SQL Agent to solve common problems. Each one of these applies the scenario to the pubs database. In addition, the examples provided here contain simplified scripts so as not to bog down the discussion with a lot of complex code.

Importing External Data

Many systems get data feeds from external sources and simply BCP the files into a database and process the results. This can have wide-ranging effects if a file is truncated during transmission or does not contain all the data it should. It's not uncommon for systems to receive data that does not match the original host files because data was dropped during transmission or because the jobs creating the files excluded data.

If at all possible, you should implement a two-phase approach to downloading data in order to achieve validation of the data volume. This is accomplished by creating a control file that follows all data transmissions. The control file has a listing of each file transmitted and the record count for that file.

When you process the data, you will BCP the data files and the control file into your staging database. The next step is to cross-check the row counts. If the counts match, you can continue to process the data. If they do not match, a notification is sent to the data center indicating that a file has been truncated in transit and needs to be retransmitted. Your job should then be reset to reprocess the data after it has been retransmitted.

One very common scenario in most environments is to have one or more files from external systems that need to be imported into SQL Server. While Data Transformation Services can accomplish some of this processing, it requires the presence of an OLEDB provider. The approach that's shown here uses BCP because every system has the capability of generating a text file. The other reason to use BCP is for speed. No other process on a SQL Server can compete with BCP for raw speed. Also new to SQL Server 7.0 is the bulk insert command, which can actually achieve a slightly higher transfer rate than BCP.

XYZ Company maintains all their sales, store, author, and publisher information on a mainframe. Every night around midnight, four files are downloaded to a network share through an SNA Server. SQL Server is then required to move the files from the share to the local machine SQL Server runs on. Because all files must be saved, after a file is moved, it is renamed by using the table name and date as an identifier. Each file is then BCPed into a processing area in SQL Server and inserted into the destination tables. One additional requirement is that a reporting table be maintained, showing aggregated sales by author.

For all BCP operations, you should consider creating a processing area. This allows you to take advantage of the speed of BCP without invalidating your transaction logs at the same time. It also allows you to dispense with format files because you can match the table structure to the external file. This can save a significant amount of time, because as anyone who has used BCP knows, the error messages generated by BCP are cryptic at best and unusable at worst.

The first thing you will do is establish a directory for the files to be moved to. This will be c:\mssql7\data\import.

Next, you need to create a table in the pubs database for the sales by author data:

```
create table salesbyauthor
(au_id      id        NOT NULL ,
 au_lname   char(40)  NOT NULL ,
 au_fname   char(20)  NOT NULL ,
 sales      money     NOT NULL)
```

You could create a view for this data, but for performance reasons, use a table instead. After creating the table, you can apply indexes that match the query patterns for this aggregated data. Had you used a view, however, some of the indexing could not have been accomplished (such as a search for the authors with aggregated sales greater than or less than a certain level).

Each file will be moved, renamed, and BCPed in separate steps in order to facilitate tracking of all actions to be performed.

The first step is to create a database, which you will call staging. Then you need to create four tables that match the file you are going to BCP in.

After that, the fun begins. You create three stored procedures to facilitate some of the processing. These procedures will insert data into pubs from staging, regenerate the salesbyauthor table, rename the files, and then clear the staging area. The moves and BCPs are accomplished directly by individual job steps.

The script to generate the stored procedures used for this job follows:

```
CREATE  procedure msp_dailyload
as
insert into pubs..authors
```

```
select au_id, au_lname, au_fname, phone, address, city, state, zip,
➥contract
from staging..authors

insert into pubs..publishers
select pub_id, pub_name, city, state, country from staging..publishers

insert into pubs..stores
select stor_id, stor_name, stor_address, city, state, zip from
➥staging..stores

insert into pubs..sales
select stor_id, ord_num, ord_date, qty, payterms, title_id from
➥staging..sales

delete pubs..salesbyauthor

insert into pubs..salesbyauthor
select a.au_id, a.au_lname, a.au_fname, sum(t.price * t.ytd_sales)
from pubs..authors a, pubs..titles t, pubs..titleauthor ta
where a.au_id = ta.au_id
and ta.title_id = t.title_id
group by a.au_id, a.au_lname, a.au_fname
GO
CREATE   procedure msp_rename
as
declare @suffix varchar(6),
            @filename  varchar(20),
            @command   varchar(255)
select @suffix = convert(varchar(2), datepart(mm,getdate()))+
        convert(varchar(2), datepart(dd,getdate())) + convert(varchar(2)),
➥right(datepart(yy,getdate()),2))
select @filename = 'authors' + @suffix + '.txt'
select @command = 'master..xp_cmdshell "rename
    c:\mssql7\data\import\authors.txt
    c:\mssql7\data\import\' + @filename + '"'
exec(@command)
select @filename = 'stores' + @suffix + '.txt'
select @command = 'master..xp_cmdshell "rename
    c:\mssql7\data\import\stores.txt c:\mssql7\data\import\'
    + @filename + '"'
exec(@command)
select @filename = 'sales' + @suffix + '.txt'
select @command = 'master..xp_cmdshell "rename
    c:\mssql7\data\import\sales.txt c:\mssql7\data\import\'
    + @filename + '"'
exec(@command)
select @filename = 'publishers' + @suffix + '.txt'
```

```
select @command = 'master..xp_cmdshell "rename
    c:\mssql7\data\import\publishers.txt c:\mssql7\data\import\'
    + @filename + '"'
exec(@command)
GO

create procedure msp_resetstaging
as
truncate table staging..authors
truncate table staging..stores
truncate table staging..sales
truncate table staging..publishers
GO
```

Now that all the prerequisites are complete, all that is left to do is define each of the job steps and the schedule. In order to help with identification in case of failures, you will define a separate job step for moving each file and BCPing the data into the staging database. This will create a set of four job steps for the move and another four for the BCP. The final three job steps will each execute one of the preceding procedures.

The type of command for the move and the BCP will be CmdExec because you are executing operating system commands or applications.

For the move, you now have much better control over the job step. Relying on external systems to send files on a particular schedule can have disastrous consequences if you rely on the data to be in your system each time the process is executed. Files can—and often do—get delayed in transmission due to a variety of factors. However, you will get around this problem through the retry attempts and the retry interval. Each of the move steps will be configured for 12 retries with an interval of 5 minutes. This means that each job step performing a move will retry the move every 5 minutes for an hour if the file is delayed. If a file is not present after retrying for an hour, you most likely have a more serious networking issue that needs to be resolved. You will want to tune this interval for your environment based on the processing window that you have.

Each of the BCPs will have no retries set. The fact you have reached the BCP indicates that valid files do exist on your system. If the BCP fails, you do not want to go any further in the process.

The only other thing to note for setting up the job is the option at the top of the Advanced tab that enables you to output to a file. You will be tempted to use a different filename for each job step, but doing so is discouraged from a manageability standpoint. For the job outlined here, this would mean having 11 files that would need to be scanned if errors occurred. In many production environments, this approach can quickly create hundreds or thousands of files. The best approach is to create a single file for each job. The first job step should be set to overwrite with subsequent steps set to append to the file. Then any output of messages that would normally go to a screen is redirected to this file.

After the data has been BCPed into the staging database, the msp_dailyload stored procedure is executed. This inserts the data into the production tables in the pubs database and regenerates the salesbyauthor table.

Upon successful completion of the load, the files will be renamed. To accomplish this, you'll use a job step of type TSQL by using `xp_cmdshell`. Alternatively, you could use a job step of CmdExec and a batch file, but the TSQL approach is much easier to understand and troubleshoot. When the files have been renamed, the staging area is cleared in preparation for the next data load.

The job steps defined for this job are shown in Figure 5.1.

Creating a Report Server

It is a very common requirement for users to be able to execute a query or report, disconnect from the system, and later be able to reconnect and pick up the results. A few reporting tools on the market provide this type of functionality, but at the cost of tens of thousands of dollars. As long as the users do not require pretty layouts, GUI displays, and a whole host of features common in today's reporting packages, you can accomplish this functionality by using your existing tools in SQL Server. This case study will explore how to construct a "poor man's" report server by using the SQL Agent and SQL Mail.

XYZ company has a group of sales reps that travel around the world selling its products. One of the needs of these users is to check on stock levels for the products they sell. Fortunately for XYZ Company, the sales reps do not need the information immediately, and as much as a twelve-hour wait time to get the information is acceptable.

The responsiveness can very easily be tuned so that nearly immediate results are returned to the sales reps. A time delay is used in this case to demonstrate some of the additional scheduling features.

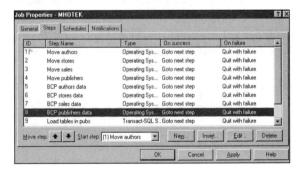

Figure 5.1 Job steps defined for batch load.

This system has worked so well for the sales reps that the management at XYZ Company has decided to expand its use into other areas of the company. With the added exposure, management has decided to add a modest amount of security to the system as well.

The security simply consists of defining which users can execute a particular query. To facilitate this and plan for easy expansion, the IS department has decided to streamline the addition of new queries to the system by creating a stored procedure for each query, which can optionally take parameters.

To accomplish the security and addition of queries to the system, two tables are created as follows:

```
create table mailqueries
(QueryID    int    identity(1,1)  not null,
MessageText  varchar(50)          not null,
ProcName    varchar(50)           not null,
Params      bit                   not null)

create table useraccess
(QueryID    int                   not null,
MailAddress  varchar(50)          not null)
```

The table called mailqueries will contain the data listed in Table 5.1.

The useraccess table simply contains an entry for each query a user is allowed to run.

Now to make a new query available, the administrators simply have to create the stored procedure and add entries into the two tables.

The entire system works as outlined in these steps:

1. You configure and start SQL Mail.

2. You create a job that uses the mail procedures to process any mail messages.

3. The users send messages to the SQL Mail mailbox indicating which query they want to run, along with any parameters.

4. When the CPU is idle, the SQL Agent processes the requests, sends the results back to the user, and deletes the message.

5. At a designated time every evening, the SQL Agent looks for unprocessed requests. If it finds any, it processes them immediately.

Table 5.1   **mailqueries Table**

Column	Description
QueryID	An identifier.
MessageText	The contents of the subject line.
ProcName	The name of the stored procedure to execute.
Params	Indicates whether any parameters can be accepted. Parameters will be entered in the body of the message.

To accomplish the processing of mail messages, you will utilize four extended stored procedures: xp_sendmail, xp_readmail, xp_findnextmsg, and xp_deletemail.

xp_sendmail is used to send mail messages to designated recipients. The syntax is as follows:

```
xp_sendmail @recipients,@message,@query,@attachments,
    @copy_recipients,@blind_copy_recipients,@subject,@type,
    @attach_results,@no_output,@no_header,@width,@separator,
➥@echo_error,@set_user,@dbuse
```

Table 5.2 details the parameters.

xp_readmail is used to read in a mail message. The syntax is as follows:

```
xp_readmail @msg_id,@type,@peek,@suppress_attach,@originator,
    @subject,@message,@recipients,@cc_list,@bcc_list,
    @date_received,@unread,@attachments,@skip_bytes,
    @msg_length,@originator_address
```

Table 5.3 details the parameters.

Table 5.2 xp_sendmail **Parameters**

Parameter	Description
@recipients	You can specify as many recipients for the message as necessary. These can be Exchange Server mailboxes or Internet email accounts.
@message	The message that will be sent.
@query	You have the ability to specify a valid query to be executed and attached to the email. This query can reference any object except the inserted and deleted tables it triggers.
@attachments	Specifies a file to be attached to the message.
@subject	The subject of the mail message.
@attach_results	Specifies that the query should be executed and sent as an attached file.
@no_header	Allows you to suppress the column headers for a query.
@set_user	Specifies the security context the query should be run under. The default is guest. If you have not enabled the guest account for access, you must specify an account that has the authority to execute the query.
@dbuser	Specifies the database context to run the query in. This should always be specified. The default is the default database for the user.

Table 5.3 `xp_readmail` **Parameters**

Parameter	Description
`@originator`	The email address of the user sending the message.
`@subject`	The subject of the message. This is normally a query that will be executed by SQL Server.
`@message`	This is either the text of the mail message or a query to execute. This variable is capable of handling only 255 characters. This can be a serious limitation and has prompted many very involved workarounds. It is best to keep messages very short.
`@recipients`	The recipients of the message.
`@skip_bytes`	The number of bytes to skip when reading the mail message. This is used to sequentially retrieve the chunks of the mail message. Fortunately, in version 7.0, a variable can be 8,000 characters. This means you can sequentially read in 255-character chunks and concatenate them in a variable. Eight thousand characters should be sufficient. If you need more, you should consider moving the query being sent from the message body to a stored procedure.
`@msg_length`	Specifies the total length of the message in bytes. This is normally used with **`@skip_bytes`** to process long messages.

To sequentially process mail messages, you would execute `xp_findnextmsg`, which has the following syntax:

```
xp_findnextmsg @msg_id,@type,@unread_only
```

When you finish processing a message, you normally want to delete that message. To do so, execute `xp_deletemail`:

```
xp_deletemail {'message_number'}
```

If you do not specify a message number, all messages in the inbox are deleted.

These four extended stored procedures define the physical mechanism for processing mail requests and returning results. The only thing left is to implement the security mechanism.

When a message comes in, the sender, subject, and message body are stored in local variables. A query is then run against the mailqueries and useraccess tables, using the subject and sender name to return the name of the stored procedure to execute. If no results are returned, the user does not have access to that query, and a message is sent back stating that. If a row is returned, the procedure is executed. If the Params column is set to 1, the message body is appended to the procedure name and executed. The results are attached to the mail message that is returned to the user, and the message that was just processed is deleted. The next message, if there is one, is located, and the whole process starts over.

After all messages have been processed, the job terminates and waits for the next idle time on the CPU to start again.

In this job, you will also take advantage of the multiple schedule feature for jobs. It is entirely possible that the CPU never goes idle on your system. Having only the CPU idle schedule available will prevent the job from ever running. So a second schedule is created to ensure that the job is executed at least once every day.

Monitoring SQL Server and Automating Tasks

One of the daily tasks of every administrator is to perform backups. Jobs within the SQL Agent are an excellent way to perform all the database and transaction log backups for the system. However, you will want to set up an additional safety net for your transaction logs.

Filling the transaction log will bring your whole system to a halt and can have a significant impact on recoverability (as just about anyone who has managed a SQL Server for very long has had the unfortunate pleasure to find out). This situation can be easily avoided with proper planning.

As was noted in previous chapters, databases and transaction logs can automatically grow and shrink. You should take advantage of this to help minimize the amount of maintenance required. However, you should not let them grow unchecked. Limiting the size of a transaction log puts you right back in a position where it can fill up and halt your applications even with proper planning for your transaction log backups, but it allows you to control the size of the log. In addition, if you do not limit the size, you run the risk of running out of disk space, which is a much more serious situation.

Before starting the system configuration, you will get the preliminary work out of the way. For each database on which you will be monitoring the transaction log, you will create a job that backs up the transaction log. You normally set this up as a backup to a fail-safe device so the automated transaction log backups can be tracked.

To prevent the transaction log from filling up, you should take advantage of the alert system by creating an alert on the SQL Server:Database Manager object and the Percent Log Used counter for the database you want to monitor. You can set this up for all databases, but it is not advisable simply because it makes things more difficult to track. Only set up an alert for those databases in which you want to automate the transaction log dumps. You will generally want to set up the alert for a Percent Log Used counter that's greater than 75 or 80.

If you set up this alert and define an operator only to notify, you still must manually intervene in the process. If the operator doesn't respond quickly enough, the transaction log can still fill up. To get around this problem, you will take advantage of the first option on the Response tab. You will select a job that was created specifically to back up the transaction log for this fail-safe method. As a result, whenever the transaction log reaches the threshold you specify, the alert system executes the job to back up the transaction log. This keeps all your databases cleaned up and prevents problems.

Whenever a job is automatically executed based on an alert, a message should always be sent to an operator. Failure to do this can cause your system to get out of hand. In a fully automated system, you can easily have dozens of alerts configured that automatically handle error events. If you are not kept abreast of each occurrence, you will never be able to uncover errors within your system or applications.

This method will protect you in normal cases. This is where the importance of notifications becomes useful. If you set up an alert for 75–80 percent full on the transaction log, you should set up an additional one for 90 percent full that does not execute a job but notifies an administrator instead. If the transaction log hits that higher threshold, the transaction log could not be backed up and flushed due to an open transaction. When this alert is raised, you should immediately check the SQL Server:Log Manager object and the Log Flush Waits counter. This counter indicates the number of committed transactions waiting to be flushed. A large number here in conjunction with a transaction log at least 90 percent full indicates that an application has left a transaction open, and is preventing any subsequent transaction from being flushed to disk or removed from the log during the backup log procedure.

To clear this open transaction from the log, you can issue a `DBCC opentran` and kill the offending spid. If that is not possible, you will have to shut down SQL Server and restart.

If the Log Flush Waits counter is a low number and the transaction log is 90 percent or more full, you have not sized the transaction log properly and will need to allow more growth for the log.

The preceding examples describe two ways you can use alerts and tasks to automate your environment. Other useful counters to monitor are noted in the section about alerts.

In addition to that, you should take advantage of the alerts on severity levels that are already configured for you. Severity levels of 19 or higher indicate a fatal situation on your SQL Server. These situations need to be handled immediately in order to protect the data.

The last thing you should note is that most administrators only scratch the surface when setting up alerts. This is because it takes quite a bit of planning, especially if multiple servers are involved, to provide a consistent and comprehensive plan. This usually takes time the administrator does not have because of all the daily fires he or she must fight. Try to resist the temptation to let setting alerts fall through the cracks. The time spent defining and setting up a complete system can save many hours in the future. The additional benefit that your organization will receive is that a single administrator will be able to manage many more servers than usual.

SQL Server has been a very stable database to run and is generally very easy to manage. If you set up alerts and jobs to fully automate your environment, SQL Server will be able to inform you when problems occur—or even better, before they occur. This enables you to take a proactive approach instead of a reactive one so you can compensate for and eliminate potential problems before they turn into real problems.

Conclusions

The SQL Agent is a simple but powerful addition to any environment. Most installations will eventually use the SQL Agent to perform periodic processing. But many of these locations will not take full advantage of the power and capabilities available. Hopefully, the three case studies presented will open your eyes to possibilities you may not have considered before.

As you learned in the first case study, the SQL Agent presents a very flexible scheduler to handle periodic processing and can control job flow to meet even the most demanding environments. The second case study showed you how to look past the simple features of the SQL Agent in order to use it as a driver for a much larger and more robust system. Being able to recognize and leverage these extended capabilities offers a finishing touch for many systems that can take them from being merely functional to being truly interactive and polished.

The lesson taught by the third case study cannot be stressed enough. The alerting mechanism in the SQL Agent will take you well beyond simple administration. Many DBAs struggle to handle the two or three active servers in their environments, whereas other DBAs manage literally dozens or hundreds of SQL Servers with just as much effort. What sets these two groups apart? The second group has automated their environments using alerts, which allows for proactive administration instead of the normal reactive method used by the first group. This also is the main driver that enables administrators to achieve almost 100 percent uptime on their systems.

6

Backup and Recovery

Chris Miller

Performing backups and preparing for recovery are the two most important jobs of a database administrator. The key to performing these tasks is to establish a routine. This chapter covers the whole routine, from the mechanics of a backup, to troubleshooting, to recovery. Here's a breakdown of how this chapter is organized:

- How Backup Works
- Configuring Automatic Backup
- Backup Strategies
- Backup Recommendations
- Disaster Recovery
- Using Third-Party Backup Utilities

Microsoft has made the mechanics for backing up a lot more flexible by introducing some new backup ideas. The first section, "How Backup Works," covers each of the types of backup, explains how each one works, and gives some ideas on how each can be used to back up a database. This chapter concentrates on the Transact-SQL syntax for performing backups. The "Configuring Automatic Backup" section concentrates on using SQL Enterprise Manager to perform and schedule backups. The "Backup Strategies" section provides some guidance on different backup scenarios and discusses the best approaches to use. The "Backup Recommendations" section contains final thoughts and recommendations on which strategies to use, as well as some other logistical concerns. The "Disaster Recovery" section goes through the other side of backup: loading and restoring databases after problems occur. The final section, "Using Third-Party Backup Utilities," covers the integration of third-party backup utilities into an overall backup and recovery strategy.

How Backup Works

This section covers the backup process at a very low level. It doesn't really delve into when backups should be done. Rather, this section exists more to provide you with information on what's going on when you hit the "OK" button to perform a backup and what restrictions and features are present in each type of backup. In this section, you'll learn about the following:

- *Backup device.* The destination for a backup, such as a disk drive, a network location, or a tape drive.

- *Database backups.* Takes all the pages that are in use in the database and writes them to specified backup media. This does *not* truncate the transaction log.

- *Transaction log backups.* Takes all the pages in the transaction log and writes them to the specified backup media. Removes all inactive (completed) transactions from the transaction log—a process that is called "truncating the log."

- *Differential backups.* Takes all of the pages that have changed *since the last full database backup* and writes them to the specified backup media. This has no impact on the transaction log.

- *File/file group backups.* Takes all the pages present in the specified file or file group and writes them to the specified backup media. This is great for backing up huge databases.

Backup Devices

Most of the backup commands require that a backup device be specified as the destination for the backup. A backup device is simply a location, such as a tape drive or a file on disk, where the backup information will be stored.

There are three types of backup devices:

- *Tape devices.* Tape drives are the most cost-effective storage media for large quantities of data. They provide a lot of storage with a long shelf life, making them ideal for archiving data. Tape drives are slower than disk media, but a combination of advances in DLT technology and the advent of tape arrays and specialized controllers make tape devices a great backup solution.

- *Disk devices.* Disk devices can be used to hold data. These include both disk drives on the local machine and network drives. A disk device name is specified all the way down to a filename, for example, C:\MSSQL\BACKUP\ PUBBACKUP.DAT.

- *Named Pipe devices.* These devices are used by third-party backup software to carry data generated during a backup to the backup software, which then writes it to the backup media (usually tape).

In every place that a backup device can be specified, a list of backup devices could be specified instead. For example, instead of listing one tape device, you could list 3 or 4 or up to 32. SQL Server will then write to these tape devices in parallel, which will significantly increase the capacity and speed of the backup. This isn't limited to tape backups; a disk backup can be split up across several different devices. The key reasons for doing this are to make the backup files more manageable and to enable multiple low-capacity disk drives to be used to keep a backup online.

Backup devices can be created and then either specified by name or specified manually. A backup device can be created by using the sp_addumpdevice system stored procedure

```
sp_addumpdevice 'device_type', 'logical_name', 'physical_name'
```

where 'device_type' is one of "disk," "pipe," or "tape"; 'logical_name' is the name of the device that will be used in SQL Server, such as "PUBS_BACKUP"; and 'physical_name' is the physical name for the device. A physical name is either a drive letter and full path for a local disk device or a UNC path for any other type of device. For a tape drive, specify the UNC path as \\.\tape0. The \\.\tape0 specifies the first tape drive in the machine, \\.\tape1 would specify the second, and so on.

To specify a dynamic backup device, use the following syntax in the command

```
'type' = 'physical_name'
```

where 'type' is "DISK," "TAPE," or "PIPE," and the physical name is the full path to the device.

Security and the Network-Based Disk Device

In order to back up to a disk device on a network drive, the SQL Server service must be running, by using an account other than the Local System account. That's because the Local System account doesn't have access to network drives because it's valid only on the local system.

Another option, which is significantly less secure, is to set up a null session share. This allows the Local System account to write across the network, but it also allows other services to access the same share. First, create the share, and then make it a null session share by adding a value to the following Registry key:

```
HKEY_LOCAL_MACHINE\System\CurrentControlSet
\Services\LanmanServer\Parameters\NullSessionShares
```

The value type should be REG_MULTI_SZ, and each share on the target machine should be on its own line. Once again, the Registry key goes on the target for the disk device and just contains the name of the share that needs to be a null session share. This will establish the share and allow outside access to it. The server must be rebooted for that change to take effect.

Backup Sets and Media Sets

Two similar-sounding yet totally different terms are tossed around liberally throughout the SQL Server documentation: "backup sets" and "media sets." This section makes it clear exactly what each means.

A *backup set* is the set of files involved in one backup. SQL Server 7.0 uses the same tape format as the Windows NT Backup software, called the Microsoft Tape Format, or MTF. That means that a SQL Server backup can be stored on the same tape as the rest of the server backup because all the tape devices supported by Windows NT are now also supported by SQL Server. However, it also means that SQL Server 6.5 database dumps are not the same format as new database backups.

So a backup set created with the Windows NT Backup utility will contain a whole lot of files. A backup set for SQL Server contains at most a whole database but may contain just a transaction log, a differential backup file, or a file/file group backup. Backup sets on a given tape are numbered starting with 1. During a restore procedure, you must specify which backup set to restore. You'll learn more about how to figure out what that number is in the section "Disaster Recovery," later in this chapter. You can give backup sets descriptive names so you can more easily find them on the tape later.

A *media set* is a collection of one or more different tapes or disk files that are used to store one or more different backup sets. So if it takes 10 tapes from five different devices to back up a database, the media set for that backup is 10 tapes. A *media family* consists of all the tapes that are used by one device. Therefore, in the preceding example, the media set could be said to contain five media families of two tapes each.

You can name media during the media format process, which will write a header on the tape. Naming the media set is a good idea because you can then specify the media set name during the backup process. If the names don't match because someone forgot to switch tapes, for example, the backups won't be accidentally overwritten.

Restriction

If you back up to a disk device and then take that disk backup and copy it to tape by using the Windows NT Backup software, you can't load it back into SQL Server from SQL Server as a tape device. Instead, you must first reload the database device back to the disk and then load the backup from disk. Remember that if you back up to a certain medium, you have to restore from the same medium.

Microsoft Tape Format Encryption

At this time, SQL Server does not support encryption of media sets. So if a media set is encrypted by using the Windows NT Backup utility, SQL Server will not be able to use that media set.

Database Backups

The database backup and the transaction log backup have been around for a long time. A database backup provides a page-by-page backup of a database and will restore a database to exactly the point in time that it was backed up. A new feature for the database backup is that a database backup will now store all the information needed to rebuild all the files and file groups that support the database. When the database is restored, it rebuilds any missing files or file groups that are needed to create the database.

In SQL Server 6.5, a database backup would consume a ridiculous amount of processor overhead. SQL Server 6.5 had a very inefficient backup scheme. Basically, it would start backing up the database from page 0. If it detected that someone wanted to change a page, it would go and back up that particular page before it was changed, and then it would resume the backup at the point of interruption. All this jumping back and forth during the backup caused a lot of overhead.

SQL Server 7.0 changes that. First, it marks the transaction log for the start of the backup. Then it starts at page 0 and backs up the database. Then it appends a backup of the current transaction log without truncating the log. During recovery, the entire database will be restored, but it will probably have partial transactions in it. Then the transaction log backup will be restored, and the transactions that are complete will be completed, and the transactions that are incomplete will be removed.

This new backup process is a lot simpler and doesn't require near as much processor overhead. Microsoft benchmarks show that a database backup now requires only about 5 percent of the total transactional volume of the server. So if the backup is done while the server is operating at 80 percent of its transactional capacity, the users won't notice any slowdowns during the backup. Although this is a very impressive advance, other database systems have employed this feature for a long time.

Restrictions

In order to maintain transactional integrity, certain operations are not allowed during a database backup. These include structural changes to the database (adding, removing, or shrinking database files), index creation, and all nonlogged operations, such as BCP or Select Into.

Syntax

The Transact-SQL syntax for backup has changed drastically. The old "Dump Database" syntax used in previous versions is now obsolete. It will still work, but it isn't guaranteed to work in any version after 7.0. The new syntax is

```
BACKUP DATABASE <database name>
TO <backup device list>
[WITH <option list>]
```

where <database_name> is the name of the database to be backed up, <backup device list> is a comma-separated list of devices to be used to back up the database, and the option list is a list of options.

Following are the options that can be specified and a brief description for each:

- **BLOCKSIZE.** The block size to use. This applies only when you're using tape backup devices; it is ignored for disk devices. For tape devices, it is used only if the FORMAT option is also specified. For Named Pipe devices, the block size defaults to 64KB; for a tape device, its default is based on the type of tape drive and media. Usually, you won't need to worry about this option. Leave it alone and let it default.

- **DESCRIPTION.** A text description, up to 255 characters, that can be added to the backup.

- **EXPIREDATE.** The date after which the backup can be overwritten.

- **RETAINDAYS.** The number of days until the backup can be overwritten. Either use EXPIREDATE or RETAINDAYS, but do not use both.

- **FORMAT or NOFORMAT.** If the FORMAT option is chosen, the device will be formatted. For a tape device, this makes all the data on the tape unusable because it overwrites the part of the tape that contains the start and stop points for the data on the tape. For disk media, this reinitializes the file but doesn't reformat the disk or do anything bad like that. The NOFORMAT option is the default, but it can be used just to make sure. The FORMAT option can be used to change which backup set the device is part of.

- **INIT or NOINIT.** INIT specifies that the backup device should be initialized before being used. This is different from the FORMAT command because this does not overwrite the media header, so the device still belongs to the same media set.

- **MEDIADESCRIPTION.** A text description that can be added to describe the entire media set, up to 255 characters.

- **MEDIANAME.** The name of the media set. If this is specified and the FORMAT option is not used, the tape that is being used must already be formatted with the correct media name. If the FORMAT option is specified, the media name is the name that will be assigned to the media set.

- **NAME.** Up to 128 characters specifying the name for the backup set. If the name is not specified, it will be left blank. If a tape contains multiple backup sets, it's a good idea to specify a name so the particular backup set you want can be found easily.

- **SKIP and NOSKIP.** Specify whether the checking of the EXPIREDATE and RETAINDAYS setting should be skipped or not. Specifying SKIP allows you to override the protection placed on a tape by the EXPIREDATE and RETAINDAYS options.

- **UNLOAD or NOUNLOAD.** For a tape device, this specifies whether or not the tape should be rewound and ejected when the tape ends or if it should just be left at the end of the tape. This defaults to UNLOAD. It is ignored for non-tape devices.

- **RESTART**. If a backup operation is stalled by a power outage or something, it can be restarted by using the RESTART option. Specify the same options as before. This can be used only for tape backups; it does not work for disk backups.
- **STATS=<percentage>**. Normally when a backup is running, you don't get any feedback until it's completed. If you use the STATS option (as in STATS = 10), you'll get feedback in periodic intervals as each 10 percent of the backup is completed.

That's the syntactical rundown. Now here's an example of how to actually use backup:

```
BACKUP DATABASE pubs
TO DISK='C:\PUBSDUMP.DAT'
WITH DESCRIPTION = "Pubs Test Backup",
     INIT,
     STATS = 5
```

This results in the following output:

```
74 percent backed up.
99 percent backed up.
Processed 160 pages for database 'pubs', file 'pubs' on file 1.
100 percent backed up.
Processed 1 pages for database 'pubs', file 'pubs_log' on file 1.
Backup or restore operation successfully processed 161 pages in 0.687
➥seconds (1.909 MB/sec).
```

Notice the percentages don't go by 5 percent increments. That's because the pubs database is too small.

To dump to a tape device, you would use this command:

```
BACKUP DATABASE pubs
TO TAPE='\\.\TAPE0'
WITH FORMAT
```

This formats a new tape, backs up the database, and provides the following output:

```
Processed 160 pages for database 'pubs', file 'pubs' on file 1.
Processed 1 pages for database 'pubs', file 'pubs_log' on file 1.
Backup or restore operation successfully processed 161 pages in 42.834
➥seconds (0.030 MB/sec).
```

It looks the same as the disk dump except for two things: percentages don't show up because the STATS option wasn't specified, and it takes a lot longer because the author has a painfully slow tape drive.

Transaction Log Backups

A transaction log backup is simply a backup of the transaction log at a particular point in time. Normally, a transaction log backup is restored over a database backup to bring the database up to the point of the transaction log backup. Also, a transaction log backup clears the transaction log, so the transaction log doesn't grow indefinitely and fill up a disk drive. The transaction log can be backed up several times, and during recovery, all the transaction log backups would need to be applied in the order they were taken to recover the database.

One of the nice features about a transaction log backup is the ability to perform point-in-time recovery. For example, suppose you ran a database backup at midnight and a transaction log backup at 5 a.m. But somebody broke into the office at 4 a.m. and deleted some critical records from a table. To recover the lost information, load the database and then load the transaction log up to the point of the deletion. The following two subsections offer information on restrictions as well as the syntax for the backup.

Restrictions

Certain rules govern how and when a transaction log backup can be used. If the Select Into/BulkCopy option is turned on, the transaction log cannot be backed up. This is because nonlogged operations can be performed in the database. To prevent users from restoring inconsistent databases, Microsoft disabled the capability to perform a transaction log backup if it was even possible to perform a nonlogged operation.

To recover from a combination of a database backup and a transaction log backup, you must have a complete database backup and a complete set of transaction log backups. Every time a transaction log is backed up, it truncates itself. So in order to recover a database to a particular point in time, all the logs have to be restored in order. SQL Server will not allow the logs to be restored out of order.

In SQL Server 6.5, a transaction log dump could be performed only on databases whose logs were on a separate device. Because all databases except the master database are now required to have transaction logs in separate files, they can all have transaction log backups.

Syntax

The syntax for the BACKUP LOG command uses the same options and format as the BACKUP DATABASE command, but BACKUP LOG introduces a new option in a new place. The command syntax is as follows:

```
BACKUP LOG <database name>
WITH {NO_LOG or TRUNCATE_ONLY}
TO <backup device list>
WITH <option list>
```

The NO_LOG or TRUNCATE_ONLY option is used if the log isn't really going to be backed up (for example, if you really just want to empty the log). This is useful if the log is full. Note, however, that both options do the same thing, so you need to specify only one or the other.

There is also a NO_TRUNCATE option, which is valid in the second option list.

The NO_TRUNCATE option backs up the log without truncating it. This should be used only during recovery, when the the log cannot be truncated because of a physical device failure. Don't use this to allow the log to grow for a long time before truncating it.

Differential Backups

Differential backups are a cool, new feature—arguably the most useful thing to happen to the backup process since the invention of the tape drive. A differential backup is a copy of all the data that has changed on a database since the last full database backup. This is different from the functionality of a transaction log backup because a transaction log provides all the changes since the last transaction log backup, whereas a differential backup provides all the changes since the last database backup. To recover from a database backup and a selection of differential backups, first restore the database backup, and then restore one differential backup that will recover the database to the required point in time.

Differential backups and transaction log backups work together to provide a combination of speedy recovery and point-in-time recovery. By overlapping a differential backup scheme with a transaction log backup schedule, multiple recovery scenarios can be used. For example, if one of the early transaction log backups is corrupted by a bad tape, a differential backup that was taken after the transaction log backup can be applied, followed by all the transaction log backups taken after the differential backup. This effectively skips the bad transaction log backup. In addition, performing differential backups reduces the number of files to be restored, decreasing the recovery time.

A full database backup requires a lot more space and a lot more time than a differential backup does. So a differential backup would be a good choice for backing up a very large database during the week, and full backups could be performed over the weekend when system use is typically lower.

Restrictions

A differential backup cannot provide the point-in-time recovery that a transaction log backup can. However, it's still a good idea to use both transaction log backups and differential backups for redundancy and speed of recovery.

Old Versus New

The NO_LOG and TRUNCATE_ONLY options are the same in SQL Server 7.0 and later, but do different things in prior versions of SQL Server. In older versions, the NO_LOG syntax meant that there was no log of the truncation being performed; however, if TRUNCATE_ONLY was specified, the log was truncated, and a record was placed in the log to record the truncation. In SQL Server 6.5, if the log was completely full, it had to be truncated with the NO_LOG option because it was full and the event could not be recorded.

Syntax

You perform a differential database backup by using the DIFFERENTIAL option with the full BACKUP DATABASE syntax. All the options that apply to a full database backup also apply to a differential backup. For example, this command

```
BACKUP DATABASE pubs
TO DISK='C:\PUBSDUMP.DAT'
WITH DESCRIPTION = "Pubs Test Backup",
     DIFFERENTIAL,
     INIT,
     STATS = 5
```

will return the following output:

```
Processed 160 pages for database 'pubs', file 'pubs' on file 1.
Processed 1 pages for database 'pubs', file 'pubs_log' on file 1.
100 percent backed up.

Backup or restore operation successfully processed 161 pages in 0.417
➥seconds (3.145 MB/sec).
```

File Group Backups

File and file group backups are used to back up pieces of a very large database. "Very large," in this case, means a database that can't be backed up without impacting production time. In general, you should design the files and file groups so they will be small enough to be backed up overnight. For more information on files and file groups, see Chapter 4, "Storage Management."

Malicious Data Loss

I think it's the nature of a person who becomes a database administrator to overlook something like malicious data loss. We get so caught up in guarding the physical security of our servers (making sure the server room is locked and making sure the backup tapes are secure) and guarding against media failures that we tend to overlook one of the major causes of data loss: people.

This type of data loss generally occurs when someone gets upset with upper management and decides to destroy some data on his way out the door by dropping a table or overwriting data. It's fairly easy to prevent a table drop, but how do you prevent someone from overwriting all the data in a database without also preventing him from making legitimate table updates?

To protect against this type of data loss, it's important that you keep a lot of point-in-time recovery backups—that means transaction log backups and differential backups. Transaction log backups are great for this type of recovery because a transaction log can actually be loaded to a particular point-in-time, so the database can be reconstructed up to the time when the data loss occurred.

Restrictions

You need to consider two very important points when performing file group backups. First of all, if a given table/index combination spans multiple file groups, all the file groups involved must be backed up at the same time. In other words, if a table is created on one file group, and the indexes are created on another file group, both the file groups involved must be backed up together. SQL Server will not allow the backup to occur otherwise, so it won't happen by accident.

The second restriction of a file group backup is that a transaction log backup must be done immediately following the file group backup or the backup set will not be recoverable. Therefore, you must always perform transaction log backups after backing up a file group.

Syntax

To back up a file group or file, use the following syntax:

```
BACKUP DATABASE <database name>
{FILE or FILEGROUP} = <file name>
TO <backup device>
WITH <option list>
```

The "FILE or FILEGROUP" part of the syntax means that you must use either the word FILE or the word FILEGROUP. The option list is the same as the option list used for a database backup.

As an example, this command

```
BACKUP DATABASE pubs
FILE = 'Pubs'
TO DISK='C:\PUBSDUMP.DAT'
```

results in the following output:

```
Processed 160 pages for database 'pubs', file 'pubs' on file 2.
Backup or restore operation successfully processed 160 pages in 0.464
➥seconds (2.824 MB/sec).
```

Notice that, unlike the full database backup shown earlier, this didn't return a status line for the log backup. The log didn't back up because it's not in the file named "pubs."

Configuring Automatic Backup

Now that you know how backup works, take a look at how to do it the easy way (through automatic backups) and then how to schedule backups so they will be run regularly. The following sections offer the details:

- Creating a Backup Device
- Performing Backups by Using SQL Enterprise Manager
- Setting Up Scheduled Backups

Automatic backups provide a routine for SQL Server and ensure that backups are performed on time. If you're attempting to run the backups by hand first thing in the morning, the day you get stuck in traffic will be the day you miss a backup. Scheduled backups provide a higher level of reliability and enable you to perform backups at times you probably don't want to be in the office.

Creating a Backup Device

A backup device is a particular tape drive or file on disk that's specified as the destination for a backup. By creating a backup device, it's easier to make sure you're hitting the right file every time. To create a backup device, open SQL Enterprise Manager, open the server you want to work with, right-click on Backup Devices, and choose New Backup Device.... The Backup Device Properties dialog box appears, as shown in Figure 6.1. Enter a name for the device. Then choose the device type (tape or disk) and the device name. For tape drives, a list of names will be provided; for disk drives, enter either a local path (if the file should be placed locally) or a UNC path (to put the backup file on another computer). Click on OK, and SQL Server responds with the message `Backup Device Created Successfully`. The new backup device will show up in the Backup Device folder.

Performing Backups by Using SQL Enterprise Manager

SQL Enterprise Manager enables you to quickly back up a database. This should be done to create a one-off backup to transfer data or to test a backup device. Here's the procedure:

1. Open the Databases folder, and then right-click on the database you want to back up.

2. From the context menu, choose Tools and then Backup Database.... The SQL Server Backup dialog box appears, as shown in Figure 6.2.

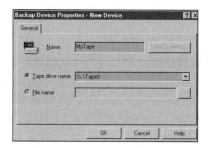

Figure 6.1   The Backup Device Properties dialog box is used to create backup devices. You can choose an available tape drive from the drop-down list, or you can open a dialog box and choose a file location.

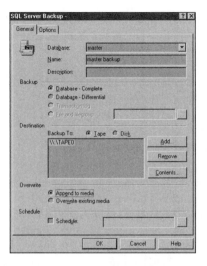

Figure 6.2   The SQL Server Backup dialog box, with the General tab showing.

3. Fill in the Description field, and then choose the backup type (Complete, Differential, Transaction Log, or File Group). Choose the destination. You can choose multiple destinations for your backups if you want to back up to multiple devices at the same time. Choose whether or not to overwrite the existing media or add a backup set to the existing media.

4. On the Options tab, shown in Figure 6.3, you'll find all the options that are available in the Transact-SQL version of the command, including options for ejecting the tape on completion and working with media sets.

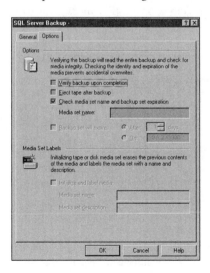

Figure 6.3   The SQL Server Backup dialog box, with the Options tab showing. These options are available in the options list for the Transact-SQL BACKUP DATABASE command.

5. Click on OK to start the backup. The backup begins. When the backup is complete, a message box appears, saying `The backup operation has completed successfully`.

The backup process will take some time, depending on the size of the database and the speed of the media being backed up to. A nice little blue bar will keep you apprised of the progress of the backup.

Setting Up Scheduled Backups

Scheduling a backup is an important part of establishing an overall backup routine. A scheduled backup can run during off-peak hours, reducing the impact on users.

To set up a scheduled backup, perform steps 1 through 3 in the preceding section and then click in the Schedule check box. This configures the backup to occur on the default recurring schedule, which is once a week on Sunday at midnight. If this is exactly what you want, you're finished. But it's probably not. To specify a different scheduled time, click on the ellipsis button (…) to open the Edit Recurring Job Schedule dialog box shown in Figure 6.4.

Choose the Recurring option, and then change the schedule to reflect what you actually want. To schedule a backup for Monday through Friday at 2 a.m., choose Weekly and check Monday through Friday. Set the time to 2 AM, and click OK.

When any kind of job is scheduled in SQL Server, it is actually handed off to the SQL Agent, which then queues up the work and processes it. That means for the scheduled job to run, the SQL Agent must be running. To monitor a job, open SQL Enterprise Manager, connect to the server that was supposed to run the job, and then open the SQL Agent. Inside the SQL Agent is the Jobs folder, which contains all scheduled jobs. You can right-click on a job and choose Job History to find the status of the last several times the job was run. (For more information on the SQL Agent and job scheduling, see Chapter 5.)

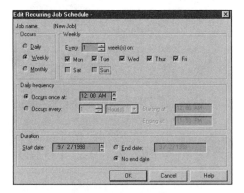

Figure 6.4   This scheduling dialog box enables you to set when recurring backups will run. This backup will happen weeknights at midnight.

Backup Strategies

Now that you know how the backup process works, and how backups should be scheduled, it's time to decide how, where, and when to back up your databases. SQL Server 7 offers a lot more options than previous versions did, so there are more decisions to make. The key things you'll learn about in this section are scheduling, tape management, and offsite logistics. This is critical to both database performance and job performance. Keep in mind that the only time you'll probably be noticed as a database administrator is when something crashes, and you'll want to be organized, be clearheaded, and have good documentation when that happens.

The general philosophy for performing backups is this: What is the replacement cost of the data? Replacement cost means three things:

1. How much will downtime cost if the database disappears?

2. How much will losing the data cost?

3. How much will reconstructing the data cost?

Don't try to overprotect things that aren't worth protecting in the first place. Tape drives, tapes, and the labor required to change the tapes daily, move the tapes offsite, and store them in a secure environment can be very costly.

Unless you are using third-party backup software that provides encryption, every piece of backup media you have is a potential security risk. If it's got proprietary or private personal information on it, take all the necessary steps to safeguard those tapes to the same level at which the servers are safeguarded. Keep the tapes in a locked secured area. If you are implementing offsite storage, pick a company that you trust to move the tapes from the server room to the storage facility.

Unless the data is relatively unimportant, always store the tapes offsite. In most areas, you can find a number of vendors who will perform this service for a small fee. There are several great reasons to store backups offsite. If a server goes down because of a drive failure, it's nice to have the backups very close. But if a server goes down because a wide-body aircraft smashes into your office building, it would probably be nice to have the tapes far, far away.

The best plan, then, is to have the tapes picked up in the afternoon. Most drive crashes and data corruption tend to happen when systems are under stress, and most systems are under stress in the morning, after all the users get in, grab a cup of coffee, and sit down to start working. If you have the tapes picked up in the afternoon, the tapes will still be around all morning in case something breaks, but the previous day's tape will be safely offsite in case of an unfortunate disaster.

As an alternative, you can duplicate the nightly backups in the morning, just in case a problem arises in afternoon. You can duplicate backups with most commercial backup software, but not with the Windows NT Backup software. These tapes can be rotated on a two-set cycle because the offsite backup is the primary method for recovery from a longer-term problem.

In the following subsections, you'll be looking more closely at backup strategies. The backup strategy you employ will be based on the volatility of the data and the size of the database. The strategies covered may not completely fit the bill in your installation, but they should provide a complete starting ground for building a backup strategy tailored to your environment.

Specifically, the following topics are covered:

- Backup strategies for read-only databases
- Backup strategies for small-to-medium databases
- Backup strategies for large databases

Backup Strategies for Read-Only Databases

A lot of the programming styles that have evolved for accessing data in databases from the World Wide Web have been geared toward distributing data to the masses, not collecting data from the masses. In most cases, this means a collection of read-only databases are used to distribute data. Keeping a database read-only has two major advantages. First, the lock manager doesn't do anything to a read-only database because there is no chance of changes being made to the database. Second, there is no need for a lot of security around a read-only database. When combined, the higher performance gained from the first part and the high security gained from the second part make read-only databases ideal for Web applications.

As a backup strategy, you should perform backups on a weekly basis. There are two reasons for doing this. It keeps a good recently built copy of the database handy in case of an emergency. Also, many of the problems that can arise in a database can be detected via backup because the backup has to read every used page in the database. Keep a copy of the database near the server in a secure area, and keep another copy offsite.

Backup Strategies for Small-to-Medium Databases

The most common type of database that SQL Server manages is probably the small-to-medium database that takes its share of both reading and writing. When backing up a small or medium database, first figure out how long it takes to perform the backup, and then determine whether that's an acceptable amount of time for the database to take the minor performance hit inherent in backing up. If one backup a day is sufficient, perform the daily backup once a day and rotate the tapes offsite the following morning. For larger databases, use differential backup.

> **How Big Is Big? How Small Is Small?**
>
> You might be wondering how to decide what constitutes a small-, medium-, or large-size database. A small or medium database is a database that can easily be backed up in an hour without any special procedures (such as parallel backup or file group backup). A large database is a database that takes longer to back up, because of either sheer size or a slow tape drive.

Keep in mind that sending a tape offsite can accomplished by copying a disk device across a WAN. In other words, for a small database, instead of backing it up to tape and moving the tapes offsite, you could back up to disk and copy the files across a WAN.

Here's a good plan for performing a weekly backup by using a differential backup scheme:

- *Day 1 (Sunday)*. Run a full backup to send offsite. Run another full backup to keep onsite.

- *Day 2 (Monday)*. Perform periodic transaction log backups during business hours and a differential backup in the evening to keep onsite. Send a copy of the full backup offsite. Send Friday's transaction log backups offsite.

- *Day 3 (Tuesday)*. Perform periodic transaction log backups during business hours. Send transaction log backups from Monday offsite. Perform a differential backup in the evening to keep onsite.

- *Day 4 (Wednesday)*. Perform periodic transaction log backups during business hours. Send transaction log backups from Tuesday offsite. Perform a differential backup in the evening to keep onsite.

- *Day 5 (Thursday)*. Perform periodic transaction log backups during business hours. Send transaction log backups from Wednesday offsite. Perform a differential backup in the evening to keep onsite.

- *Day 6 (Friday)*. Perform periodic transaction log backups during business hours. Send transaction log backups from Thursday offsite. Perform a differential backup in the evening to keep onsite.

- *Day 7 (Saturday)*. In the evening, perform a differential backup, followed by whatever database diagnostics are prudent.

This brings up a few things to which you need to pay particular attention. First of all, at no point is the database not recoverable from data onsite. For example, if the database crashed on Wednesday right after the tapes went offsite, it would be necessary to restore the full backup from Sunday, the differential backup from Tuesday night, and the transaction log backups up to the point of failure.

At the same time, if the building got hit by a meteorite, your replacement could set up the new server, restore the offsite copy of the Sunday night full backup and the transaction logs from Monday and Tuesday. That provides recovery up through business hours on Tuesday, which means all that would be lost is Wednesday's data. If it's critical that you are able to recover up to the Wednesday data in this example, it might be wise to contract with one of the Internet-based data repositories and send them the transaction log backups when they are complete. Then even if the building is hit by a meteorite, the data is safe somewhere else but is still retrievable. It might be advisable, however, to encrypt the data by using any well-known encryption software to keep prying eyes out.

Also, notice that this recovery scheme doesn't really have a single point of failure that will prevent recovery to at least the last day. If one or more of the transaction log backups were to become corrupt, you would have the differential backups. If one of the differential backups were corrupt, you would have to use the differential backups that work and then cover the rest up with transaction log backups.

Another possibility is to perform a full database backup every night, and then every day, send the previous night's backup offsite. This is a simpler system that, if combined with differential or transaction log backups through the day, can provide a little more redundancy. Although this still doesn't have the redundancy of the system described previously, it keeps data offsite and provides good backups.

Backup Strategies for Large Databases

For a large database, the backup strategy has to be a little different. Larger databases tend to be busier, and they tend to require more backup time even though they actually have less time to perform the backup.

The first bit of advice to offer is to try all the techniques mentioned in the small-to-medium database section first. Don't try to estimate how long a database backup will take based on past experience with SQL Server backup. The new backup system in SQL Server 7 is much faster and has less processor overhead. Unless the server is fully engaged in processing transactions, it can probably handle a backup almost anytime. Also, don't forget the early evening hours. In most 9 to 5 operations, the most overlooked time to perform backups is right after almost everyone goes home for the night but before the nightly batch processing starts. If the backup can be started at 4 in the afternoon without affecting performance, run the backup at 4 in the afternoon until it finishes. Think outside the "it must be done during the wee hours of the morning" box if possible.

Tape Rotation

A lot of good references are available on how to rotate tapes before overwriting them. Open up any consumer-packaged backup tape, and there's usually an insert on how to do a 2-week or 4-week rotation. Here are a few points to consider about tape rotations.

Some industries require that records be kept for a long period of time—3 or 4 years. Make sure that the media you choose to store backups on is stable enough to handle that. Most magnetic tapes have very long media life, up into the 8-to-10-year area. Keep track of the tapes with a numbering scheme, and if the records need to be kept for more than half the life of the media, refresh the media at the halfway point for the shelf life of the media. For example, for a tape with a 6-year shelf life, recopy the data on the tape to a different tape after 3 years. It doesn't necessarily have to be a new tape, it is usually just necessary to rewrite the data to maintain it.

If it's not necessary to keep data around for archival purposes, don't use more than a 2-week rotation schedule. There are two reasons for this. First of all, fewer tapes mean less expense. Also, fewer tapes mean less stuff to juggle around. What good is four-week-old data anyway? Probably not much.

Another factor is to buy tapes that are easier to care for and less likely to be damaged in an accident. For example, a DLT tape is in a fairly rugged container, and the tape is sheltered from dust and small spills. A 4mm tape is less rugged because the tape is exposed on the underside.

The second thing to try is to use parallel backup systems. Attach three, four, or five tape drives to a server to speed up data transfer time. Add tape drives to the system to match the capacity of the data bus and tape drives. For an old 10MB per second data bus, adding five drives that can process 10MB per second each won't improve throughput. Don't overload the data bus. At the same time, don't put the tape drives and the disk drives on the same data bus, for the same reason. Remember, the data has to come off the disk drive, go to the processor, be processed, and go back to the tape drive. If both the tape drive and the disk drive are on the same bus, getting data across may not be an easy task.

If none of those steps can be completed in the amount of time you have to perform a backup, you'll need to use some advanced techniques to get the data backed up in a timely manner. This is a two-step process. First, if you are using the technique of placing indexes in a separate file from their corresponding tables, you'll need to split the files up further into file groups (see Figure 6.5). As long as the objects and indexes are kept in the same file group, they can be backed up and restored as a unit, making it possible to back up an entire database in intervals instead of all at once.

Keep in mind also that when a file group is backed up, the transaction log backups have to be kept current. That means that if a file or file group method of backup is used, the transaction log backups have to be kept current and up-to-date with no loss.

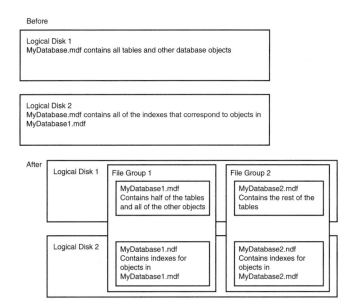

Figure 6.5 This diagram shows a suggested layout for breaking a database into two file groups across two different logical devices, which might be physical disk drives or RAID arrays.

One nice feature of a file group backup is that if one file group in the database is destroyed but the others remain intact, it is necessary to load only the backup for the file group that was destroyed and all the transaction logs that were backed up after the file group backup. That may be beneficial in very large databases.

Here's an example of a weekly backup plan using file group backups with two file groups defined as File Group A and File Group B:

- *Day 1 (Sunday).* Perform a full backup.

- *Day 2 (Monday).* Perform transaction log backups during business hours. Send a full backup offsite. At night, back up File Group A.

- *Day 3 (Tuesday).* Perform transaction log backups during business hours. Send the previous night's file group backup and the previous day's transaction log backups offsite. At night, back up File Group B.

- *Day 4 (Wednesday).* Perform transaction log backups during business hours. Send the previous night's file group backup and the previous day's transaction log backups offsite. At night, back up File Group A.

- *Day 5 (Thursday).* Perform transaction log backups during business hours. Send the previous night's file group backup and the previous day's transaction log backups offsite. At night, back up File Group B.

- *Day 6 (Friday).* Perform transaction log backups during business hours. Send the previous night's file group backup and the previous day's transaction log backups offsite. At night, back up File Group A.

- *Day 7 (Saturday).* At night, back up File Group B. Perform any prudent database diagnostics.

This doesn't provide a lot of redundancy. In case of failure, you will almost certainly have to have copies of all of the transaction logs kept locally or have the tapes brought back from storage. It does keep a good solid backup, however, and it provides two recovery paths.

There are two ways to perform recovery given this backup plan. First, you can restore the Sunday full backup and all the transaction logs up to the point of failure. Alternatively, you could also restore the two most current file group backups (one from File Group A and one from File Group B) and then restore all the transaction logs taken since the backup of the older of the two file groups. So if the database went down during the day on Thursday, it would be necessary to load the Tuesday night backup of File Group B, the Wednesday night backup of File Group A, and then all the transaction logs from Tuesday and Wednesday and up to the crash on Thursday.

There is one single point of failure in this instance: the transaction logs. For this to work, the transaction log backups have to be rock solid, with none missing, and they all have to be restored in order. This may take a while. As a matter of fact, the complexity introduced by this type of backup scheme makes the case for not using this type of scheme unless it is absolutely necessary.

Backup Recommendations

Here are a few closing thoughts on the topic of backups before you get into disaster recovery. First of all—and this can't be stressed enough—no backup plan is worth anything unless it is completely tested and thoroughly documented. Second, if you haven't tested your backup, you really don't have a backup. If it hasn't been documented and tested, how do you know a backup will work? Finally, the fewer backups needed to restore the data, the better. If you can restore a database from a database backup, an incremental backup, and one transaction log backup, you are much better off than if you had to restore one database backup and 24 transaction log backups.

To test a backup, either use a spare server or borrow one from a server vendor. Large corporations have a fairly easy time of this. Smaller companies may need to do a little arm-twisting. The server onto which you're restoring data doesn't have to be the same make, model, or spec as the one you're restoring from. As a matter of fact, it might be best if it is a different server so you can make sure there are no oddities in tape drives or drivers. Perform a full restore of all the data at several different places in the scheme. First, try just a database restore from tape, and then apply transaction logs. Then start over and try it again with differential backups.

The documentation you produce should enable someone with an equal amount of knowledge in SQL Server but no knowledge of your particular environment to restore your server from backup without your help. In other words, it should cover everything: database names, tape labeling conventions, character sets, sort orders, and scheduled jobs. Test the documentation if possible by giving it to someone else and seeing whether she can follow it when you aren't around to help.

Always back up the master database and, if necessary, the msdb database on a regular basis, preferably nightly. Master and msdb both contain data that is critical to operations. If one of these becomes corrupt, it's a real bear of a problem trying to recover them by reinstalling SQL Server. Do yourself a favor and have a backup on hand. Remember, the master database contains all the information that SQL Server uses to find all other databases, along with security information. Without the master database, SQL Server can't start any other database. The msdb database contains critical information about backups, as well as the entire setup for your replication scheme and your scheduled tasks. These databases are critical to database operation.

Always, always, always label your backup tapes. Invent and follow a naming scheme that allows you to figure out what day a particular tape was created, how many times the tape has been used, and where the tape fits into your backup scheme.

It also bears repeating that backup media should be treated with the same security measures servers are given. Don't leave tapes lying around. Keep them locked up. A little paranoia is a good thing.

A Documentation Checklist

Keep the software part of the documentation and a printed copy in a binder next to the server. Keep another binder at another location, such as a home office. A good set of documentation contains the following:

- A CD containing the current version of the server operating system (including all applied service packs and hot fixes) and boot floppies if necessary.

- A *current* emergency repair disk.

- A current Registry backup of the SQL Server Registry entries. Use the utility REGREBLD.EXE in the \MSSQL7\BINN directory to create a Registry backup. Use the command `regrebld -backup <directory name>` to place a copy of the SQL Server Registry entries in a directory for use later during recovery.

- Current versions of all hardware drivers (SCSI, display, and network) on CD.

- A copy of SQL Server 7, with all appropriate service packs.

- A document outlining the contact list for the server (whom to call if the server catches fire in the middle of the night). This should be laminated and then taped to the front of the server. Consider using bright yellow paper with black type.

- A document thoroughly describing the server hardware, including amount of RAM; number, type, and speed of each processor; network interface type; and device I/O bus type (SCSI, Fast/Wide Ultra Super SCSI 3, or whatever).

- A document describing the disk layout of the server and what is supposed to go where, with drive letters. This document should describe all the disks on the system and their functions, and then it should describe all the partitions on the system and their functions.

- The following phone numbers: Microsoft Product Support, the hardware manufacturer's support line, the network hardware vendor's support line, and the electric company's customer service number.

- A document describing each database. It should contain all the files in the database, with their current sizes and estimates of row counts in at least all of the major tables.

- A document describing the security on each database.

- A document describing the backup procedures for each database, with descriptions of how to determine which tapes are needed to recover each database. This document should also describe the tape labeling scheme.

- A hard copy of the current output from sp_configure and sp_helpsort, which can be used to help restore the server to its original configuration.

This is a good minimum list. Record all this documentation and save it somewhere. Then print out a dozen or so copies and hide them about your work environment. All the electronic copies in the world won't do you any good if you can't get the server up because you don't remember the settings for the SCSI controller.

Disaster Recovery

Disaster recovery is the one thing that no database administrator wants to go through. It's tense after a disaster, and while you are trying to clean things up and get them operational, every individual on the corporate food chain between you and the CEO will be watching you, probably over your shoulder. If you have a good manager, this is his or her opportunity to shine by keeping everyone out of your hair so you can do your job. Then you just take a deep breath and get started.

In this section, you delve into disaster recovery, covering the following specific topics:

- Damage assessment
- Alternatives to restoring backups
- Exploring disaster recovery steps
- Recovering databases
- Recovering from failures in the master database

The key to being a hero during disaster recovery is planning what to do before things go wrong. So, instinctively, you'll know exactly what to do when the server decides to take a few days off.

Damage Assessment

Imagine this scenario: The frontline help desk takes a call, enters some description of the problem, attempts to fix it, makes the problem worse (usually), and then sends it to you. And the description of the problem often includes the phrase, "It won't work."

Very profound and totally useless.

To solve any problem, you need a good grasp on exactly what's broken. It does very little good to restore backups if the disk controller is spitting useless data onto the disks.

To perform good damage assessment, you must look in several places. First, examine the SQL Server error log. To do so, open the file with Notepad (the file will be located in \MSSQL7\LOG). Multiple files there start with the name "Errorlog." Notice that they are numbered: The most recent doesn't have an extension, the next most recent is "Errorlog.1," the next is "Errorlog.2," and so on. Open the error logs and make two immediate determinations:

- Is SQL Server up and running?
- Were any databases not recovered?

It's easy to tell whether SQL Server is still running because if it shut down the last time it started, the log will say so. It's also easy to tell if there were databases that could not be recovered: Just search for the word "suspect."

A suspect database is a database that SQL Server could not recover when it started or one that developed severe problems while SQL Server was running. SQL Server marks the database as suspect because it suspects problems running the database.

If SQL Server is up and running, the master database must be okay, and one of the other databases will probably be marked as suspect. If one or more databases are marked suspect, note which databases they are and try to figure out why they are suspect.

The reasons that databases are marked suspect fall into two categories. Either SQL Server has some sort of internal data corruption that it can't fix, or the hardware or physical media is bad. It is important to distinguish between the two types of problems. A SQL Server internal problem means that the database can probably be restored from backup without replacing any hardware. If there was a hardware problem, that problem will have to be resolved before you can restore any data.

The problem is figuring out whether the problem is a software or hardware problem. The easiest way to go about this process is to eliminate hardware from the picture. Open the Windows NT Event Log and look at the system log. Usually, if there are hardware problems, it will report events generated from Windows NT or even from the hardware drivers, which will supply some data that will help you determine the nature of the problem. Look for timeout problems generated from the driver (most likely the source of the messages will be the software driver itself). For IDE drives, the driver will almost always be called "atdisk," but for SCSI drives, it will vary. For Compaq disk arrays, for example, the driver will usually be "cpqarray." Look for any messages in the Event Log that may point to a hardware problem.

Renaming Errorlogs

Most of the time, a database is marked suspect as a result of a developing problem. SQL Server is very good at "living with" a problem for a while and reporting errors on it so a database administrator can take prompt corrective action. Check the logs on critical servers at least daily. You may also want to consider adding a stored procedure into the automatic execution stored procedure set to clean things up. To do so, create a stored procedure that renames the errorlog file with a time/date stamp, and then make it a startup stored procedure. The stored procedure would contain the following command:

```
Create procedure sp_RenameErrorLog
As
begin
declare @ExecStr varchar(255)
select @ExecStr = 'ren d:\mssql7\log\errorlog.1 errorlog.' +
➥convert(varchar, getdate(), 102) + '.' + convert(varchar,
➥datepart(hh, getdate()))
➥ + '.' + convert(varchar, datepart(mm, getdate()))
exec xp_cmdshell @ExecStr
end
```

Then run the sp_procoption stored procedure to make the stored procedure run at startup:

```
sp_procoption sp_RenameErrorLog, startup, true
```

This resets the stored procedure so it will run after SQL Server starts. Be sure to clean out the MSSQL7\LOG directory periodically.

If it is a hardware problem, fix it according to the manufacturer's specified procedures. Then you can think about repairing the databases. Or, if available, start restoring the databases to another server.

Alternatives to Restoring Backups

If the databases that are corrupt are corrupt because of a SQL Server problem as opposed to a hardware problem, you can try a few alternative solutions before starting the restoration process. At least read through these suggestions and evaluate whether or not they would be helpful.

The first thing to do is to make sure that SQL Server really means the database is suspect. One of the reasons SQL Server marks a database as suspect is if there was not enough space in the database to complete auto-recovery (see the sidebar entitled "What Is Auto Recovery?" at the end of this section). Remember that databases will now automatically grow as needed to hold the data that is put into them. What would happen if the data being put into the database was logged, but before it could be written to disk by the lazy writer, the server stopped? Well, if there isn't enough space to commit all the data in the transaction log, and there isn't enough space to enlarge the database device, the database will be marked suspect. How do you fix that? First, free up some disk space on the volume where the data devices for the database reside. Then tell SQL Server the database isn't suspect anymore. The following steps give you specific instructions:

1. If SQL Server is running, stop it.

2. Open a Windows NT command prompt.

3. If there is a chance that other users may be trying to attach to the SQL Server, reach back and unplug the network cable from the server.

4. At the command prompt, type **sqlservr -m**. This will start SQL Server in single-user mode with the Allow Updates option turned on. After a short delay, the command shell window will begin to fill with all the messages that are coming out of SQL Server, as shown in Figure 6.6. This text is also written to the ERRORLOG file, so don't panic if you can't read it fast enough. Notice the warning line at the bottom; that means the server is in override mode, and you can directly update system tables.

5. Start ISQL/w. *Don't* use SQL Enterprise Manager. When SQL Server is in single-user mode, only one connection is allowed. Because SQL Enterprise Manager uses several connections in order to maintain status information to the server, it enables you to get the necessary status information without connecting with a query window.

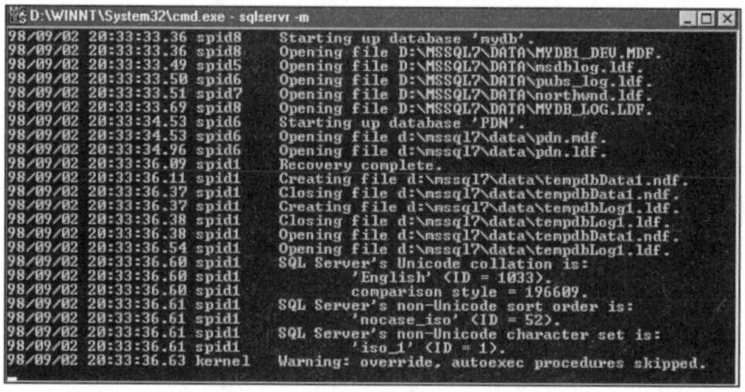

Figure 6.6   This is what it looks like when SQL Server is run from a command shell (looks like the ERRORLOG file, doesn't it?).

6. In ISQL/w, perform the following tasks:

■ Begin a transaction by typing the following:
begin transaction

■ Substitute the name of the database for <dbname>. For example:
Update sysdatabases set status = status - 256 where name =
➥**'pubs'**

■ If you get the message 1 row(s) affected, run the following command:
Commit transaction

If SQL Server doesn't reply with 1 row(s) affected, run this command
Rollback Transaction

and then try to figure out what you misspelled.

7. Execute the shutdown command in ISQL/w. This stops the server. Alternatively, you can pull the command shell back up and press Ctrl+C.

What did you just do? The status field in the sysdatabases table governs the status of databases. It is an integer field in which each bit is a different piece of status information (such as Select Into/BulkCopy and the rest of the options that can be turned on with the sp_dboption stored procedure or with the database properties window). There are some bits that you aren't normally allowed to change, and one of them is the bit that governs whether or not a database is suspect. So basically, you just told SQL Server that the database it thought was suspect really isn't, and that it should really try to recover it again, please. Restart SQL Server and watch for error messages. If the error messages come up again, it's time to recover from backup.

Take Heed

Changing entries in system tables (discussed in this section) can be a very bad thing. This is like editing the Registry in Windows NT, but without enough documentation to understand what you're really doing. In short, don't screw around with this; you might put someone's eye out or something.

Exploring Disaster Recovery Steps

Performing database recovery involves several steps, each of which is covered in detail in this section or elsewhere in the chapter:

1. Get the operating system up and running with no errors.

2. Clean up the mess: Back up all the error logs and event logs if possible. Make sure that all the data you'll need to figure out exactly what went wrong has been archived and sent somewhere else, so you can clearly see any new error messages that may occur during the recovery process.

3. Get the master database up and running.

4. Restore the databases that need to be restored, starting with the smallest database first.

5. Restart the server and make sure everything comes up clean.

6. Check the data for reasonableness.

The upcoming subsections take a general look at each of these steps. The key step—restoring databases—is explored in greater detail following the more general coverage.

What Is Auto Recovery?

Automatic recovery is a process that SQL Server goes through whenever it starts. Basically, when SQL Server starts, it checks the Registry and figures out where the master database is. Then it opens the master database, performs some rudimentary checks to make sure the master database is okay, and opens the table sysdatabases and starts recovering databases.

The database recovery process goes like this. First, SQL Server gets the information from sysdatabases on which databases it will attempt to open. If a database is marked suspect, SQL Server will not recover it. For each database, it opens all the associated files for the database. If that succeeds, it goes through the transaction log and makes sure all the transactions that are marked completed but that haven't already been written to the disk by the lazy writer are written to disk. This is where automatic recovery usually fails, either because the transaction log is corrupted or because the database is corrupted and can't be written to. Any transactions that aren't complete are removed from the transaction log (rolled back). Then SQL Server writes a record into the transaction log to show that the database was recovered successfully and the transaction log is caught up, which is called a checkpoint. At that point, the database is up and running.

If any of these steps fails, the database is marked suspect. This usually happens for one of two reasons. The aforementioned problem of not being able to apply transactions is the first. The second reason is that SQL Server tries to open a file and cannot, either because the file isn't there or because of a disk, controller, or driver problem. If the problem occurred because the file didn't exist and you can make the file exist again in the same place, you may want to try the process outlined previously for revoking the suspect status from a database.

Get the Operating System Running

If there is a media problem, it will probably manifest itself first by locking up Windows NT or by preventing it from starting after a reboot. The first order of business is to get Windows NT up and running again. You may need to restore from your Windows NT backup, or you might have to reinstall the operating system. In any case, and even if there wasn't a media problem, make sure the operating system is starting with no errors in the Windows NT Event Log.

Clean Up the Mess

If you didn't have to reinstall the operating system, make a clean backup to disk of all the Windows NT Event Logs and SQL Server error logs. Also, SQL Server may have produced some dump files from internal access violations. Save all of those to a different directory so you can look at them later to find out more exactly what went wrong or in case Microsoft wants them at some point in the future. If SQL Server created any dump files, they will be located in either the MSSQL7\LOG directory or the WINNT directory.

Make sure all the drives are formatted and ready. If this is definitely going to be a restore operation, make sure all the databases that are going to be restored are completely and thoroughly removed by moving their files to another directory (if possible) or by deleting them (as a last resort). Try to keep them around just in case.

Get the Master Database Up and Running

This step involves getting SQL Server up and running cleanly, with no errors. If the operating system had to be reinstalled, this is where you need to reinstall SQL Server. Hopefully, you wrote down what character sets and sort orders to use. Otherwise, you'll be in for a very long day. If there was a problem that destroyed Windows NT but left SQL Server intact, use the REGREBLD utility with the -RESTORE option to restore the lost Registry entries. Then restart the server.

Start SQL Server and make sure the error log doesn't show any major problems. If SQL Server is still trying to open the databases that are suspect and you've already decided to restore, go ahead and delete the databases. From the SQL Enterprise Manager, right-click on the databases and choose Delete from the context menu.

It is very important for you to make sure that both SQL Server and Windows NT are operating perfectly before you restore the databases. Data recovery is a very complex process, and throwing in a few more variables—such as a bad driver or an outdated system file—only complicates matters. In the event of a master database crash, go to the section "Recovering from Failures in the Master Database," later in this chapter.

Restore Databases

An entire upcoming section covers how to restore databases, so that topic won't be covered here in tremendous detail. The only thing that needs to be covered here is the order in which databases should be restored. Always restore user databases from the smallest to the largest because smaller databases will be restored faster, and if there are lingering problems with the hardware, they will probably manifest themselves during the recovery process. By restoring smaller databases first, you may be able to uncover the lingering problems before you spend a huge amount of time recovering a large database.

Restart the Server

Always reboot the server after recovery. This may just be superstition on the part of the author, but it's a good idea to see the whole recovery process complete at least one time from beginning to end before allowing users to put more data on the server.

Check the Data for Reasonableness

Try to keep a good idea of how many records are in the major tables in each database, so you can make sure all the data is there. Always keep track of some important numbers. For example, if it is an employee tracking database, always make sure the CEO and CIO's data are intact. If anybody's records will be incorrect in the database, it will be a high-profile record (Murphy's law).

Also, have someone familiar with the data take a look to make sure things look right. If everything went smoothly, this second pair of eyes won't find any problems, but it will help you sleep a little better.

That covers the general overview of database recovery. Next up, a more in-depth look at recovering databases.

Recovering Databases

Having covered it in general terms, you're now ready for a detailed look at what it actually takes to recover a database from scratch. Recovering a database from backup as part of backup recovery should not be taken lightly; it is a process that should be planned out in advance. This section is broken into three main parts:

- Recovery Basics
- Recovering a Database by Using T-SQL
- Recovering a Database by Using SQL Enterprise Manager

If at all possible, use SQL Enterprise Manager to recover your databases. SQL Enterprise Manager automatically hooks into MSDB and figures out exactly what backups you need to restore, and it will actually generate options for database recovery. This is a very helpful feature.

Recovery Basics

In general, a database recovery works like this. First, find all the media necessary to load the backups. If you are loading from a database backup, load the most recent database backup first, then the most recent differential backup, and then the transaction logs that span between the last differential backup and the crash. Figure 6.7 shows a database backup scheme that uses full backups, incremental backups, and transaction log backups for recovery. In this scheme, a recovery that happened on Thursday in the late afternoon (before the incremental backup) would require you to restore the full backup from Sunday, the incremental from Wednesday night, and the transaction log backups from Thursday.

If you are loading from a file or file group backup, restore the file groups from oldest to newest. That means if you have three file groups and you backed up file group A on Monday, file group B on Tuesday, and file group C on Wednesday, and the crash happened on Thursday, you should restore file group A, then file group B, and then file group C. Then restore all the transaction logs since the backup of file group A. When everything is loaded, you can recover the database. Figure 6.8 shows this database backup scheme. If the database crashed on Thursday afternoon in this case, the file group A backup from Tuesday would need to be loaded, followed by the file group B backup from Wednesday, and then the transaction logs from Wednesday and Thursday.

Recovering a Database by Using T-SQL

You can use Transact-SQL to recover a database by using the `RESTORE` command. The `RESTORE` command is actually used anytime you need to read data that SQL Server wrote to backup media (disk backups or tape backups), including when you just need to see a catalog of what's on a given tape.

To get a listing of the contents of a backup device, initiate the following command:

```
RESTORE HEADERONLY
FROM <backup device>
WITH NOUNLOAD or UNLOAD
```

Sunday Full Backup	Monday Transaction Logs plus Incremental	Tuesday Transaction Logs plus Incremental	Wednesday Transaction Logs plus Incremental	Thursday Transaction Logs plus Incremental	Friday Transaction Logs plus Incremental	Saturday Transaction Logs plus Incremental

Figure 6.7   This illustration shows the full database backup scenario, with incremental and transaction logs. A crash on any weekday would require a restore of the full backup, then a restore of the previous night's incremental backup, plus a restore of all transaction logs created since the incremental.

Sunday	Monday	Tuesday	Wednesday	Thursday	Friday	Saturday
Filegroup A plus transaction logs	Filegroup B plus transaction logs	Filegroup A plus transaction logs	Filegroup B plus transaction logs	Filegroup A plus transaction logs	Filegroup B plus transaction logs	Filegroup A plus transaction logs

Figure 6.8   This illustrates the file group backup scenario. Any crash would require you to load the most recent file group backup for each file group, followed by all the transaction logs created since the oldest file group backup.

This command will return a result set of all the backups on a given piece of media. If you have a high-capacity tape or a slow tape drive, this command will take a while. To get a quick snapshot of the tape description, use the `RESTORE LABELONLY` command, which will show only the description information for the tape. If you need to find out what logical filenames are used on a tape so you can move the files to a new location, use the `RESTORE FILELISTONLY` command. Both the `RESTORE LABELONLY` and `RESTORE FILELISTONLY` commands work just like the `RESTORE HEADERONLY` command.

The syntax for the `RESTORE DATABASE` command is similar to that of backup. There is one important difference between the SQL Server 7 restore command and the one provided in earlier versions of SQL Server: The specifications for the files used by the database are stored in the backup file. The restore process includes building these files. That's just one fewer thing you'll have to keep track of when rebuilding the database.

There are three different forms for the `RESTORE` command: database, filegroup, and log. This section starts out with the database syntax.

The `RESTORE DATABASE` command has the following syntax:

```
RESTORE DATABASE <database name>
     FROM <backup device list>
     WITH <options>
```

The *<database name>* part should be obvious by now. The *<backup device list>* is the same list and format specified by the `BACKUP DATABASE` command. The only real differences are in the options:

- **DBO_ONLY.** This sets the database to dbo use only; in other words, only the sa and the database owner will have access to the database after it is created.

- **FILE = File Number.** The number of the backup set on tape. If the backup set you want to restore is the fourth on the tape, use FILE = 4. To find the backup set number, use the `RESTORE HEADERONLY` command.

- **MEDIANAME = Media Name.** If a media name was specified during the backup process, the name can optionally be specified during the restore. This can prevent you from accidentally restoring the wrong backup.

- **MOVE 'logical file name' TO 'operating system file name'.** The restore process will automatically attempt to generate all the files it needs to the same locations they were in when the backup was created. If it's necessary to move the files to a new drive as part of the restore process, you can do so. This option can be specified multiple times in order to move multiple files. To find the logical file names, use the `RESTORE FILELISTONLY` command.

- **NORECOVERY or RECOVERY or STANDBY = undo file name**.
  Only one of these can be used in a given restore statement. Specifying
  NORECOVERY means that SQL Server will not perform the steps associated with
  auto-recovery after the load is complete. Specify RECOVERY, and SQL Server will
  immediately perform recovery steps, and the database will be placed online.
  STANDBY will bring the database online without recovering it so you can check
  the status of the database in between restores. The undo file part allows the last
  recovered item (either a transaction log or differential backup) to be removed
  without removing the entire database.

- **NOUNLOAD or UNLOAD**. Specifies that the tape should be rewound and
  (if possible) ejected.

- **REPLACE**. If this is specified and another database with the same name as the
  one being restored already exists, the existing database will be completely deleted before the incoming database is restored. Also, if the database name that is
  specified in the RESTORE DATABASE command is different from the one found on
  tape, the restore will not work unless REPLACE is specified.

- **RESTART**. If a restore operation is interrupted, the RESTART command will
  attempt to resume the restore where it stopped. This works only on restores
  from tape that use multiple tapes.

- **STATS = percentage**. Just like the BACKUP command, the STATS option periodically shows how far along the backup is.

That syntax will load either a full database backup or a differential backup on top
of an existing full backup. For example, to load the Northwind database from tape,
you could use this command:

```
RESTORE DATABASE NorthWind
FROM TAPE='\\.\TAPE0'
WITH STATS = 5, UNLOAD
```

Then, if there was a differential backup on the next tape that you wanted to load,
you could just pop in the tape and use the exact same command.

To restore a transaction log, use the RESTORE LOG command, which uses the same
options as the RESTORE DATABASE command, with one interesting addition. The STOPAT
option allows you to select the time of the last transaction to be logged. For example,
if you are recovering a database because someone accidentally dropped a table at 11:30
a.m. on Monday, October 26, 1998, you first load the database, and then load all the
logs up to the last one prior to the accident. Then use this syntax:

```
RESTORE LOG MyDB
FROM TAPE = '\\.\TAPE0'
WITH FILE=4, STOPAT="October 26, 1998 11:30"
```

This loads a transaction log from the fourth backup set on the tape, but does not
load any transactions that start after 11:30 a.m. on October 26.

That leaves one case yet to discuss. To load a file or file group, you use the RESTORE DATABASE command with the NORECOVERY option to load each file, and then you use the RESTORE LOG command to load each transaction log. For this example, assume that you need to load two files, both on the same tape in backup set 1 and backup set 2, as well as the transaction logs, which are dumped twice a day. Here's the command syntax you would use:

```
RESTORE DATABASE MyDB
FILE = 'File1'
FROM TAPE = '\\.\TAPE0'
WITH FILE=1, NORECOVERY
GO
RESTORE DATABASE MYDB
FILE = 'File2'
FROM TAPE = '\\.\TAPE0'
WITH FILE=2, NORECOVERY
GO
(switch tapes here)
RESTORE LOG MYDB
FROM TAPE '\\.\TAPE0'
WITH FILE = 1, NORECOVERY
GO
RESTORE LOG MYDB
FROM TAPE '\\.\TAPE0'
WITH FILE = 2, NORECOVERY
GO
RESTORE LOG MYDB
FROM TAPE '\\.\TAPE0'
WITH FILE = 3, NORECOVERY
GO
RESTORE LOG MYDB
FROM TAPE '\\.\TAPE0'
WITH FILE = 4, RECOVERY
GO
```

This restores the database. Notice that the NORECOVERY option is used on every restore except the last one. After the last restore is complete, the database will come back online.

Some troubleshooting notes on these procedures. First of all, any attempt to load transaction logs out of order will fail. It won't cause any damage; SQL Server will check to see whether the log being loaded is correct before it loads. That also means, however, that if you are missing any logs, you will be able to restore only up to the missing log. The second thing to watch out for is the NORECOVERY statement. A database will not be usable until it has recovered, and it won't recover until you tell it to. If you forget to put a WITH RECOVERY option on the last transaction log, you can use this command to perform recovery:

```
RESTORE DATABASE MyDB
WITH RECOVERY
```

This prompts SQL Server to recover the specified database. This doesn't load any data, it just performs the recovery steps on the database that are normally performed during startup. Restarting the server won't work, however, because the database is marked by SQL Server as nonrecoverable until you successfully complete this task.

Recovering a Database by Using SQL Enterprise Manager

SQL Enterprise Manager provides some extremely nice tools for performing data recovery. Something that hasn't been mentioned up to now is that SQL Server keeps track of all backups that are made of every database. It keeps all this information in the msdb database (another great reason to back up msdb). It can then use this information to present you with a list of all the alternatives you have for restoring your database. This is especially handy for performing file group restores. The key to doing any of this, however, is proper tape labeling. If the tapes aren't labeled right, this won't work.

To restore a database backup, open SQL Enterprise Manager and expand the server you want to work with. Then right-click on the Databases folder, choose Task, and then choose Restore Database.... This brings up the Restore Database dialog box shown in Figure 6.9. Choose the database you want to restore from the drop-down list at the top of the window.

There are three main options in this dialog box. The Restore Database and Transaction Logs option is used to restore database, differential, and log backups. If you choose this option, a list of all available database, differential, and log backups appears at the bottom of the window.

The Restore Filegroups or Files option allows you to restore file groups or files. When you select this option, all available file or file group backups appear at the bottom of the window.

The last option, Restore Backup Sets from Device, enables you to manually enter a device path and restore from that device. This is the option to use if you are restoring from a backup created on a different server, or if you are restoring after losing the msdb database. As a matter of fact, if SQL Server doesn't have a record of any backups of the database specified at the top of the dialog box, this will be the only option available.

If you are restoring transaction logs, you can optionally enter a time and date to restore to in the Point in Time Restore text box.

The Options tab, shown in Figure 6.10, contains all the options included in the options list of the `RESTORE DATABASE` statement. From here, you can eject the tape at the end of the restore, force an overwrite (similar to the `REPLACE` option), rename the database after the restore (also similar to the `REPLACE` option), or relocate the files created by the load. Also, you can choose to recover the database at the end of the restore by choosing the Leave Database Operational option, or you can postpone recovery by choosing the Leave Database Nonoperational option, or you can choose the Leave Database Read-Only option to check the status after each step.

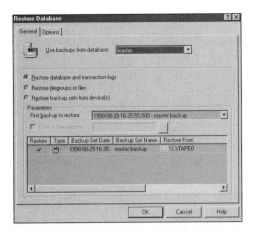

Figure 6.9   This is the Restore Database dialog box. Notice the list of available backups in the bottom part of the window.

After choosing all the options you want, click on OK, and SQL Server starts prompting you to insert tapes. After the process is complete, check all the data and make sure it looks right.

Recovering from Failures in the Master Database

The master database contains all the information about what databases are in what files, as well as information on how those files are linked together. The master database is the first database opened when SQL Server starts, and if it can't be opened for some reason, SQL Server will not start.

What happens when the master database is lost, but all the other databases are either still intact or in an unknown state? At that point, you need to load a backup copy of the master database, but in order to start SQL Server and perform that operation, you must have a good working master database.

To restore the master database, first you create a master database by using SQL Server Setup. Then stop SQL Server and restart it in single-user mode, as discussed earlier in this chapter. Use either the ISQL program or the ISQL/W program to access SQL Server. *Don't* use Enterprise Manager. Then execute the RESTORE DATABASE statement to reload the master database.

If you don't have a current backup of the master database, go ahead and use SQL Server Setup to build a new master database, and then pull up ISQL/W and start reattaching the databases. Fortunately, this is significantly less traumatic than in previous versions of SQL Server. To reattach a database, you need to know the full path and name of every file associated with the database. Then use the sp_attach_db stored procedure:

```
Sp_attach_db 'database name', 'file 1', 'file 2'...
```

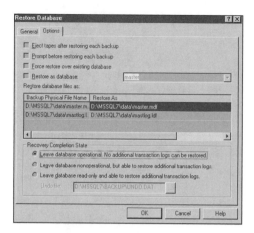

Figure 6.10 The Options tab of the Restore Database dialog box allows you to select many options, such as whether to eject the tape, how to handle the media set information, and where to restore the database to.

Unfortunately, this works only for databases with 16 files or fewer. For databases with more than 16 files, you'll have to call Microsoft Product Support and have them help. Also, you'll have to perform this operation for each of the databases on the server.

Third-Party Backup Utilities

Many backup solutions available from third parties can be used to perform backup and recovery. These tools usually integrate some very nice features, including the ability to automatically catalog tapes for easy recovery. In this section, you'll take a look at the pros and cons of using a third-party backup package.

The big advantage of using a third-party backup package is convenience. A single product that can back up an entire Windows NT Server regardless of what software is running on it is very appealing. Several vendors offer packages that will back up Windows NT files and Registry information, along with Exchange Server and SQL Server, in one integrated one-stop backup solution. In addition, most of these solutions work great over networks by using end-to-end compression, so one monster tape drive can back up a whole bunch of servers.

If you get to choose which product to use, get evaluation copies and test them thoroughly on both the backup and restore process. Several software packages available will produce very quick clean backups. But how long will it take to figure out how to restore from the tapes? There are so many standard features anymore that all the packages are basically the same. All the backup software utilities use the same technology to access SQL Server (remember that bit about Named Pipes and backup devices earlier), so there really aren't any advantages there.

Enterprisewide backup solutions are very convenient and may help control costs and reduce restore times by keeping better track of tapes. Many have built-in tape rotation schedules, so you can choose when to back up and how long to keep tapes before overwriting them.

The disadvantages of using third-party backup software are few. One is expense. SQL Server comes with perfectly adequate software for performing scheduled backups; do you really need more? Also, if a serious problem occurs during recovery, how well is the person at Microsoft Product Support going to know the third-party product? Chances are they will know the big players in the market (such as Seagate and Cheyenne), but they may not know any of the others. This may cause some delays in getting problems resolved. Finally, if an entire server goes down, in order to restore that server, you'll have to install the third-party backup software onto the server after installing the operating system and then installing SQL Server. This adds more time to the restore process—and it's one more step you might forget or one more CD-ROM you might misplace.

Conclusions

This chapter covered one of the most important topics for any database administrator: backup/recovery. A few key ideas need particular emphasis. First, always test your backups. You should do this for two reasons: It validates your backup media, hardware, and procedures, and it is simply a very good practice. The next thing to keep in mind is that you really need to be able to restore databases by using the Transact-SQL syntax. What happens if you need to restore a master database, and you have only one connection? Enterprise Manager won't be around to save you. To avoid that predicament, learn the Transact SQL commands.

The last and most important point to remember is to document everything. That means document which files are used by which databases, which tapes go with which servers and which databases, and so on. Good documentation also includes clearly labeling servers, tape drives, and tapes so they match the documentation. Complete and thorough documentation will keep people from calling you when the database crashes (which will inevitably happen while you are on vacation).

7

Database Maintenance

Chris Miller

ATINY PART OF THE LIFETIME of a database is spent being designed, created, and built. The rest of the time the database is being used or is down. Consider that a good database design for a simple database might take a day, and implementing that design might take another day, and then the database goes into production for years and perhaps even decades. Maintaining that database is an ongoing task that will consume a considerable amount of time over the lifetime of a database. This chapter covers the kinds of things that need to be done actively to maintain clean and reliable databases. It also describes how to automate processes for maintenance. This chapter offers very detailed information on how the various database consistency checking options can be used to maintain and correct problems in the database.

Preventive Maintenance

Databases require certain maintenance tasks to be performed on a regular basis to ensure top performance and reliability. Modern cars have computers in them that perform diagnostics on startup and during operation to detect problems. SQL Server has many of the same features built into it that keep it running reliably and help detect problems before they become critical. This section covers the types of checks you can perform. Automation of those tasks is covered at the end of the chapter in the section "Proactive Maintenance with the Database Maintenance Plan Wizard." The key topics covered in this section include the following:

- Hardware Maintenance
- Checking Server Logs
- Ensuring Database Consistency

Hardware Maintenance

Many IT shops have a nice clean room with filtered air and filtered power to keep everything nice and clean. Some IT shops put servers in environments that aren't quite as nice. This section is simply a reminder to dust everything out periodically, to check to make sure the uninterruptible power supply (UPS) is really not interruptible, and to clean up the physical area in which the server lives. Although a lot of this seems like housework, and it's very easy to pawn these tasks off as "someone else's job," it's the database administrator who will be paged when a component overheats and dies prematurely or when the power goes out and the server crashes. Checking these things out periodically will help keep minor problems from becoming major.

Dust causes major problems inside computers. Not only does it prevent heat from dissipating, which can cause overheating, it also can get into contacts inside servers and prevents the contacts from passing signals properly. Keep the inside and outside of the server cabinet clean.

Server Monitoring Software

Most high-end servers, such as those from Compaq or Hewlett-Packard, come with advanced monitoring software that will keep an eye on things such as airflow, internal temperature, and disks that are developing bad sectors. Insight Manager from Compaq, Intel's LanDesk, and HP NetServer all provide this functionality. It's highly recommended that you use these tools to detect problems and fix them before they cause an outage.

Always Check Your Filters: A True Story

I was working on a SQL Server at a client site. The server wasn't in a server room, but it was encased in a dustproof industrial cabinet with its own ventilation system. In order to apply some service packs, I opened the case and put in the CD-ROM containing the software. Immediately, I noticed that the inside of the cabinet was a little warm, and air didn't seem to be moving properly. I started the upgrade and proceeded to check the ventilation system.

Pulling the filter off, I saw that the filter appeared to be in good order. Then I touched the filter surface, and my finger came away coated in dried black goo. I took the filter to the nearest bathroom sink and washed it out, dropping a huge amount of this gunk into the sink. After replacing the filter, the fan ran much quieter, and the air was moving inside that case.

The moral of the story is that filters don't do any good at all if they aren't periodically cleaned or replaced.

You should check out your UPS on a basis recommended by the manufacturer, usually every month or quarter. The safest way to test a UPS is to shut down Windows NT but leave it at the "It is now safe to turn off your computer" window. Run whatever diagnostics are provided by your UPS vendor. If all those diagnostics turn out okay, consider performing the good old manual test if possible. Unplug the UPS from the utility power or flip the circuit breaker. By performing these diagnostics, you can find and resolve problems with a UPS without having to wait for the next thunderstorm.

Many buildings and computer rooms maintain a supply of clean uninterruptible power through the combined use of batteries, generators, and redundant failover technologies to prevent loss of power. Check with the computer room owner and see whether this is available, and then make sure you're on the list of people to be notified prior to generator tests.

Keeping the server clean makes the server more reliable. Keeping the server free of dust and ensuring adequate cooling will help components run cooler so they last longer. Make sure that the server is clean, especially the ventilation holes. Keep the case on, and make sure it fits properly. Cases that don't fit properly don't encourage proper ventilation and can cause dust to build up in places where dust shouldn't build up.

Checking Server Logs

Very few sudden errors occur in SQL Server. Most of the problems that happen tend to creep up slowly. By watching event logs and error logs for problematic events, you can head off little problems before they evolve into big problems.

SQL Server stores error messages in two different places:

- Text error log file
- Windows NT Event Log

Text Error Log File

All messages, regardless of severity, are stored in the errorlog. The errorlog is stored in \mssql7\log. Seven logs are usually stored here: the current log, called just errorlog,

More Than Seven Error Logs

If you really want more than seven error logs, you can have them. Modify the Registry key HKEY_LOCAL_MACHINE\Software\Microsoft\MSSQLServer\MSSQLServer\NumErrorLogs and set it to the number you want.

Seven error logs are usually sufficient to trace back any errors. During maintenance or disaster recovery, when the server is going to go down and come up a lot, it might be a good idea to bump this up so if a problem arises, the complete list of errorlogs will be available for use in tracking the error.

and the files named errorlog.1 through errorlog.6. These plain text files can be opened either with Notepad or from inside the SQL Server Enterprise Manager console. To use the latter, open the server group, open the server, and then open SQL Server Logs. Click on the error log you want to view, and it shows up in the right side of the console.

SQL Server error logs always start the same way. Individual servers will have different messages and possibly a different order. Here's a sample errorlog taken from SQL Server right after startup. Breaking up the following listing are parenthetical notes to keep you updated on what's going on.

```
98/07/11 12:18:15.71 kernel   Microsoft SQL Server  7.00 - 7.00.583
➥(Intel X86)
     Oct 1 1998 16:07:26
     Copyright (c) 1988-1997 Microsoft Corporation
98/07/11 12:18:15.75 kernel   Copyright © 1988-1997 Microsoft Corporation.
98/07/11 12:18:15.75 kernel   All rights reserved.
```

(That's just the normal copyright and version information. The build number—7.00.583 in this case—changes as service packs are applied.)

```
98/07/11 12:18:15.75 kernel   Logging SQL Server messages in file
➥'D:\MSSQL7\LOG\ERRORLOG'
```

(The name and location of this errorlog file.)

```
98/07/11 12:18:15.77 kernel   initconfig: number of user connections
➥limited to 30
```

(Number of user connections; this may go away with gold code.)

```
98/07/11 12:18:15.77 kernel   SQL Server is starting at priority class
➥'normal'(1 CPU detected).
```

(This means the server can be pre-empted by other threads. On multiprocessor machines, the server can be started in priority class "real-time," which means that SQL Server is active on at least one processor at all times.)

```
98/07/11 12:18:15.84 kernel   User Mode Scheduler configured for thread
➥processing
98/07/11 12:18:17.03 server   VLM extensions not found.
```

(Very Large Memory extensions have to be applied to Windows NT Server Enterprise Edition to allow large—> 2GB—amounts of memory to be used.)

```
98/07/11 12:18:17.11 server   Using dynamic lock allocation. [8361] Lock
➥Blocks, [16722] Lock Owner Blocks
```

(Lock configuration is here.)

```
98/07/11 12:18:17.11 kernel   Attempting to initialize Distributed
```

```
Transaction Coordinator
98/07/11 12:18:19.55 spid1      Starting up database 'master'
98/07/11 12:18:19.56 spid1      Opening file D:\MSSQL7\DATA\MASTER.MDF.
98/07/11 12:18:19.57 spid1      Opening file D:\MSSQL7\DATA\MASTLOG.LDF.
98/07/11 12:18:19.70 spid1      Loading SQL Server's default sort order and
➥character set
```

(For each database, SQL Server will print a `Starting up database` line, followed by two or more `Opening file` lines while it opens the files involved in the database. Older versions of SQL Server would report when a given database's recovery was complete, but SQL Server 7 does not. The preceding shows the "master" database being opened, and then the default sort order and character set starting to load.)

```
98/07/11 12:18:19.84 spid1      Starting up database 'model'
98/07/11 12:18:19.84 spid1      Opening file D:\MSSQL7\DATA\MODEL.MDF.
98/07/11 12:18:19.92 spid1      Opening file D:\MSSQL7\DATA\MODELLOG.LDF.
```

(The startup of the "model" database.)

```
98/07/11 12:18:20.02 spid1      Clearing temp db
98/07/11 12:18:20.03 spid1      Creating file D:\MSSQL7\DATA\TEMPDB.MDF.
98/07/11 12:18:20.15 spid1      Creating file D:\MSSQL7\DATA\TEMPLOG.LDF.
98/07/11 12:18:20.45 spid1      Opening file D:\MSSQL7\DATA\TEMPDB.MDF.
98/07/11 12:18:20.59 spid1      Opening file D:\MSSQL7\DATA\TEMPLOG.LDF.
98/07/11 12:18:22.42 spid1      Starting up database 'tempdb'
98/07/11 12:18:22.42 spid1      Opening file D:\MSSQL7\DATA\TEMPDB.MDF.
98/07/11 12:18:22.50 spid1      Opening file D:\MSSQL7\DATA\TEMPLOG.LDF.
```

(It says `Clearing temp db`, but what it actually does is delete and rebuild tempdb every time SQL Server starts. The "model" database will always recover before tempdb because "model" contains the basic structures needed to rebuild tempdb.)

```
98/07/11 12:18:22.76 spid1      server name is 'INTREPID'
98/07/11 12:18:22.76 kernel     Using 'SQLEVN70.DLL' version '6.00.000'.
98/07/11 12:18:22.77 kernel     Using 'OPENDS70.DLL' version
➥'7.00.00.0583'.
98/07/11 12:18:22.78 ods        Using 'SSMSSH70.DLL' version '7.0.583' to
➥listen on ''.
98/07/11 12:18:22.80 ods        Using 'SSNMPN70.DLL' version '7.0.583' to
➥listen on '\\.\pipe\sql\query'.
98/07/11 12:18:22.81 ods        Using 'SSMSSO70.DLL' version '7.0.583' to
➥listen on '1433'.
98/07/11 12:18:22.81 ods        Using 'SSMSRP70.DLL' version '7.0.583' to
➥listen on 'INTREPID'.
```

(Now all the server-side network libraries and other DLLs start.)

```
98/07/11 12:18:24.77 spid6      Starting up database 'msdb'
98/07/11 12:18:24.77 spid6      Opening file D:\MSSQL7\DATA\MSDBDATA.MDF.
98/07/11 12:18:24.77 spid7      Starting up database 'pubs'
```

```
98/07/11 12:18:24.77 spid7    Opening file D:\MSSQL7\DATA\PUBS.MDF.
98/07/11 12:18:24.78 spid8    Starting up database 'Contacts'
98/07/11 12:18:24.78 spid8    Opening file
➥D:\MSSQL7\DATA\CONTACTS_PRIMARY.MDF.
98/07/11 12:18:25.02 spid8    Opening file
➥D:\MSSQL7\DATA\CONTACTS_LOG.LDF.
98/07/11 12:18:25.02 spid6    Opening file D:\MSSQL7\DATA\MSDBLOG.LDF.
98/07/11 12:18:25.05 spid8    Opening file
➥D:\MSSQL7\DATA\CONTACTS_SECONDARY.NDF.
98/07/11 12:18:25.07 spid7    Opening file D:\MSSQL7\DATA\PUBS_LOG.LDF.
98/07/11 12:18:25.70 spid1    Recovery complete.
```

(`Recovery Complete` means that each database has been opened and either has opened successfully or has been marked suspect.)

```
98/07/11 12:18:25.70 spid1    SQL Server's default sort order is:
98/07/11 12:18:25.70 spid1        'nocase_iso' (ID = 52)
98/07/11 12:18:25.70 spid1    on top of default character set:
98/07/11 12:18:25.70 spid1        'iso_1' (ID = 1)
```

(This is helpful information if the sort order and character set have been forgotten.)

```
98/07/11 12:18:25.77 spid1    Launched startup procedure 'sp_sqlregister'
```

(This is a procedure that will run after recovery is complete. It's user definable.)

Let's take a closer look at just one log entry:

```
98/07/11 12:18:24.77 spid6    Opening file D:\MSSQL7\DATA\MSDBDATA.MDF.
```

The date and time, obviously, are the first entries. Those are followed by the SPID, or process ID, of the process that's involved with the message, and then the message itself. There are three special process IDs:

- kernel
- server
- ods

The kernel process is involved in the very basic startup procedures, such as opening generic DLL files and printing the version of SQL Server. The server SPID is used for setting memory options, such as loading VLM and handling lock memory allocation. The ods SPID is for Open Data Services and opens all the ODS DLL files, which include all the server-side network libraries.

When a server is in normal operation, it might be a good idea to keep a copy of a "normal" startup, so a startup that isn't normal can be fully and easily diagnosed.

Windows NT Event Log

In addition to the text error log file, SQL Server also uses the Windows NT Event Log for more urgent events. The Event Log also contains some additional information

from the network libraries. The previous sample error log generated some Windows
NT Event Log messages, which are shown in the following listing and pictured in
Figure 7.1.

```
➥Mesg 17052 : Microsoft SQL Server  7.00 - 7.00.517 (Intel X86) Jun 19
➥1998 17:06:54 Copyright (c) 1988-1998 Microsoft Corporation Standard
version on Windows NT
Mesg 17162 : SQL Server is starting at priority class 'normal'(1 CPU
➥detected).
Mesg 17052 : 7 transactions rolled forward in database 'master' (1).
Mesg 17052 : 0 transactions rolled back in database 'master' (1).
Mesg 17026 : Using 'SQLEVN70.DLL' version '6.00.000'.
Mesg 17026 : Using 'OPENDS70.DLL' version '7.00.00.0583'.
Using 'SSNMPN70.DLL' version '7.0.583' to listen on '\\.\pipe\sql\query'.
Using 'SSMSSO70.DLL' version '7.0.583' to listen on '1433'.
Using 'SSMSRP70.DLL' version '7.0.583' to listen on 'INTREPID'.
RPC NETLIB Listening on: ncalrpc:INTREPID[WMSG000000D6.00000001]
RPC NETLIB Listening on: ncacn_ip_tcp:10.1.1.13[1033]
RPC NETLIB Listening on: ncacn_np:\\\\\INTREPID[\\pipe\\000000D6.001]
Mesg 17052 : Recovery complete.
```

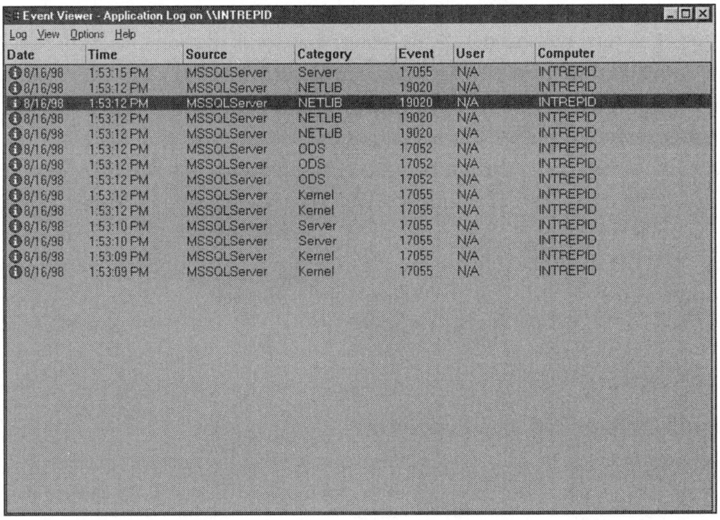

Figure 7.1   The Windows NT Event Viewer after a SQL Server 7.0 startup.

The last three messages are involved with RPC starting up and describe how RPC
is going to listen for different protocols. The Windows NT Event Log also tracks some
things that are "beneath" SQL Server, such as problems accessing disk drives and

network connections. These problems will be described in greater detail in the Windows NT Event Log because they are more truly Windows NT events than they are SQL Server errors.

So after reading through the Windows NT and SQL Server logs, it would be nice if you could have some kind of notification of the occurrence of a critical event. For example, if SQL Server experienced some kind of bad error message, it would be ideal if you could receive an alert describing the error—and possibly even notification via a text page. The upcoming chapter on the SQL Agent describes how to do exactly that.

Ensuring Database Consistency

Database consistency checks are a primary part of database maintenance. If you perform database consistency checks, the database will perform better and be more reliable. A *database consistency check* ensures that the physical and logical structures that hold data are intact. All the pointers point to the right kinds of things, and all the allocation in the database is correct.

Imagine a large fishing net. The net is consistent if all of the lines are knotted together properly in the normal grid fishnet pattern, and can be said to be inconsistent if the net is tangled or if some of the lines are cut. If the lines are cut or the net is tangled, the performance of the fishing net will be diminished, or it may foul up the machines used to retrieve the net. SQL Server has tools that enable it to check every one of the knots and lines in the database and determine that they are connected properly. When you ensure database consistency, you also ensure the performance of the database and the reliability of the database for storing data.

All the SQL Server tools for checking database consistency are accessed through the DBCC commands. DBCC stands for DataBase Consistency Checker; however, through the revisions of SQL Server, a lot of nonconsistency-related commands have been added to DBCC. Table 7.1 lists the commands that will be covered in this section. A complete list of all the DBCC commands, consistency-related or otherwise, can be found in SQL Server Books Online.

Database Consistency and Data Consistency

Database consistency from the SQL Server perspective means that the database structures are intact. It doesn't mean that the actual data makes any sense. In other words, it's up to the dba and the database programmers to ensure that the data put into SQL Server is correct and that the relationships between tables are correct. In this section, the structure of the database is the primary concern.

Table 7.1 **DBCC Commands for Checking Consistency**

Command	Description
DBCC CHECKTABLE	Checks individual table structure
DBCC CHECKDB	Checks database structures
DBCC CHECKCATALOG	Checks system tables
DBCC CHECKALLOC/NEWALLOC	Checks space allocation
DBCC TEXTALLOC/TEXTALL	Checks text/image data
DBCC CHECKIDENT	Checks and corrects Identity columns
DBCC CHECKFILEGROUP	Examines file groups

DBCC CHECKTABLE

The DBCC CHECKTABLE command is used to check the structures supporting an individual table, including all the data, index, and text-type (text, image, or ntext) pages. The syntax for this command is as follows:

```
DBCC CHECKTABLE('table', [Index option] [Repair Level]) [WITH
NO_INFOMSGS]
```

The table name should appear in quotation marks, but they're optional. The Index option can be NOINDEX (don't check any indexes), blank (check all the indexes for the table), or a specific index. The Repair Level specifies what type of repairs SQL Server should attempt to perform, for which the default is to not repair anything and just report problems. The WITH_NOINFOMSGS suppresses the printing of informational messages, but all errors will still be displayed. Without the switch, DBCC CHECKTABLE will print nice informational messages. For example, this command

```
Dbcc checktable('authors')
```

returns:

```
Checking authors
There are 23 rows in 1 pages for object 'authors'.
DBCC execution completed. If DBCC printed error messages, see your System
➥Administrator.
```

If NO_INFOMSGS is used, the command

```
Dbcc checktable('authors') with no_infomsgs
```

returns:

```
DBCC execution completed. If DBCC printed error messages, see your System
➥Administrator.
```

There's a lot less data to wade through by using the NO_INFOMSGS option, but it might be nice to know how many data pages are being used.

SQL Server also provides some new and improved options for repairing database problems you find with DBCC CHECKTABLE or DBCC CHECKDB:

- `REPAIR_REBUILD`. This option tells SQL Server that it should attempt to repair errors found during the CHECKTABLE process, such as removing values from nonclustered indexes that aren't present in the table, rebuilding indexes overall, and fixing the links between indexes and tables. This command will not perform any fixes that may result in data loss, and it may take a while to run because it can involve rebuilding indexes.

- `REPAIR_FAST`. This option specifies that any "fast" repairs, such as removing values from nonclustered indexes, should be performed, but that larger or more time-consuming problems should be ignored.

- `REPAIR_ALLOW_DATA_LOSS`. This option specifies that SQL Server should perform any repair possible, even if it means losing data from the table in question. This means that SQL Server may reallocate and deallocate pages into or out of the table in order to make the table consistent. This can (and should) be done as part of a transaction. Perform the fix, run a query to make sure the level of data loss is acceptable, and then either commit the changes or issue a rollback.

These options are specified as part of the option list as shown in the syntax at the top of the section. Only one of them can be specified in the command, for example:

```
DBCC CHECKTABLE ('authors', REPAIR_REBUILD)
```

This command will check the 'authors' table and fix any problems it finds as long as the fix doesn't cause data loss.

DBCC CHECKDB

Although the `DBCC CHECKTABLE` command is very useful, usually it's a good idea to check all the tables in a database. Instead of writing a complex script and repeatedly running `DBCC CHECKTABLE`, you can use a command called `DBCC CHECKDB`, which will perform exactly that operation. `DBCC CHECKDB` also runs `DBCC CHECKALLOC` to check the database space allocations. With one convenient package, you can check all the tables in a database and the corresponding space allocations. Here's the syntax for `DBCC CHECKDB`:

```
DBCC CHECKDB('database'[, NOINDEX] [Repair Level]) [WITH NO_INFOMSGS]
```

The NOINDEX option skips checking all of the indexes, the Repair Level option works just like it does in `DBCC CHECKTABLE`, and the WITH NO_INFOMSGS skips all the informational messages just like it does in the `DBCC CHECKTABLE` command. For example, this command

```
Dbcc checkdb('pubs')
```

returns

```
Checking pubs
Checking sysobjects
There are 88 rows in 1 pages for object 'sysobjects'.
Checking sysindexes
```

```
There are 45 rows in 1 pages for object 'sysindexes'.
Checking syscolumns
There are 458 rows in 6 pages for object 'syscolumns'.
Checking systypes
There are 27 rows in 1 pages for object 'systypes'.
Checking syscomments
There are 127 rows in 15 pages for object 'syscomments'.
Checking sysfiles1
There are 2 rows in 1 pages for object 'sysfiles1'.
Checking syspermissions
There are 50 rows in 1 pages for object 'syspermissions'.
Checking sysusers
There are 13 rows in 1 pages for object 'sysusers'.
Checking sysdepends
There are 214 rows in 1 pages for object 'sysdepends'.
Checking sysreferences
There are 10 rows in 1 pages for object 'sysreferences'.
Checking sysfilegroups
There are 1 rows in 1 pages for object 'sysfilegroups'.
Checking sysallocations
There are 1 rows in 1 pages for object 'sysallocations'.
Checking authors
There are 23 rows in 1 pages for object 'authors'.
Checking publishers
There are 8 rows in 1 pages for object 'publishers'.
Checking titles
There are 18 rows in 1 pages for object 'titles'.
Checking titleauthor
There are 25 rows in 1 pages for object 'titleauthor'.
Checking stores
There are 6 rows in 1 pages for object 'stores'.
Checking sales
There are 21 rows in 1 pages for object 'sales'.
Checking roysched
There are 86 rows in 1 pages for object 'roysched'.
Checking discounts
There are 3 rows in 1 pages for object 'discounts'.
Checking jobs
There are 14 rows in 1 pages for object 'jobs'.
Checking pub_info
There are 8 rows in 1 pages for object 'pub_info'.
Checking employee
There are 43 rows in 1 pages for object 'employee'.
CHECKDB found 0 errors in database pubs
DBCC execution completed. If DBCC printed error messages, see your System
➥Administrator.
```

Now you'll see why the `NO_INFOMSGS` option was created. The same command with the `NO_INFOMSGS` option returns:

```
DBCC execution completed. If DBCC printed error messages, see your System
➥Administrator.
```

which is the "No news is good news" approach to messages. Notice in the first sample output that SQL Server checked all the system tables in the database. Although it checks the system table integrity, it doesn't actually check the system tables to ensure that the data in the tables is correct. That operation is performed by `DBCC CHECKCATALOG`.

DBCC CHECKCATALOG

The `DBCC CHECKCATALOG` command checks the system tables that keep track of objects and columns to ensure that they are correct. Specifically, `DBCC CHECKCATALOG` confirms that every object (row in the *sysobjects* table) contains at least one column (a row in the *syscolumns* table) and that every column has a valid data type (a row in *systypes*). You run `DBCC CHECKCATALOG` with the following command:

```
DBCC CHECKCATALOG ('database') [WITH NO_INFOMSGS]
```

For example:

```
Dbcc checkcatalog ('pubs')
```

returns:

```
Checking pubs
DBCC execution completed. If DBCC printed error messages, see your System
➥Administrator.
```

The WITH NO_INFOMSGS option makes only one difference here: The `Checking pubs` line disappears. If this runs successfully, it means all the tables are valid and have corresponding entries in the system catalogs. How can you run a similar check to ensure that all the allocation pages are correct? Use `DBCC CHECKALLOC`.

DBCC CHECKALLOC and DBCC NEWALLOC

The `DBCC CHECKALLOC` command is used to determine space allocation. The `DBCC CHECKALLOC` command and `DBCC NEWALLOC` are functionally identical, but `DBCC NEWALLOC` may not be supported in future versions, so don't use it in any new scripts. The `DBCC CHECKALLOC` command performs a subset of the checks performed by `DBCC`

DBCC Performance

With prior versions of SQL Server, many DBAs didn't run DBCC on a regular basis because it caused a serious performance problem. Even on quality hardware, it could take 10–12 hours to perform checks on large (10GB plus) databases. In SQL Server 7.0, DBCC has been rewritten to run significantly faster—up to 60 times faster—than before. So if you weren't using DBCC before, give it a try now and start using it on a regular basis.

CHECKDB. Therefore, it's not necessary to run both; run only DBCC CHECKDB.

Run DBCC CHECKALLOC with this command syntax:

```
DBCC CHECKALLOC ('database'[, NOINDEX] [Repair Level]) [WITH NO_INFOMSGS]
```

This command has the same options that have been covered before. To run this command on the pubs database, for example, use this command:

```
Dbcc checkalloc('pubs')
```

which returns about three pages of output. (Some of the output has been removed to conserve space.)

```
Checking pubs
****************************************************************
TABLE: sysobjects           OBJID = 1
INDID=1       FIRST=(1:5)    ROOT=(1:16)    DPAGES=1    SORT=0
     Data level: 1.  2 Data  Pages in 2 extents.
INDID=2       FIRST=(1:112)  ROOT=(1:112)   DPAGES=1    SORT=0
     Indid    : 2.  1 Index Pages in 1 extents.
INDID=3       FIRST=(1:120)  ROOT=(1:120)   DPAGES=1    SORT=0
     Indid    : 3.  1 Index Pages in 1 extents.
TOTAL # of extents = 4
****************************************************************
TABLE: sysindexes           OBJID = 2
INDID=1       FIRST=(1:24)   ROOT=(1:56)    DPAGES=1    SORT=0
     Data level: 1.  2 Data  Pages in 2 extents.
INDID=255     FIRST=(1:96)   ROOT=(1:96)    DPAGES=0    SORT=0
     Indid    : 255.  5 Index Pages in 1 extents.
TOTAL # of extents = 3
****************************************************************
TABLE: authors              OBJID = 117575457
INDID=1       FIRST=(1:296)  ROOT=(1:304)   DPAGES=1    SORT=0
     Data level: 1.  2 Data  Pages in 2 extents.
INDID=2       FIRST=(1:440)  ROOT=(1:440)   DPAGES=1    SORT=0
     Indid    : 2.  1 Index Pages in 1 extents.
TOTAL # of extents = 3
****************************************************************
TABLE: publishers           OBJID = 197575742
INDID=1       FIRST=(1:312)  ROOT=(1:320)   DPAGES=1    SORT=0
     Data level: 1.  2 Data  Pages in 2 extents.
TOTAL # of extents = 2
****************************************************************
TABLE: titles       OBJID = 261575970
INDID=1       FIRST=(1:328)  ROOT=(1:336)   DPAGES=1    SORT=0
     Data level: 1.  2 Data  Pages in 2 extents.
INDID=2       FIRST=(1:472)  ROOT=(1:472)   DPAGES=1    SORT=0
     Indid    : 2.  1 Index Pages in 1 extents.
TOTAL # of extents = 3
```

```
****************************************************************
Processed 40 entries in Sysindexes for dbid 5.
Alloc page (1:2) (# of extent=67 used pages=140 ref pages=95)
         (1:2) (# of mixed extents=9  mixed pages=68)
    OBJID 1 INDID 1 data extents=2 pages=2 mixed extent pages=0
    OBJID 1 INDID 2 index extents=1 pages=1 mixed extent pages=0
    OBJID 1 INDID 3 index extents=1 pages=1 mixed extent pages=0
    OBJID 2 INDID 1 data extents=2 pages=2 mixed extent pages=0
    OBJID 2 INDID 255 index extents=1 pages=5 mixed extent pages=4
    OBJID 117575457 INDID 1 data extents=2 pages=2 mixed extent pages=0
    OBJID 117575457 INDID 2 index extents=1 pages=1 mixed extent pages=0
    OBJID 197575742 INDID 1 data extents=2 pages=2 mixed extent pages=0
Total (# of extent=67 used pages=140 ref pages=95) in this database
      (# of mixed extents=9  mixed pages=68) in this database
CHECKALLOC found 0 errors in database pubs
DBCC execution completed. If DBCC printed error messages, see your System
➥Administrator.
```

Notice that the first two system tables and the first two user tables are all that's left in the output. The first section of output, which has rows of asterisks in it, provides data on each table in the database, how many pages are in use, and which pages are in use. The second part of the output is the index processing, which shows how and where each index is stored. Finally, the line starting with TOTAL gives summary information for the database, showing that 140 pages in 67 extents are used and that there are 9 mixed extents (extents that hold data from multiple tables) and 68 mixed pages (pages that hold data from multiple tables).

DBCC TEXTALLOC and *DBCC TEXTALL*

The DBCC TEXTALLOC and DBCC TEXTALL commands have been superseded by functionality available in DBCC CHECKTABLE and DBCC CHECKDB, respectively. However, these commands may not be available in future versions of SQL Server, so don't use them in any new scripts. These two commands are used to check strictly the text pages of either a table (DBCC TEXTALLOC) or all the text pages in a database (DBCC TEXTALL). (In this case, "text pages" refer to pages of type IMAGE, TEXT, or NTEXT.) The two commands have the same syntax as DBCC CHECKTABLE and DBCC CHECKDB.

> **SQL Server Data Storage**
>
> Why does SQL Server put 140 pages on 67 extents? 67 extents hold 530 pages, and 140 pages could fit on as few as 18 extents. The answer is that SQL Server doesn't fill all the extents or all the pages. Why not? Spreading the data around the disk into a larger number of extents enables SQL Server to find the data it needs faster than if all the data were located in one small section of the database. Also, because the extents and pages aren't full, there is more space available to add data before an extent split is necessary.

DBCC CHECKIDENT

The DBCC CHECKIDENT command checks the identity column of a specified table and corrects it if necessary. It modifies only the *seed value*, which is the value that the next row in the table will receive. The DBCC CHECKIDENT command checks to see whether any values in the identity column are higher than the current seed value. If it finds any that are higher, it resets the current seed value to the next value.

The command runs in two modes, NORESEED, which will not correct any errors, and RESEED, which will either set the seed value to the next correct value or set it to a user-supplied value. The syntax follows one of these formats:

```
DBCC CHECKIDENT ('table', NORESEED)
```

or

```
DBCC CHECKIDENT ('table', RESEED[, value])
```

The first syntax option returns the current seed value. If no value is specified, the second syntax checks to see whether the seed value is less than any of the identity values, and if it is, the value is reset. That means that if the seed value is one million above the highest value in the identity column, the seed value will not be reset, and those million keys will be lost. If the value parameter is included, the seed value will be set to the value parameter.

One strategy for reducing the number of lost keys is to reset the seed value to zero and then use DBCC CHECKIDENT with the RESEED option but not include a value for resetting the seed to the next valid value. The following is an example of such using the pubs database.

First, insert a bunch of duplicate data into the "jobs" table:

```
insert into jobs (job_desc, min_lvl, max_lvl)
select job_desc, min_lvl, max_lvl from jobs
(14 row(s) affected)
```

Then say "oops" and delete the duplicate data:

```
delete jobs where job_id > 14
(14 row(s) affected)
```

Then check the seed value without resetting it:

```
dbcc checkident(jobs, NORESEED)
Checking identity information: current identity value '28', current
➥column value '14'.
DBCC execution completed. If DBCC printed error messages, see your System
➥Administrator.
```

The current identity value, or seed value, is 28, and the current highest value in the identity column is 14. So there are 14 missing keys.

Take a look at what DBCC CHECKIDENT does with just the RESEED option:

```
dbcc checkident(jobs, RESEED)
Checking identity information: current identity value '28', current
➥column value '28'.
DBCC execution completed. If DBCC printed error messages, see your System
➥Administrator.
```

That didn't do much, so reset the seed value to zero:

```
dbcc checkident(jobs, RESEED, 0)
Checking identity information: current identity value '28', current
➥column value '0'.
DBCC execution completed. If DBCC printed error messages, see your System
➥Administrator.
```

That resets the seed value to zero. Check to make sure that it is really set to zero with this command:

```
dbcc checkident(jobs, NORESEED)
Checking identity information: current identity value '0', current column
➥value '14'.
DBCC execution completed. If DBCC printed error messages, see your System
➥Administrator.
```

It looks like it really is reset to zero. Now reset the seed value to the correct value by using this command:

```
dbcc checkident(jobs, RESEED)
Checking identity information: current identity value '0', current column
➥value '14'.
DBCC execution completed. If DBCC printed error messages, see your System
➥Administrator.
```

Then check to make sure the seed value actually was reset correctly:

```
dbcc checkident (jobs, NORESEED)
Checking identity information: current identity value '14', current
➥column value '14'.
DBCC execution completed. If DBCC printed error messages, see your System
➥Administrator.
```

That little exercise completely erases the mistake of inserting duplicate data. When you reset the seed value, the rest of the data will be inserted correctly. This could also be used to "fill" a hole in identity values by resetting the seed value to the beginning of the hole and allowing the users to fill in the hole. If any of these seed modification techniques is ever done in a production environment, it should be encapsulated within a transaction or done while the database is in single-user mode to prevent user interference.

DBCC CHECKFILEGROUP

The DBCC CHECKFILEGROUP command ensures the integrity of a specified file group and the objects residing in that file group. In other words, it performs the same checks as DBCC CHECKDB, but only on a specified file group. Remember that a file group is a group of one or more files, and that a file group always belongs to a specific database. So the DBCC CHECKFILEGROUP command checks all the structures that belong to a given database and are in a given file group.

If a file group contains nonclustered indexes, DBCC CHECKFILEGROUP will check the nonclustered indexes, and as part of that check, it will scan the tables even if the tables are in another file group. The integrity of an index relies on the integrity of the base table. However, the reverse is not true: If a table is checked and a nonclustered index is in another file group, the index will not be checked.

DBCC CHECKFILEGROUP uses the following syntax:

```
DBCC CHECKFILEGROUP (['filegroup name' ¦ filegroup id][, NOINDEX]) [WITH
➥NO_INFOMSGS]
```

Filegroup id is the id from the table *sysfilegroups* that corresponds to the file group to be checked. If neither a file group name nor a file group id is specified, the default file group in the current database will be checked. If the NOINDEX option is specified, indexes will not be checked at all. This is helpful because it reduces the amount of time spent checking the file group.

Here's what the command looks like when it is run on the default file group in the pubs database:

```
Use pubs
Dbcc checkfilegroup
```

That command returns the following:

```
Checking pubs
Checking sysobjects
There are 88 rows in 1 pages for object 'sysobjects'.
Checking sysindexes
There are 45 rows in 1 pages for object 'sysindexes'.
Checking syscolumns
There are 458 rows in 6 pages for object 'syscolumns'.
Checking systypes
There are 27 rows in 1 pages for object 'systypes'.
Checking syscomments
There are 127 rows in 15 pages for object 'syscomments'.
Checking sysfiles1
There are 2 rows in 1 pages for object 'sysfiles1'.
Checking syspermissions
There are 50 rows in 1 pages for object 'syspermissions'.
Checking sysusers
There are 13 rows in 1 pages for object 'sysusers'.
Checking sysdepends
There are 214 rows in 1 pages for object 'sysdepends'.
Checking sysreferences
There are 10 rows in 1 pages for object 'sysreferences'.
Checking sysfilegroups
There are 1 rows in 1 pages for object 'sysfilegroups'.
Checking sysallocations
There are 1 rows in 1 pages for object 'sysallocations'.
Checking authors
There are 23 rows in 1 pages for object 'authors'.
Checking publishers
```

```
There are 8 rows in 1 pages for object 'publishers'.
Checking titles
There are 18 rows in 1 pages for object 'titles'.
Checking titleauthor
There are 25 rows in 1 pages for object 'titleauthor'.
Checking stores
There are 6 rows in 1 pages for object 'stores'.
Checking sales
There are 21 rows in 1 pages for object 'sales'.
Checking roysched
There are 86 rows in 1 pages for object 'roysched'.
Checking discounts
There are 3 rows in 1 pages for object 'discounts'.
Checking jobs
There are 14 rows in 1 pages for object 'jobs'.
Checking pub_info
There are 8 rows in 1 pages for object 'pub_info'.
Checking employee
There are 43 rows in 1 pages for object 'employee'.
CHECKFILEGROUP found 0 errors in database pubs
DBCC execution completed. If DBCC printed error messages, see your System
➥Administrator.
```

If the NO_INFOMSGS option had been turned on, only the last message would have been returned. Notice that the output from this looks suspiciously similar to the output from DBCC CHECKDB run on the pubs database.

If you use the DBCC commands and monitor the Windows NT event log and SQL Server errorlog, you will get as much warning as possible of impending doom in a database. Microsoft recommends that you run DBCC commands prior to nightly backups to ensure the integrity of the backups. This is usually conducted with the Database Maintenance Plan Wizard, which you'll learn about later in this chapter.

Maintaining Performance

The previous section dealt with ensuring the accessibility of SQL Server, but it did not deal with keeping performance tuned to the highest possible levels. This section deals with maintaining the desired performance of the database by ensuring that indexes are kept live and that data pages are packed full of good data and not empty space. This section is not going to delve into how to design databases for performance because that's beyond the scope of this book. This section does provide advanced theories and practices on how to make SQL Server databases return the same data with a predictable delay. In this section, you'll discover how to update statistics and how data fragmentation impacts a database.

Updating Statistics

When a query is executed, a module within SQL Server called the *query processor* takes the query apart and determines how it will be executed. That means the query processor picks indexes on each table mentioned in the query to use to find the data. It determines which index to use by examining the query and figuring out what conditions are placed on the query, which is usually outlined in the WHERE clause of a SELECT statement. For example, if a query is looking for a last name, the query processor uses the index on last names.

First, let's lapse into database design a little bit. A good index has high selectivity. That means that a given value for the index will return a very small number of rows. Take the example of a mailing list table containing last name, first name, street address, and gender. Street address is probably a good field to index on, because a small percentage of the people on a mailing list will live at the same address. The combination of last name and first name tends to be a good choice as well because a very small percentage of people will have the same last name and first name. Gender is not a good index field because on a normally distributed list, any value of gender will return half the table.

In order to select indexes quickly, the query processor uses index statistics that measure the selectivity of a given index. Index statistics are based on the number of times values repeat inside of the columns used in an index. If the selectivity is low, that index field will never be used. If the selectivity is high, SQL Server will use that index field to perform the query.

Unfortunately, the statistics kept on an index are fairly static. In other words, as data is added to the table, the distribution of data in the table may change, but the statistics will not. So anytime a large amount of data is added to or removed from a table, the statistics need to be updated. As the statistics become less accurate, the query analyzer may quit using certain indexes, which will cause a sudden drastic performance problem. It's a good idea to update statistics on a fairly regular basis.

Statistics have to be updated either on a table-by-table basis or by using the Database Maintenance Plan Wizard, which is covered later in this chapter. The command to use, amazingly enough, is called UPDATE STATISTICS, and its syntax is as follows:

```
UPDATE STATISTICS table [(index list)] [WITH options]
```

The table parameter is the name of the table to update. The index list is optional; if it's not provided, statistics for all indexes on the given table will be updated. The index list options include the following:

- FULLSCAN or SAMPLE. FULLSCAN means the whole table will be scanned to find the statistics. SAMPLE followed by a number and then the keyword ROWS or PERCENT means that either a certain number of rows or a certain percentage of the table will be scanned and used to generate statistics. SQL Server may sample more than the suggested amount if it decides the amount is too small to be statistically relevant. The default behavior is to perform a sample with the smallest statistically significant set.

- NORECOMPUTE. SQL Server will automatically recompute statistics on tables when the statistics become out of date. If you use the NORECOMPUTE option, SQL Server will not recompute the statistics on the given index or set of indexes.

- COLUMNS or INDEX or ALL. Specifies which statistics are being updated. SQL Server maintains statistics on certain columns and all indexes, so using this option turns on checking for a specific column, or index, or for both.

For example, the following command recomputes all indexes on the "authors" table by reading every row in the table, and then it turns off recomputing for that index:

```
Update statistics authors with fullscan, norecompute
```

Here's another example, this time updating statistics on the "titles" table and using only 30 percent of the rows to compute statistics:

```
Update statistics titles with sample 30 percent
```

Both of these commands return the message The command completed successfully.

Because it's not extremely convenient to run the update statistics command on every single table in a given database, SQL Server offers a system stored procedure called sp_updatestats that you can run to update all the statistics for all the indexes in the current database.

Automatically Updating Statistics

Realizing that the process for maintaining statistics was not very clean, Microsoft introduced a new process that will automatically maintain statistics for tables. This process compensates for tables where the statistics tend to change slowly over time. When a table changes significantly over a short period of time—during a batch update, for example—it's a good idea to manually run UPDATE STATISTICS. In the case of a table that is being used "normally," the automatic generation of statistics is suffi-cient.

To prevent the automatic regeneration of statistics for a given set of indexes on a table or for just one index, use the sp_autostats stored procedure:

```
sp_autostats 'table_name' [, 'Stats_Flag'] [, 'Index_Name']
```

If none of the optional arguments is specified, the procedure will return the status of automatic statistics regeneration for the specified table. The 'Stats_Flag' argument can be set to either ON or OFF. The 'Index_Name' argument specifies which index should have the automatic generation of statistics turned on or off. If the index is not specified, the setting in 'Stats_Flag' will be applied to all the indexes on the specified table.

Generating Statistics on Columns

The COLUMNS option of the UPDATE STATISTICS command can be used to generate and maintain distribution statistics for a given column or combination of columns. This can be used either as raw statistical information on the table or to determine whether the combination of columns might be a good selection for an index. For example, consider this command:

```
UPDATE STATISTICS authors(au_lname, au_fname)
    WITH COLUMNS
```

This creates statistics for the "authors" table in the pubs database on the columns au_lname and au_fname. The data returned from this can be displayed by using DBCC SHOW_STATISTICS to determine whether an index on the two columns would be selective enough to be valuable.

Dealing with Index and Data Fragmentation

Data and index information in SQL Server is stored on 8KB pages. For an index, when the index page becomes full, the page splits, a new page is added to the index, and some of the data from the original page is copied to the new page. If this process sounds complicated, it is. In addition to copying the data from the old page to the new page, SQL Server has to make sure both pages are repointed to the correct places.

To avoid page splits, it is possible to specify a fill factor when creating an index. A *fill factor* determines how full the index pages will be when an index is created. Fill factors range from zero to 100. A fill factor of 100 means that SQL Server will attempt to fill an entire index page with data. This is the desirable state in a read-only (or read-mostly) database, where the number of page splits will be very low due to low transaction volume. A fill factor of zero is similar to a fill factor of 100, but some of the top pages in the index tree will be left partially empty to improve performance.

For tables that receive frequent updates, filling the index pages will result in a large number of page splits, which will have a detrimental impact on performance. By using a lower number for the fill factor (say 75 percent), you can increase the amount of space used by the index by 25 percent, and the number of page splits will be reduced as well, improving overall performance. Using a very low fill factor wastes not only the space on disk, but space in memory as well. SQL Server caches data by the page. So if the page is only 75 percent full, 25 percent of the space used by that page is wasted in memory as well as on disk. For more information to help you figure out where to draw this particular line, see Chapter 11, "Performance Tuning and Optimization."

That's how index fragmentation can be managed. What about fragmentation on data pages? For heaps, which are tables without indexes, there is no way to handle data fragmentation. As rows are deleted, the space might get reused—or it might not. The data is stored somewhere "out there," with no particular order to it.

So how can data become defragmented and whole again? Well, remember clustered indexes? In a clustered index, the data is stored as the leaf nodes of the index, in sorted order. So if there is a clustered index on a table, you can defragment the table by rebuilding the index with the same options and fill factor.

How is fragmentation determined? The command `DBCC SHOWCONTIG` has nothing to do with database consistency, but it reports both the amount of space allocated to a given table and the amount actually in use by the data in the table. It takes only two parameters: the ID of the table and the ID of an index to check (which is optional). If the index is specified, fragmentation information will be provided for only the given index.

To find the ID for an object, run the following query

```
Select object_name("authors")
```

replacing "authors" with the name of the table.

To find the ID for an index, run the following query:

```
Select indid, name from sysindexes where object_name(id) = "authors"
```

Replace "authors" with the name of the table for which you want to find the indexes. The query returns the name and ID for each index on the given table.

Anywhere an ID is specified in this book, it is the ID that was found on the author's SQL Server installation. The ID used on your installation will be different.

The `DBCC SHOWCONTIG` command for checking all of the indexes on the authors table is this

```
dbcc showcontig (117575457)
```

which will return the following:

```
DBCC SHOWCONTIG scanning 'authors' table...
[SHOW_CONTIG - SCAN ANALYSIS]
------------------------------------------------------------------
Table: 'authors' (117575457)  Indid: 1  dbid:5
TABLE level scan performed.
- Pages Scanned...............................: 1
- Extents Scanned............................: 1
- Extent Switches............................: 0
- Avg. Pages per Extent......................: 1.0
- Scan Density [Best Count:Actual Count].......: 100.00% [1:1]
- Logical Scan Fragmentation .................: 0.00%
- Extent Scan Fragmentation ..................: 0.00%
- Avg. Bytes free per page...................: 6008.0
- Avg. Page density (full)...................: 25.77%


(11 row(s) affected)

DBCC execution completed. If DBCC printed error messages, contact your
➥system administrator.
```

This report shows the number of pages scanned (1) and the average page density (25.77%). In other words, the table uses only a quarter of a page. For larger tables, the average page density will be significantly higher. To get a better feel for the fragmentation in the table overall, check the Scan Density item, which reports 100%. This figure means that the database is 100% not fragmented. As this number goes down, the total amount of fragmentation in the table goes up.

Rebuilding indexes can be a lengthy task. To correctly rebuild all the indexes, you would have to generate all the SQL for all the index drops and rebuilds and then encapsulate it inside a transaction to make sure either that the drop and rebuild both occurred or that neither occurred.

To make the process of rebuilding indexes simpler, SQL Server provides the command `DBCC DBREINDEX`. The `DBCC DBREINDEX` command has absolutely nothing to do with the database consistency checker, but it is, nonetheless, a DBCC command. The syntax is as follows:

```
DBCC DBREINDEX (table[, index[, fill factor]]) WITH NO_INFOMESSAGES
```

The table can be a table name, with or without quotation marks, or a fully qualified name in the format database.owner.table, which must have quotation marks around it. The index name is optional; the default is to rebuild all the indexes on the table. Fill factor is also optional and can be supplied only if the index is also supplied. The default for fill factor is zero.

The other nice thing about `DBCC DBREINDEX` is that it will rebuild all the indexes, but first it rebuilds the clustered index, followed by any nonclustered indexes. Also, any indexes that are part of a primary key unique constraint can be rebuilt without having to rebuild the constraint.

That's all fine, but it's still an inconvenience to build a script to run DBCC on each table in a database with more than 100 tables. There must be an easier way. Read on.

Proactive Maintenance with the Database Maintenance Plan Wizard

The Database Maintenance Plan Wizard is one of the new wizard tools in SQL Server 7.0 that will create scheduled jobs for automating routine database tasks, such as rebuilding indexes and ensuring database consistency. The Database Maintenance Wizard will also schedule jobs to occur at regular intervals, making maintenance much simpler.

Using `DBCC DBReindex`
Like all the other DBCC commands, the `DBCC DBREINDEX` command has been performance optimized so it will run significantly faster than it did in prior versions. Also, `DBCC DBREINDEX` will automatically rebuild indexes that are part of foreign key or primary key constraints, without having to use `ALTER TABLE` to remove and then replace the constraint.

Maintenance Plan Wizard Components

The purpose of the Database Maintenance Plan Wizard is to create jobs that can be scheduled to run on a daily or weekly basis that include steps necessary to maintain the integrity and performance of a database. The wizard breaks the tasks down into four steps:

1. *Update Data Optimization Information.* Updating statistics, rebuilding indexes, and removing "dead space" from the database.

2. *Run Data Integrity Tests.* Checking space allocations (DBCC CHECKALLOC) and database integrity (DBCC CHECKDB).

3. *Specify the Database Backup Plan.* Database backup.

4. *Specify the Transaction Log Backup Plan.* Transaction log backup.

Each of these steps can be scheduled independently for each database or for the collection of databases. The scheduling is the normal SQL Server scheduling that has become the standard for how flexible scheduling should work. There are options for Daily, Weekly, or Monthly events, each of which can occur at a set time or at specified intervals throughout a day. To get an idea about how all this works, walk through the following Database Maintenance Plan Wizard steps:

1. Open SQL Enterprise Manager, open the server that you want to work on, and then click on Database Maintenance Plans. Choose Action, New Plan (see Figure 7.2).

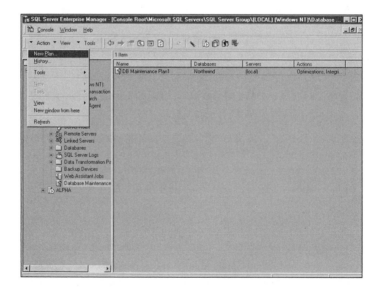

Figure 7.2   The SQL Server Enterprise Manager's Action menu, where you start the Database Maintenance Plan Wizard.

2. Click on Next on the introduction window.

3. In the Select Databases window, choose the Northwind database, and then click on Next.

4. On the Update Data Optimization Information page, choose to rebuild the indexes with the original amount of free space, to update statistics, and to remove unused space from the database file, as shown in Figure 7.3.

5. To schedule the job to occur every other week on Monday, Wednesday, and Friday, click on the Change button by the Schedule box, and then click the Change button in the Edit Schedule dialog box. Choose a Weekly job that occurs every two weeks on Monday, Wednesday, and Friday at 1:00 a.m. (see Figure 7.4). Click OK to close the Edit Recurring Job Schedule dialog box. Then name the schedule "BiWeekly MWF" so the schedule can be used in other plans. Click on OK to save the schedule and return to the Update Data Optimization Information page of the wizard. Click on Next.

6. The Run Data Integrity Tests page appears next. The Perform Internal Data Integrity Tests item will run checks on system tables. The other major option, Perform Database Integrity Tests, will check all tables. Selecting the Exclude Indexes item is the same as specifying the NOINDEX option, and Attempt to Repair Any Minor Problems sets the Repair Level to REPAIR_REBUILD to fix problems without losing data.

7. Next you see the Specify the Database Backup Plan page of the wizard. Select a schedule for performing the database backup and click on Next.

8. On the Specify the Transaction Log Backup Plan page of the wizard, specify a schedule for performing transaction log backups. Then click on Next.

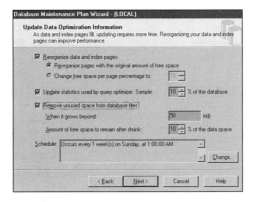

Figure 7.3 The Database Maintenance Plan Wizard enables you to update indexes and data storage.

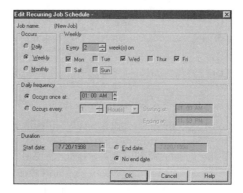

Figure 7.4 The scheduler window for the Database Maintenance Plan Wizard. All scheduler windows look the same for all the steps of the plan. This picture shows the setup discussed in step 5.

9. The Reports to Generate window appears next. These options are covered in the section "Creating and Analyzing Plan Output" later in the chapter. Click on Next.

10. The Maintenance History window enables you to save the output from maintenance jobs for future review or study. The history can be stored on the local server or sent to a remote server for collection. Click on Local Server and limit the rows in the table to 10,000 so it doesn't take over a hard disk (see Figure 7.5).

11. Click on Next to review all the selections you made. This provides a nice plain-English review of all the selections you made during the wizard. Click on Finish to save the plan.

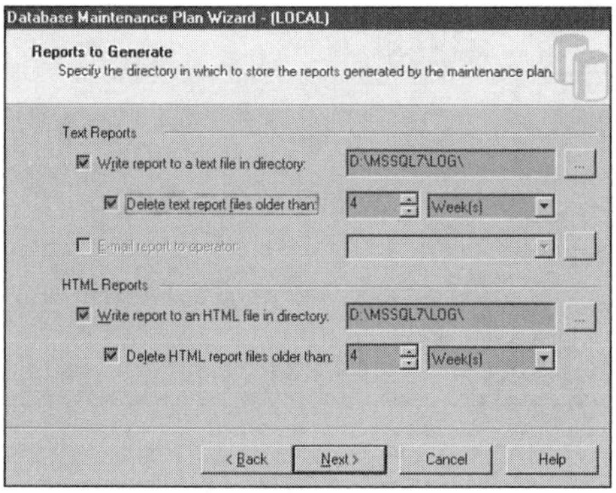

Figure 7.5 From the Reports to Generate screen, you can choose to write both a plain text file and an HTML formatted report.

Those are the basic steps involved in creating a plan and the types of things a plan can do. After you've created the plan, the only thing left to do is to monitor the plan output.

Using the Database Maintenance Plan Wizard to Perform Backups

The Database Maintenance Plan Wizard can be used to perform both transaction log and full database backups on a scheduled basis, while providing the same level of reporting as other maintenance tasks. Simply schedule the backups to run, and then monitor the results. It is a good idea to run database integrity checks prior to backups so the wizard can be configured to either run the database integrity checks on a scheduled basis or run them immediately prior to backup. To run them prior to backup, choose the Perform These Tests Prior to Backing Up the Database or Transaction Log option in the Database Maintenance Plan Wizard.

Modifying Existing Database Maintenance Plans

To modify an existing database maintenance plan, open the Database Maintenance Plans folder and double-click on the plan you want to edit. A tabbed window appears, with one tab for each of the steps in the Database Maintenance Plan Wizard. Here you can change scheduling, along with all the rest of the details of a plan. You might edit a plan, for example, if it is running over into production hours or if it is not taking very long to add more steps to the plan.

Running a Database Maintenance Task on Demand

To kick off a database maintenance task manually, start the SQL Agent, and then expand Jobs. Each step in the maintenance plan is displayed in this window. Right-click on the job you want to run and click on Start, and the job kicks off. Watch the Status column of the job you started to determine when the job is complete. Right-click on the job and choose Job History to see the status of the job up close and to see how long it took to run. Figure 7.6 shows an example.

Creating and Analyzing Plan Output

One of the biggest problems with an automated maintenance routine is monitoring the maintenance to ensure that the plan executed successfully and did not find any problems the database administrator should be aware of. In previous versions of SQL Server, it was very cumbersome to get a full report of any problems that occurred during a maintenance job. By default, SQL Server reported only the success or failure of the job. However, SQL Server 7 displays the output of the job in an easy-to-read format and saves the job output into a table so reports can be created more easily.

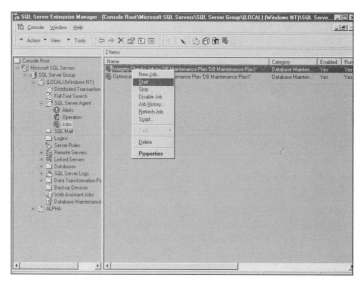

Figure 7.6 Starting a database maintenance plan job manually. Notice the job is split into the backup portion and the index optimization job.

There are four ways to get reports out of SQL Server 7 when a maintenance job ends:

- The Maintenance Plan Wizard can write a text report out of the maintenance job.

- The Maintenance Plan Wizard can write out the same report in HTML.

- The Maintenance Plan Wizard can write out the same report into a table on the local database.

- The Maintenance Plan Wizard can write out the same report into a table on a linked server.

Reports put into a text file or an HTML document will be named with the format "DB Maintenance Plan12_199807191514." This example represents the output from the DB Maintenance Plan run on July 19, 1998 (19980719) at 3:14 PM (1514). The extension will either be .TXT for a text report or .HTM for an HTML report. These reports can be saved anywhere, so they could all be placed on a network drive. However, problems can occur if multiple servers all write to the same drive, because it's not obvious from the filename which server wrote the report. So text files and HTML documents are helpful for keeping track of a single server, but for multiple servers something a little more centralized would be nice.

SQL Server also provides the capability to save the report into a table, either on the local server (good) or on a linked server (excellent). On the local server, the data can be used to generate home-grown reports. By consolidating all the servers' reports back to a single server, the data can be collected at one point and analyzed in one place to check for problems. The exact same data that is found in the report is in the table, and all the servers can report to the same table. The table is in the msdb database and is called *sysdbmaintplan_history*. Table 7.2 provides a description of that history table.

Table 7.2 **Structure of the Maintenance Plan History Table**

Column Name	Datatype	Description
sequence_id	int	Primary key
plan_id	uniqueidentifier	ID number of plan being executed
plan_name	sysname	Name of plan
database_name	sysname	Name of database
server_name	sysname	Name of server
activity	nvarchar	Type of plan
succeeded	bit	1 if Successful, 0 otherwise
start_time	datetime	When the plan started
end_time	datetime	When the plan completed
duration	int	How long the plan took to run
error_number	int	Return code of any errors
message	nvarchar	Message from any errors

Given that description, the following query will extract any of the reports that were not successful:

```
Select server_name, database_name, activity from sysdbmaintplan_history
➥where succeeded=0;
```

It would be easy enough to write a battery of queries that pull data such as plans that took too long to run or plans that have started but not finished at the current time to get the broad spectrum of issues that might pop up. By executing these queries after each reporting interval, the database administrator can be assured that the Maintenance Plan Wizard is running correctly.

```
Select server_name, database_name, activity from sysdbmaintplan_history
➥where duration > 3600
```

```
Select server_name, database_name, activity from sysdbmaintplan_history
➥where end_time is null
```

If you run this handful of queries on a centralized table, it's much easier to track the maintenance plan progress on all the servers in an entire organization with a minimum of overhead for each server. This is also a good way to make sure that the maintenance plan jobs are not impinging on production time.

Recommendations

Microsoft used to strongly recommend the use of database integrity checks on a very regular basis to ensure reliability and performance of databases. Very few database administrators took the time to set up basic check tasks such as the ones outlined in this chapter, and data and time are lost because of it. Microsoft no longer recommends these checks in SQL Server 7.0, but they're still a very good idea.

The maintenance schedule you use should evolve from and with the size of the databases you are maintaining. If you can integrate a full spectrum of integrity checks and index rebuilds with your backup schedule and run them in a few hours, you might as well run them all every night. If the database is so large that not all of the checks can be run in a given night, split the tasks up and schedule them independently. Run database integrity checks on Monday, Wednesday, and Friday, and run index maintenance on Tuesday and Thursday, for example.

If you are balking at this much maintenance because of bad experiences in which the jobs took too long under SQL Server 6.5, give them a shot again. SQL Server 7.0 implements a lot of fundamental changes that will speed up almost all database diagnostics. Maintenance should run significantly faster than it did in SQL Server 6.5.

One good way you can set up maintenance in an environment that doesn't require 24-by-7 uptime is to run as much stuff as possible during the maintenance window. In 24-by-7 situations, you can run backups on a nightly basis when activity is low and schedule `DBCC CHECKALLOC`-type diagnostics nightly as well. The `DBCC CHECKDB` tends to use a lot more resources, so put it off until the weekend. The key is to analyze the business, figure out how long different parts of maintenance take, and then set up a schedule to accommodate both.

Monitoring daily maintenance is critical. If SQL Server tells you that something is wrong but you skip checking out the reports on that one particular day and miss out, you could be in for a fun day sometime in the future. Always spend the first few minutes of every day checking logs and running through reports from the previous night's activity. Some shops even track the duration of maintenance to help track trends in data growth.

The big deal about maintenance is that it is a proactive approach to dealing with major problems. By performing scheduled maintenance, you buy yourself time to react to problems before they impact users or cause data loss. Database backup and restoration will help you recover from a disaster, but good maintenance may help prevent a disaster in the first place.

Conclusions

Database maintenance is critical. If you perform maintenance according to a regular, scheduled maintenance cycle and you monitor the results of the maintenance tasks, database server downtime can be reduced, and the users (or at least the users' bosses) will be much happier. Database maintenance helps find small problems before they become big user-impacting problems. Fixing small problems is a lot less exciting than fixing big problems, but we all need a little less of that kind of excitement in our lives.

Less Frequent Activities

8

Data Import/Export

Sean Baird

Many SQL Servers today operate in environments where SQL Server is not the primary data store. Mainframes, other relational database systems (such as Oracle), flat files, desktop databases, and email servers are all examples. Having data spread among different repositories is a hindrance to many businesses, but consolidating this information is often difficult because of costs or logistical reasons.

Often, the solution to the distributed data problem revolves around the periodic transfers of data. Consider some of the following examples:

- Loading mainframe data into a SQL Server to support a client/server system or to support ad hoc queries and reports
- Moving or copying data from a transaction processing system into a data warehouse
- Pulling information from multiple heterogeneous data repositories (such as email systems, network monitoring agents, and so on) for analysis purposes
- Maintaining mission-critical business data among multiple company sites (using either tight or loose consistency)
- Exporting information from a database for batch processing on a mainframe
- Exporting information from a database for use in other data analysis tools, such as a spreadsheet

Fortunately, SQL Server 7.0 offers a variety of methods for transferring data into and out of a database. In fact, the available options are much better than what existed in versions 6.5 and earlier. Unfortunately, with so many options to choose from, choosing the most appropriate method can be challenging.

This chapter begins by providing an overview of the available data transfer options and provides some guidelines for choosing one. The remainder of the chapter is devoted to in-depth information on the three main data transfer options.

Exploring Transfer Methods

The suite of data transfer features available in SQL Server 7.0 consists of these three main options:

- Bulk copy libraries
- Distributed queries
- Data transformation services

Bulk Copy Libraries

The bulk copy libraries are the most well-established of all the data transfer methods. The bulk copy libraries are a set of API and object libraries that provide functions for importing and exporting data into and out of SQL Server. These libraries are the most efficient of all the data transfer options, providing support for the rapid transfer of very large amounts of data. The following libraries are available in SQL Server 7.0:

- *DB-Library.* DB-Lib, as it's often known, is the original API library used for programmatic access to SQL Server. DB-Lib contains a set of function calls used primarily for submitting queries and retrieving the results for those queries. It also contains a set of function calls used for importing and exporting data. DB-Lib is most easily used from C++, but it can also be used with Visual Basic.

  Although DB-Lib is supported in SQL Server 7.0, it does not support many of the new features of this product. Other API libraries have now superseded DB-Lib.

- *SQL-DMO.* SQL-DMO (SQL-Distributed Management Objects) is the broad term used for the object library used for manipulating all aspects of a SQL Server, from administrative tasks to querying for and retrieving data. SQL-DMO was introduced in SQL Server 6.0. The most well-known front-end built on SQL-DMO is SQL Server's own Enterprise Manager. Beginning with version 6.5, SQL-DMO supports bulk copy operations.

Replication As a Distributed Data Solution

Although replication is a common solution to many distributed data problems, it is a large enough topic to warrant its own chapter (Chapter 9, "Replication"). The Distributed Transaction Coordinator (DTC), which is useful for maintaining tight consistency between multiple databases, is more of a developer topic and thus is outside the scope of this book.

- *ODBC API.* The ODBC API library has been around as long as ODBC itself, and it provides many of the same features as DB-Lib. Again, most access to SQL Server from the ODBC API is accomplished from C++ programs. Beginning with ODBC version 3.5, the SQL Server ODBC driver provides bulk copy functions.

- *OLE-DB.* OLE-DB is Microsoft's newest data access library. OLE-DB is SQL Server 7.0's native data connectivity library, and it is designed to eventually replace DB-Lib and ODBC. The SQL Server OLE-DB driver provides bulk copy functions.

These libraries are commonly used from specialized client applications written in C++ or Visual Basic, but because this book is geared toward system administrators, this chapter focuses on the two bulk transfer options provided by Microsoft: BCP and the BULK INSERT SQL statement. Both features are built on top of the aforementioned SQL Server libraries.

The Bulk Copy Program (BCP) has been around as long as DB-Lib and was originally built on the DB-Lib API. It is a command-line utility used from a DOS session to import and export data. Beginning with SQL Server 7.0, BCP uses the ODBC bulk copy functions. Note that BCP doesn't do any of the actual work of bulk copying data; that is accomplished by the ODBC library. BCP is just a command-line interface to the bulk copy library. Many administrators and developers avoid BCP because of its many command-line switches and sometimes cryptic error messages. In addition, because it is a DOS-based utility, incorporating BCP into automated scripts can be challenging. Nonetheless, BCP still provides an extremely fast way to transfer data into and out of SQL Server.

The BULK INSERT SQL statement is new for SQL Server 7.0, providing a way to import data from a Transact-SQL query statement instead of the command line.

Distributed Queries

Distributed queries are a powerful new feature of SQL Server 7.0. The SQL Server query processor now supports OLE-DB, Microsoft's new data access standard. OLE-DB is a replacement of sorts for ODBC, and it supports native data access to a wide variety of relational and non-relational data. For instance, OLE-DB providers exist or will exist for such diverse data sources as ISAM and VSAM files on mainframes, Microsoft Exchange message stores, and the Active Directory in Windows NT 5.0. In addition, an OLE-DB provider exists for ODBC, which gives you access to any ODBC data source. Distributed queries can be used to copy data from an OLE-DB data source into a SQL Server table. And distributed queries can expose external data as a sort of "virtual table" for use by a query.

SQL Server 7.0 supports the concept of *linked servers*, which is similar to the idea of a linked table in Microsoft Access. A SQL Server linked server provides a well-defined name that points to another OLE-DB data store. Data structures in the linked data store may then be referred to in a query by name. In addition, queries can use the OPENQUERY and OPENROWSET keywords to retrieve external data on an ad hoc basis.

Data Transformation Services

Data Transformation Services (DTS) is a combination of several technologies that provide fast, robust, and flexible data transfers to and from SQL Server. DTS can be used to import and export data from and to any OLE-DB data source. Unlike BCP, which offers a command-line interface, DTS provides an easy-to-use graphical interface for defining data imports and exports.

DTS really shines when used for data warehousing applications. In addition to its basic import and export features, DTS provides a way to define data transformation "packages" that can pull data from multiple data stores, transform data types, create aggregate or calculated fields, and then store the resulting data in a new schema in SQL Server.

After a DTS import, export, or transformation package is defined, it can be stored in a SQL Server or central repository for later use. It is then easy to create a backup copy of the package by backing up the msdb database or the repository. In addition, the DTS process can easily be included in automated scripts run by the SQL Agent or in command-line scripts (by using the DTSRUN.EXE utility).

Choosing a Transfer Method

Which transfer method you use depends largely on your comfort level with the different tools available. All offer similar features, with a few exceptions. Use the following questions to determine which transfer method is right for your needs.

1. *Will you be importing or exporting data?*

   BCP, DTS, and distributed queries can both import and export data. The BULK INSERT command can be used only for importing data.

2. *For imports, where does the external data reside? For exports, where do you want to put the data?*

   BCP and BULK INSERT can be used only with operating system files. Distributed queries work only with OLE-DB data sources. DTS can be used with operating system files, ODBC data sources, or OLE-DB data sources.

3. *What are the performance requirements for the transfer?*

   Because BCP and BULK INSERT use the bulk copy APIs with a minimum of overhead, these two methods provide the best performance. In addition, both of these utilities may be run from multiple client machines to load data in parallel, further improving performance.

   DTS adds some complexity to the transfer process, especially if data conversion scripts are used. However, DTS still uses the bulk copy API for physically moving the data, and so it retains much of the performance found in BCP. The performance of distributed queries is largely dependent on the performance of the source data store, and because distributed queries do not take advantage of the bulk copy API, this is the slowest of the data transfer options.

4. *Will the transfer be a simple import/export, or is more complex data scrubbing required?*

BULK INSERT and distributed queries are often best used for simple single-table imports. BCP imports or exports data only one table at a time, but multiple BCP operations can be scripted together. With these three methods, additional scripts or stored procedures can be scheduled to run after the transfer to perform additional data scrubbing. However, DTS packages provide a way to consolidate data transfer and data scrubbing. This consolidation makes it easier to administer complex data transfers.

5. *Will the transfer be ad hoc or scheduled?*

Any of the transfer methods can be scheduled by using the SQL Agent. DTS excels for scheduled transfers because of the robustness you can design into DTS packages. As for ad hoc transfers, any of the methods may be used; use whichever you feel most comfortable with.

6. *Do you prefer a graphical or command-driven user interface?*

The DTS wizards and package designer provide the most user-friendly interface of any of the transfer methods. The remaining three are command-line interfaces or use Transact-SQL commands and are, therefore, more difficult to learn.

So, as with most of today's complex products, making the right design decisions is not a straightforward task. Carefully consider your needs and preferences when deciding on a transfer method.

Now that you have been introduced to the various data transfer methods supported by SQL Server, take an in-depth look at each one. You'll begin with BCP.

Using BCP and *BULK INSERT*

BCP has been around for a while, and you may be faced with maintaining a transfer process that uses this utility. In addition, BCP remains a viable alternative to some of the newer transfer tools available in SQL Server 7.0. This next section will familiarize you with all aspects of BCP, beginning with the basic concepts and terms, then moving to common usage, and finally touching on some advanced concepts.

Introduction to BCP

Understanding the basics of how BCP operates will help you use this utility effectively. The next few subsections will familiarize you with how BCP behaves when importing and exporting data.

BCP Terminology

BCP uses a lot of specialized terminology. Not knowing the terminology can make learning this utility much more difficult. Fortunately, none of the concepts are very difficult. The following are some of the more common terms you will encounter when using BCP:

- *Data file.* This is the operating system file that contains the data to be imported into SQL Server, or the file that contains exported data. You will often see this called a "source file" when the data is to be imported. The data may be in either native or character format.

- *Character format.* BCP can import from or export to a *character* (or text) file. These files use the standard ASCII character set to store information, and they are often used when transferring data between heterogeneous sources (such as a SQL Server and a mainframe). Columns in a character file are divided by delimiters (such as a comma or a Tab character) or are defined to be of a certain size (a fixed-width file). You can use a text editor such as Notepad to view the contents of a character file.

- *Native format.* BCP can also import from or export to a *native* file. Native files are binary files that contain the data in the same format that SQL Server uses to store data internally. Native files are generally used to transfer data between SQL Servers.

- *Unicode character format.* This file format is new to SQL Server 7.0. In a Unicode character file, each character is represented by two bytes (as opposed to one byte for standard ASCII files). Unicode character files are useful for transferring character data that may be in different languages or for transferring character data that uses an extended character set, such as Chinese or Japanese characters.

- *Unicode native format.* This file format is new to SQL Server 7.0. It is similar to a native format file, except that character data is transferred in the Unicode format, which is useful for multilanguage transfers.

- *Format file.* When transferring data into or out of a character data file, you can use a *format file* to specify the column and row delimiters used in the data file. Format files are also useful for importing only parts of the data file into a table. You'll learn more about the format file later in this section.

- *Batch size.* By default, BCP loads all rows from the data file into SQL Sever in a single transaction. By specifying a batch size, you can tell BCP to load the data in smaller "chunks." See the next section, "BCP Data Transfer Behavior," for more information on batches.

Using Native Format Files

When you're transferring data between SQL Servers, native format files are the best format choice because SQL Server can process them most efficiently.

- *Source table/destination table.* These terms are often used to describe the table from which data will be exported and the table to which data will be imported, respectively.

BCP Data Transfer Behavior

Knowing how BCP transfers data into and out of SQL Server can save you hours of frustration. The first thing to remember is that when data is imported into a table, rows are appended to the table, and existing rows are left untouched. The destination table must already exist in SQL Server. When data is exported to a file, the destination file is overwritten if it already exists.

When importing data into a database, by default BCP inserts all rows in a single batch. This means that all rows are imported in a single transaction. If the copy fails for any reason, none of the rows are inserted. The BCP utility allows you to specify a batch size on the command line (see the section "Command Line Syntax" for details). When you specify a batch size—say 100,000 rows—BCP imports each group of 100,000 rows in a single transaction. So if a 500,000 row import fails at row 347,000, the destination table will contain only 300,000 rows (because three batches completed successfully).

Why use batches? Wouldn't it be easier to clean up from a failed BCP if the transaction was rolled back? Well, yes, but that isn't the primary reason for using batches. When BCP imports data into a table, it generates log records (see the next section, "BCP Performance Issues") in varying quantities. If BCP attempts a very large import with an inadequately sized transaction log, the log may fill up. This can occur even if the import database has the Truncate Log on Checkpoint option set, because the truncation applies only to committed transactions in the log. During a single-batch import, the transaction remains open for the duration of the import, and the log can fill up. Breaking the data load into smaller batches allows the transaction log to be cleared out periodically by the checkpoint process.

When BCP is importing data into a table, other users in the database can be using that table. The rows inserted by BCP become visible after a batch has been completed. (Remember that by default, the entire contents of the data file are loaded in a single batch.) In addition, when BCP is exporting data from a table, other users can be using the table as well. However, BCP exports a "snapshot" of the table as it existed when the BCP was started, and data modifications made by users after the BCP has started are not reflected in the data file. For this reason, you may want to prevent users from accessing the database (or at least the table) while data is being exported. To do this, you can hold an exclusive lock on the table for the duration of the export, as explained later in this chapter.

Selecting a Batch Size

When specifying a batch size, use the largest practical size that does not cause the transaction log to fill up. This will improve the performance of the import.

To use the BCP utility, you must have a valid logon ID on the SQL Server and a valid user ID in the database involved in the data transfer. In addition, you must have the permissions described here:

- If the data file resides on an NTFS partition, you must have permission to read from the file (for imports) and to create or modify the file (for exports).

- When importing data, you must have INSERT permission on the destination table. If you own the table, you will automatically have INSERT permission; otherwise, the table owner will have to grant INSERT permission to your database user ID.

- When exporting data, you must have SELECT permission on the source table. The table owner has the permission to select data and can grant that permission to other database users.

BCP Import Performance Issues

The performance of a BCP import is affected by a number of factors. The factor that has the greatest impact on performance is whether or not BCP operates in logged or nonlogged mode. In a logged BCP, each row inserted into a table is written to the transaction log, much like it would be during an INSERT statement. During a nonlogged BCP, only extent allocations are logged as the table is expanded to accept the new data. (So technically, the term "nonlogged" is somewhat of a misnomer, because BCP always logs *something* to the transaction log.)

Because of the reduced logging function, a nonlogged BCP is much faster than a logged BCP, often by an order of magnitude. Nonlogged operations are thus the preferred method for transferring large amounts of data. For a nonlogged BCP to take place, the following conditions must be met:

- The Select Into/Bulkcopy option must be turned on for the database receiving the imported data.

- The destination table cannot have triggers.

- The destination table cannot be marked for replication.

If any of these conditions is not met, a logged BCP takes place.

Use Caution When Performing Nonlogged Operations

If you permit nonlogged operations in a database, you lose the ability to perform up-to-the-minute recovery with the transaction log; only the full database can be backed up and restored. (SQL Server will still perform automatic recovery in the event of a system failure, however.)

For this reason, you should perform a full or differential backup of a database (if it has data) before importing large amounts of data. After the data load is complete, you can perform another full or differential backup and turn off the Select Into/Bulkcopy option.

When BCP is importing data into a table, data types, null options, and default constraints are observed for each column. For example, BCP will not allow you to import character data into a numeric field or to import a null value into a column that does not allow nulls. However, importing a null value into a non-nullable column with a default constraint is permissible, because default values are provided during an import. PRIMARY KEY and UNIQUE constraints are also enforced during a BCP import.

In SQL Server 7.0, you have the option of telling BCP to enforce other constraints on the table, such as REFERENCE or CHECK constraints. To do so, you use the `CHECK_CONSTRAINTS` hint at the command line. Keep in mind, however, that enforcing constraint checking will degrade the performance of the import. For more information about using hints with BCP, see the next section, "Command-Line Syntax."

In SQL Server 7.0, a table's indexes need not be dropped for a fast or nonlogged load to take place. However, when loading large amounts of data into a table, the updates to the table's indexes may degrade the performance of the data load. As a general rule of thumb, if you are loading a large percentage of rows in comparison to the number of rows that already exist in the table, it is often more efficient to drop the table indexes before the load and then re-create them after the load is complete. If you are creating a scheduled transfer process, you may want to test the load with and without indexes to get the best performance.

If the data in the source file is already sorted by one or more columns, you can use a hint to tell BCP which columns are sorted in the source file. Sorting the source file can improve the performance of the bulk load, especially if indexes exist on the sorted columns. For more information on providing this hint to BCP, see the next section, "Command-Line Syntax."

Another way to improve performance is to exclusively lock the table during the data import. This reduces the number of locks SQL Server has to hold on the table, thus reducing the overhead for the operation. Be careful when using this option, however, because it reduces concurrency; other database users will be unable to use the table for the duration of the load. To exclusively lock a table during a BCP import, specify the `TABLOCK` hint in the BCP command line or turn on the Table Lock on Bulk Load option for the table by using the system stored procedure `sp_tableoption`.

Nonlogged Does Not Mean "No Logging"

Recall from the previous section that it is still possible for BCP to fill the transaction log, even with the minimal logging used by a "nonlogged" BCP. If you find that the transaction log is filling up during a nonlogged BCP, use a smaller batch size as described in the previous section.

Considerations for Table Triggers

Table triggers are always ignored by BCP, except when they're used to make the determination for a logged or nonlogged import. If you use triggers to perform referential integrity or other data validation checks on a table, you must manually perform these checks with a T-SQL query (or queries) after the data has been imported.

When loading extremely large data sets into a table, BCP can load the data *in parallel*, that is, from multiple clients running BCP. In this scenario, you would partition the source file into a number of smaller files (say, taking a 10 million row source file and splitting it into two files of 5 million rows each). You could then load both files into the same table at the same time from two different machines running BCP. For a parallel data load, all the requirements for a nonlogged BCP must be met. In addition, the table cannot have any indexes.

Command-Line Syntax

The executable file BCP.EXE is located in the BINN subdirectory under the SQL Server installation directory. The syntax for the BCP command-line utility is as follows:

```
bcp [[database_name.]owner.]table_name {in ¦ out ¦ format} datafile-name
➥[options]
```

where the following are true:

[[database_name.]owner.]table_name is the qualified name of the table (or view) that's to supply exported rows or receive imported rows.

{in ¦ out ¦ format} specifies the direction of the data transfer; if a format is specified, a format file is generated for the given table or view.

Datafile-name is the path and filename of the source or destination file. UNC names are supported.

[options] represents the use of one or more of the following options:

BCP Locking

By default, an exclusive table lock is not held during a BCP load. BCP will hold extent locks as it adds rows to the table, however.

Not Everyone Can Participate in a Parallel Data Load

Only clients using the ODBC or the OLE-DB bulk copy API routine can participate in a parallel data load. This would exclude clients using SQL-DMO and DB-Lib, which are common in earlier versions of BCP.

Check Your Case

Command-line options are case sensitive, so /f and /F are different options. Options can be preceded by a front slash (/) or a hyphen (-). Only the most common BCP options appear in the following list; for a complete list, consult the SQL Server Books Online.

Restriction

The /N and /w options cannot be used with versions of SQL Server prior to 7.0.

Option	Description
/m	Specifies the maximum number of errors that can occur before the transfer is cancelled. If this option is omitted, BCP fails after ten errors.
/f	Specifies the name of the format file, if one is used. This option is required if the Format Transfer option is specified.
/E	Specifies a file in which BCP will store any rows that cannot be transferred.
/F	Specifies the number of the first row to copy. If this option is omitted, BCP starts transferring with the first row in the data file or source table.
/L	Specifies the number of the last row to copy. If this option is omitted, BCP ends the transfer with the last row in the data file or source table.
/b	Specifies the number of rows per batch.
/n, /N	Specify that the data file is a native format file or that the data file created from an export should be in native format. /n specifies a native data file; /N specifies a native Unicode data file.
/c, /w	Specify that a character format data file will be used for the transfer. /c is used for ASCII data files; /w is used for Unicode data files. The default column delimiter is a tab, and the default row delimiter is a newline character (carriage return/linefeed combination).
/E	Specifies that the BCP transfer will be importing data into a table with an identity column, and that the values for the identity column will be explicitly provided in the data file. This option has no effect if data is being exported.
/t	Specifies a column (or field) terminator other than the default tab character for a character format data file.
/r	Specifies a row terminator other than the default newline character for a character format data file.
/U	Indicates that BCP is to log in to the SQL Server in mixed security mode. It specifies the name of the database user ID to use for the transfer.
/P	Indicates that BCP is to log in to the SQL Server in mixed security mode. It specifies the password of the database user ID given with the /U parameter.
/T	Indicates that BCP should log in to the SQL Server with a trusted security connection.
/S	Specifies the name of the SQL Server that is participating in the data transfer. This option can be omitted if the data file resides on the actual SQL Server machine. If possible, you should perform data transfers on the machine that hosts SQL Server; this reduces the overhead generated by sending data across the network.

/a   Specifies the network packet size used when BCP loads data into a SQL Server over the network. Microsoft recommends a packet size in the range of 4,096 to 8,192, but larger packet sizes can sometimes improve performance; experiment to find the best size.

/h   Specifies hints for the bulk copy. The syntax for this setting is /h "hint1 [,hint2[,...hintN]]", where "hint" is one of the following:

CHECK_CONSTRAINTS—This enables you to specify that the table's constraints should be checked during the bulk load of data.

KILOBYTES_PER_BATCH = kk—When the /b option is not specified, this allows you to define the size of a batch in kilobytes instead of number of rows.

ORDER (column1 [ASC ¦ DESC] [,...column]—When the data to be imported is sorted in the source file, you can use this hint to tell BCP which columns are already sorted and in what order.

ROWS_PER_BATCH = rr—When the /b option is not specified, this allows you to define the size of a batch in number of rows.

TABLOCK—This enables you to specify that the entire table should be locked during the duration of the bulk load. This can improve performance, especially when data is being loaded in parallel.

All of these hints can affect the performance of BCP. For more information, see the section "BCP Import Performance Issues," earlier in this chapter.

The following list offers some simple examples of how you might use BCP to transfer data into and out of the *pubs* database.

■ This example exports data from a table called authors into a character file called C:\authors.txt. The file's columns are tab-delimited, and each row starts on a new line. A trusted connection is used to connect to the local server:

```
Bcp pubs..authors out C:\authors.txt /c /T
```

The results of this command will look something like this:

```
Starting copy...
23 rows copied.
Network packet size (bytes): 4096
Clock Time (ms.): total =     20 Avg =      0 (1150.00 rows per
➥sec.)
```

Hints Are New

The hint option can be used only when loading data into SQL Server 7.0 or later. Earlier versions of SQL Server and BCP do not support hints.

■ This example imports the data file from example #1 back into the authors table in the pubs database:

```
Bcp pubs..authors in C:\authors.txt /c /T
```

Because data already exists in the authors table, this import attempts to insert duplicate data. Therefore, BCP returns the following error message:

```
Starting copy...
SQLState = 23000, NativeError = 2627
Error = [Microsoft][ODBC SQL Server Driver][SQL Server]Violation of
➡PRIMARY KEY
constraint 'UPKCL_auidind'. Cannot insert duplicate key in object
➡'authors'.
SQLState = 01000, NativeError = 3621
Warning = [Microsoft][ODBC SQL Server Driver][SQL Server]The
➡statement has been aborted.
23 rows copied.
Network packet size (bytes): 4096
Clock Time (ms.): total        922 Avg        40 (24.95 rows per sec.)
```

■ This example exports the contents of the authors table into a native format file called C:\authors.dat:

```
Bcp pubs..authors out C:\authors.dat /n /T
```

If you have difficulty using BCP, you might want to check out the "Common BCP Issues" section of SQL Server Books Online. Several common problems and solutions are listed there. In addition, you can check the Knowledge Base at `http://www.microsoft.com/support/` for information on specific BCP-related issues.

Using Format Files

BCP format files allow you to fine-tune how data files are imported into a table or how a table's data is exported into the data file. You can specify different column or row terminators, adjust the length of the data transferred, or rearrange the order in which table columns are transferred. You will most often create a format file when importing a text file into SQL Server. Figure 8.1 shows a sample format file that might be used to import data into the jobs table in the pubs database. Each part of the format file is marked so that you can distinguish among the different parts used.

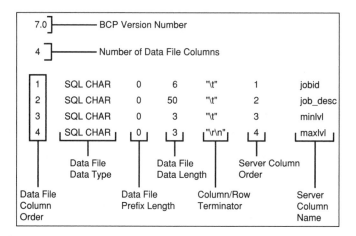

Figure 8.1   Example format file for the jobs table, illustrating the various sections of a format file.

Next, look at the structure of a format file. Then you'll see an example of how to use a format file.

Format File Syntax

The following list outlines the purpose of each part of the format file:

- *Version*. This is the version number of the BCP program. This is always "7.0" for SQL Server version 7.0.

- *Number of columns*. This is the number of columns in the data file.

- *Data file column order*. This defines the order in which the columns appear in the data file. They are usually listed in sequential order.

- *Data type*. This entry specifies the data type of the column in the data file. For text files, always use SQLCHAR. For native format files, use the name of the table column's data type, such as SQLSMALLINT for a smallint column. (See SQL Server Books Online for a complete list of native data types for use with BCP.)

- *Prefix length*. This value is used with native format files to specify a storage area in the file that's used to hold the length of the data in the column. For text files, always use 0.

- *Data length*. This value specifies the actual length of the data in the data file for a particular column. For text files, this is the maximum length of a column; for instance, when the max_lvl column is represented as characters, the number may range from 0 to 255 because it is a tinyint. The maximum length for this field would be 3 characters.

- *Terminator.* The terminator column enables you to specify column terminators for all but the last column and a row terminator for the last column. Typically, tabs (\t) or commas are used to delimit columns, and a newline (\r\n) character is used to delimit rows.

- *Server column order.* This specifies the column that SQL Server should insert into or retrieve from in the destination or source table.

- *Server column name.* The name of the column in the source or destination table. SQL Server does not actually use this to determine which column data will be inserted to or retrieved from, so you can enter any value here. However, you cannot leave this column blank.

The next section shows you one example of using a format file; other examples are available in the SQL Server Books Online.

Example: Using a Format File to Import a Text File with String Delimiters

Format files are useful not only when the columns in the source file and database table differ, but also when the contents of the source file are in a format that BCP has difficulty dealing with. This comes in handy when you have no control over the format of the source file.

One of the more common problems with "misbehaving" source files is the use of double quotation marks to delimit strings. BCP has no native way to strip the quotation marks from the string during an import, so the quotes often end up in the database. The example in this section shows you how to use a format file to get around this problem.

First, look at a relatively simple table that into which you want to import data. It contains an Employee ID, a last name, and a first name. The SQL Statement for creating the table follows:

```
CREATE TABLE EmployeeTest (
      EmployeeID   int         NOT NULL,
      FirstName    varchar(30) NOT NULL,
      LastName     varchar(30) NOT NULL
)
```

And this is the file that you're trying to import:

```
1,"Press","Jon"
2,"Noel","David"
3,"Graziano","William"
4,"Miller","Chris"
```

Notice that, in the source file, the columns are in the order EmployeeID, LastName, FirstName. In the destination table, the columns are in the order EmployeeID, FirstName, LastName. In addition, the columns are comma delimited, and the rows are newline delimited. Knowing this information, you can develop the following format file:

```
7.0
3
1    SQLCHAR    0    10    ","    1    EmployeeID
2    SQLCHAR    0    30    ","    3    LastName
3    SQLCHAR    0    30    "\r\n" 2    FirstName
```

Note that the last name and first name columns changed positions as previously described.

Now, to import the file, you use the following BCP command (with the assumptions that you created this table in the pubs database, the name of the source file is EmployeeTest.Txt, the name of the format file is employeeTest.Fmt, and you're using a trusted connection on the local server):

```
BCP pubs..EmployeeTest in EmployeeTest.txt -fEmployeeTest.fmt -T
```

Take a look at the results of the import:

```
SELECT * FROM pubs..EmployeeTest

EmployeeID  FirstName              LastName
1           "Jon"                  "Press"
2           "David"                "Noel"
3           "William"              "Graziano"
4           "Chris"                "Miller"

(4 row(s) affected)
```

As you can see, BCP doesn't know that the double quotation marks are text delimiters and should be ignored. However, the problem is easily corrected with a few tweaks to the format file.

Look at the following single line while you're thinking about the problem:

```
2,"Noel","David"
```

The only thing you can really control in the format file that will take care of the problem is the column terminator. To strip the trailing quotation mark off the Last Name column, you can tell BCP that the column terminator is the combination of a quotation mark and a comma (",) instead of just a comma. In the format file, this would look like "\",". (Because the double quotation mark is used in the format file, you have to tell BCP that you mean the double quotation mark character, which you do by preceding it with the backslash character, otherwise known as the escape character.)

To strip off the opening quotation mark on the Last Name column, you can tell BCP that the row terminator is the combination of a comma and a quotation mark (,"), which would look like ",\"" in the format file.

Using these two concepts, you can create the following format file:

```
7.0
3
1   SQLCHAR   0   10    ",\""     1   EmployeeID
2   SQLCHAR   0   30    "\",\""   3   LastName
3   SQLCHAR   0   30    "\"\r\n"  2   FirstName
```

Unfortunately, when you try this, BCP gives you an unexpected EOF encountered in host data file error. Adding the quotation mark to the end of the delimiter string doesn't cause the problem (as in the example ",\""). However, as soon as you add the quotation mark to the beginning of the delimiter string ("\",\""), you encounter the problem. It's not entirely clear why this happens; perhaps BCP misreads the format file.

So, you know that you can strip off the beginning quotation marks on the two-string columns by using the following format file:

```
7.0
3
1   SQLCHAR   0   10    ",\""     1   EmployeeID
2   SQLCHAR   0   30    ",\""     3   LastName
3   SQLCHAR   0   30    "\r\n"    2   FirstName
```

This gives you the following results:

```
SELECT * FROM pubs..EmployeeTest

EmployeeID  FirstName               LastName
1           Jon"                    Press"
2           David"                  Noel"
3           William"                Graziano"
4           Chris"                  Miller"
```

Now you must find a way to dispose of the trailing quotation marks on the string columns. You can use another BCP format file trick: the ability to indiscriminately discard a certain number of characters or a specific set of characters by setting the Server Column Order field to 0.

First, take another look at a single line from the data file:

```
2,"Noel","David"
```

What if you could tell BCP that the column delimiter for the FirstName and LastName columns was really the quotation mark character? All you would have to do then would be to somehow discard the other characters separating the data—in this case, a comma and quotation mark between LastName and FirstName and a CRLF after FirstName. Examine the following format file:

```
7.0
5
1   SQLCHAR 0   10    ",\""    1   EmployeeID
2   SQLCHAR 0   30    "\""     3   LastName
3   SQLCHAR 0   2     ""       0   EatCommaQuote
4   SQLCHAR 0   30    "\""     2   FirstName
5   SQLCHAR 0   0     "\r\n"   0   EatCRLF
```

Note that line 2 of the format file says the LastName column really ends with a quotation mark. You then need to strip off the following comma and quotation mark before the data in the FirstName column. Line 3 accomplishes that: When you specify a data length of 2 with no delimiter, BCP treats that comma and quotation mark as a new two-character column. Setting the Server Column Order to 0 means that BCP will discard that information, which takes care of your quotation mark problem.

Line 5 demonstrates the same concept, except that instead of stripping off the two characters, the line instructs BCP to find the next CRLF and discard it.

Fortunately, handling quote-delimited strings is about the most difficult thing you'll have to attempt with a format file. (Remember that more examples are available in the Books Online.) As you will see later in this chapter, DTS thankfully handles quote-delimited strings in text files quite easily.

Using the T-SQL *BULK INSERT* Statement

The `BULK INSERT` statement provides the same features as BCP as far as importing data is concerned. However, because it is a Transact-SQL command, it can be executed directly from a query window. This makes the `BULK INSERT` statement especially useful for ad hoc imports of data. In addition, using `BULK INSERT` instead of a BCP command can make small data loads easier to implement: All functionality can be contained in a SQL batch or stored procedure.

The data transfer behavior of `BULK INSERT` is identical to that of a BCP import. For a detailed discussion on this topic, see the section "Introduction to BCP," earlier in this chapter.

The basic syntax for the `BULK INSERT` command is shown in the following code. To learn the full syntax, see the "Transact-SQL Reference" section of Books Online.

```
BULK INSERT [['database_name'.]['owner'].]{'table_name' FROM data_file}
[WITH
(
[ BATCHSIZE [ = batch_size]]
[[,] CHECK_CONSTRAINTS]
[[,] DATAFILETYPE [ = {'char' ¦ 'native'¦ 'widechar' ¦ 'widenative'}]]
[[,] FIELDTERMINATOR [ = 'field_terminator']]
[[,] FIRSTROW [ = first_row]]
[[,] FORMATFILE [ = 'format_file_path']]
[[,] KEEPIDENTITY]
[[,] LASTROW [ = last_row]]
[[,] MAXERRORS [ = max_errors]]
[[,] ORDER ({column [ASC ¦ DESC]} [, ...n])]
[[,] ROWTERMINATOR [ = 'row_terminator']]
[[,] TABLOCK]
)
]
```

You should recognize all of the options from the previous section that outlined the BCP command-line syntax. In its simplest form, the BULK INSERT command looks like this:

```
BULK INSERT pubs..authors FROM 'C:\authors.txt'
```

The preceding command would bulk load data from the authors.txt file into the authors table in the pubs database.

When no options are specified, BULK INSERT assumes that you want to import a character file that uses tabs as the column delimiter and the newline character as the row delimiter.

So far, you've studied BCP and BULK INSERT in depth. For the most part, these technologies existed in SQL Server 6.5. Now you'll get to look at some of the newer distributed data transfer technologies, namely, distributed queries and DTS.

Using Distributed Queries

The new distributed query feature in SQL Server 7.0 can be used to query any OLE-DB data source from within a Transact-SQL statement. While this has obvious uses beyond data transfer, this section of the chapter focuses on how distributed queries can be used to load data into a SQL Server database by use of the SELECT INTO and INSERT..SELECT statements. A distributed query can also be the target of INSERT, UPDATE, and DELETE statements—provided that the OLE-DB data store permits these data modifications. In this way, you can export SQL Server data to an external store or modify data in an external store based on SQL Server data.

There are basically two ways to access distributed data from SQL Server. The first involves creating a linked server; the second involves using passthrough queries or ad hoc connections created by the OPENQUERY and OPENROWSET T-SQL functions.

Remember that distributed queries are not as efficient as other transfer methods and, therefore, may not be a good choice when large quantities of data are involved.

Cannot Save Untransferred Rows

Note that BULK INSERT does not support an option that is functionally equivalent to the \e option in BCP. In other words, you will not be able to save rows that are not transferred.

SQL Server Data Not Required

Distributed queries don't necessarily have to use SQL Server data at one end. It would be completely valid to move data from an Access database to an Oracle database, for example.

Linked Servers Versus Remote Servers

Do not confuse linked servers with remote servers. *Remote servers* are an older feature of SQL Server used primarily for executing remote stored procedure calls. *Linked servers* provide transparent access to other OLE-DB data stores.

This section gives you an overview of how you can use distributed queries in your data transfer strategy. For more detailed information, consult the SQL Server Books Online.

Using Linked Servers

Microsoft Access gives you the ability to "link" a table to a remote ODBC data source. After a remote table is linked, you can use the data in that table transparently from within Access. The concept of linked servers in SQL Server is very similar. Instead of linking to a single table, however, you can link to an entire OLE-DB data store (such as an Oracle or Access database).

When a server is linked, you can query its catalog information (if the OLE-DB data provider supports this feature) to obtain a list of tables in the data store. In addition, you can control access to the data store by mapping SQL Server users to users in the remote database.

To create a linked server, you can use SQL Server Enterprise Manager or the `sp_addlinkedserver` system stored procedure. For example, to create a linked server that points to the Access 7.0 Northwind sample database, you would execute the following query:

```
Exec sp_addlinkedserver
     @server = 'AccessNwind',
     @srvproduct = '',
     @provider ='Microsoft.Jet.OLEDB.4',
     @datasrc = 'c:\nwind.mdb'
```

Having linked to the remote data store, you can reference any of its tables by using the notation

```
server.[catalog].[schema].object
```

where the following statements are true:

`server` is the name of the linked server as defined in `sp_addlinkedserver`.

`catalog` refers to the specific database on the linked server. This is used only if the linked RDBMS supports multiple databases. For instance, for an Oracle server, you would need to specify the catalog/database; for an Access database, you would not.

`schema` refers to the object owner, where appropriate.

`object` is the name of the object (such as a table or view) in the database.

To load information from the external table into SQL Server, you could use a `SELECT INTO` statement or an `INSERT` with `SELECT` statement, as shown in the following examples:

More on Linked Servers

For detailed information on the setup and advanced features of linked servers, see the SQL Server Books Online.

```
SELECT  RemoteCustomers.*
INTO    mySQLCustomers
FROM    AccessNwind...Customers AS RemoteCustomers

INSERT mySQLCustomers
SELECT RemoteCustomers.*
FROM    AccessNwind...Customers AS RemoteCustomers
```

In the first example, a SQL Server table is created from the Customers table in the Access database. (This assumes that the Select Into\bulkcopy option is turned on for the destination database.) The second example populates a preexisting SQL Server table with the contents of the Customers table in the Access Database.

Using *OPENQUERY* to Perform Passthrough Queries

You can use the OPENQUERY statement in conjunction with a linked server name to pass a query to the linked server. The linked server (not SQL Server) processes the query and returns the results in an OLE-DB rowset that SQL Server treats as a table.

OPENQUERY is useful when the linked server uses a different SQL Syntax from SQL Server or when, in the case of nonrelational data stores, the linked server does not support SQL Queries at all. You can pass the command to open the desired rowset to that server for processing. The following example is equivalent to the first example shown in the previous section:

```
SELECT RemoteCustomers.*
INTO mySQLCustomers
FROM
    OPENQUERY (AccessNwind,'SELECT * FROM Customers') AS RemoteCustomers
```

Remember that the OPENQUERY statement returns a rowset that SQL Server treats as a table, so it can be given a table alias like any other table. In this case, the remote table is given an alias of RemoteCustomers. Aliases come in handy if you need to join the external table to another table, external table, or view.

Using *OPENROWSET* to Connect to a Remote Data Store

OPENROWSET is similar to OPENQUERY in that it returns a rowset that SQL Server interprets as a table. Instead of using a linked server name, however, you pass the OLE-DB connection string to the OPENROWSET statement. SQL Server then opens a connection, retrieves the data, and disconnects.

The OPENROWSET connection is not as full-featured as a linked server connection, so it is better suited to ad hoc queries against external data stores.

The following query uses the OPENROWSET statement, which is equivalent to the first example shown in the section "Using Linked Servers":

```
SELECT RemoteCustomers.*
INTO    mySQLCustomers
FROM
    OPENROWSET('Microsoft.Jet.OLEDB.3.51','c:\Northwind.mdb';'admin';'',
➥Customers)
    AS RemoteCustomers
```

Using Data Transformation Services (DTS)

Given all the advanced functionality it provides, DTS is surprisingly easy to use. DTS provides three main feature sets:

- The ability to export and import data to and from a SQL Server
- The ability to write robust complex data transfers (packages) from any OLE-DB provider to another
- The ability to transfer database objects (tables, views, stored procedures, and so on) between SQL Server 7.0 databases

These feature sets are covered in the remainder of the chapter. Incidentally, DTS is fully controllable from other applications through an object-oriented interface. Because this book is geared more toward system administrators, however, only the Enterprise Manager DTS tools are discussed here.

DTS Import and Export

Although Enterprise Manager provides two separate wizards for import and export, they are functionally equal. In other words, regardless of which wizard you use, you can copy data from any OLE-DB or ODBC data source to any other OLE-DB or ODBC data source. What the wizards are really doing is walking you through the steps of creating a DTS package. DTS packages are discussed in more detail in the section titled "DTS Packages."

Regardless of which wizard you use, you will follow a series of basic steps to define the data transfer. These are the steps, in order:

1. *Choose the source data provider.* In this step, you choose the source for the data to be transferred. For some data sources, you may also have to enter information about the format of the stored data. For instance, if you are using a text file as your data source, you will need to specify the delimiters for the data columns and rows.

2. *Choose the destination data provider.* In this step, you choose where the data should be stored as it is transferred. The wizard may require additional information on how the data should be stored in the destination data store.

3. *Specify the data to copy.* The wizard will ask you several questions in this step in order to determine what data you would like to copy. This step appears only if multiple sets of data can be stored in the source data store, which would be typical in a database or Excel spreadsheet. The wizard skips this step if only a single set of data is stored in the source, which would be typical with a text file. When transferring data from a database, you will typically be asked to select one or more tables to transfer; you can also create a query that specifies the data you would like to transfer.

4. *Specify the destination for the data and any data transformations for the data.* This step allows you to specify the destination table for the transferred data, which source

columns are to be transferred, and any transformations needed for the source columns. A number of transformations may be performed; for more information, see the next section, "Transformation Scripts."

5. *Run, save, and schedule the transfer.* After the wizard has gathered all the information it needs to perform the transfer, you can choose whether to run the transfer immediately, save the transfer package, schedule the package's execution for a later time, or all three. (In order to schedule the package for later execution, you must save it.)

If you understand the first four steps, you are well on your way to defining more complex data transfers. When the import and export wizards no longer suffice, you can use the DTS package designer to create even more complex transfers. See the section "DTS Packages" later in this chapter for more information on the package designer.

Transformation Scripts

Transformation scripts are a powerful feature of DTS that allows you to transform and validate source data as it is copied to the destination. Scripts may be written in Visual Basic Script, JavaScript, PerlScript, or other custom scripting languages. You can script any of five basic transformations:

- Modifying the source data by changing the data type or format.
- Splitting a single source column into multiple destination columns. For instance, splitting a Name column into first name and last name columns.
- Combining multiple source columns into a single destination column.
- Transforming a source column value into a different value by way of a lookup table.
- Validating a source column or columns to meet custom business rules.

DTS provides three objects for use in a DTS script:

- *DTSSource.* This object provides access to all the columns in the source table. The syntax to access a source column is as follows:
    ```
    DTSSource("<column_name>")
    ```

- *DTSDestination.* This object provides access to all the columns in the destination table. The syntax to access a source column is as follows:
    ```
    DTSDestination("<column_name>")
    ```

- *DTSLookups.* This object is used to perform code-table lookups for data transformations.

Scripts sometimes return error codes that tell DTS how to behave. For instance, you could abort processing if an invalid source row was encountered.

The following are excerpts from a transformation script. All are written in VBScript.

- **Changing the format of a source column.** This example shows how to convert an address to all uppercase:
  ```
  DTSDestination("Address") = Ucase(DTSSource("Address"))
  ```

- **Splitting a source column into multiple destination columns.** This example shows how to split a date field into month, day, and year fields:
  ```
  DTSDestination("Month") = DatePart(mm,DTSSource("MyDate"))
  DTSDestination("Day") = DatePart(dd,DTSSource("MyDate"))
  DTSDestination("Year") = DatePart(yyyy,DTSSource("MyDate"))
  ```

- **Combining multiple source columns into a single destination column.** This example shows how you could combine first name and last name columns into a full name column in the format <lastname>,<firstname>:

  ```
  DTSDestination("FullName") = DTSSource("LastName") & "," &
  ➥DTSSource("FirstName")
  ```

Sample Transfer

At the beginning of this chapter, examples were given as to why you might need a data transfer. One example was for "exporting information from a database for use in other data analysis tools, such as a spreadsheet." This section uses that example to demonstrate how to use the data transfer wizards.

In the following example, you will export some information out of the SQL Server Northwind sample database into an Excel spreadsheet so an executive can analyze sales trends. You will export the contents of the Orders table and its associated tables (Customers, Order Details, and Employees) into a flat listing of Orders that lists the Customer Name, Sales Rep Name, Order Date, Shipping Region, and total Dollar Amount. Then you could create a pivot table on the data in Excel.

To create the transfer, follow these steps:

1. *Start the Data Export Wizard.* From Enterprise Manager, connect to a SQL Server and choose the Data Transformation Packages folder. Right-click on the folder and select All Tasks, then Export Data…, as shown in Figure 8.2. Click Next when the introduction screen appears.

2. *Choose the source data source.* The source data provider will be SQL Server itself, so you must set the options necessary to connect to the local SQL Server and pull data from the Northwind sample database (see Figure 8.3). When you finish setting the options, click Next to continue with the wizard.

3. *Choose the destination data source.* The destination data provider will be Microsoft Excel, so you must set the options necessary to write the data to an Excel work-book (see Figure 8.4). When you finish setting the options, click Next to continue with the wizard.

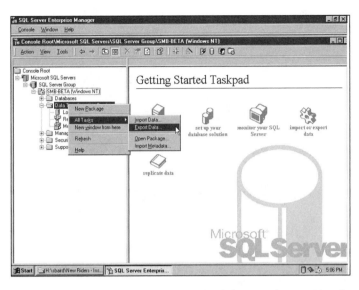

Figure 8.2 Start the DTS Export Wizard by right-clicking on the Data Transformation Packages folder.

4. *Select the data to copy.* Because you want the data for the export to come from multiple tables, you will use a query to provide the data to copy. Select the option Use a Query to Specify the Data to Transfer, and then click Next. The next wizard screen allows you to enter a query, as shown in Figure 8.5. Enter the query given here, and then select Next to continue with the wizard.

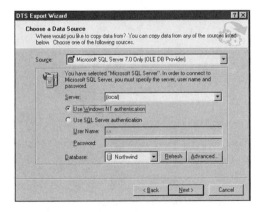

Figure 8.3 Select the local SQL Server Northwind database as the Source data provider.

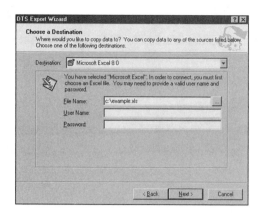

Figure 8.4 Specify an Excel worksheet as the destination for the exported data.

```
SELECT Employees.FirstName, Employees.LastName,
Customers.CompanyName,
            Orders.OrderDate, Orders.ShipRegion,
            Sum(OrderDetails.UnitPrice * OrderDetails.Quantity)
➡OrderTotal
FROM Orders JOIN [Order Details] OrderDetails
        ON Orders.OrderID = OrderDetails.OrderID
JOIN    Employees
        ON Orders.EmployeeID = Employees.EmployeeID
JOIN    Customers
        ON Orders.CustomerID = Customers.CustomerID
GROUP BY Employees.FirstName, Employees.LastName,
                Customers.CompanyName, Orders.OrderDate,
➡Orders.ShipRegion
```

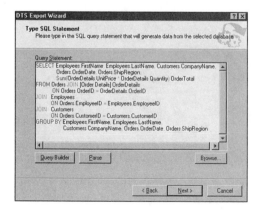

Figure 8.5 Use the given query to selectively copy data from multiple tables.

5. *Transform the copied data.* Now that you have specified the data to transfer, you must specify where you want to put the data in the destination data source. Place the results of the transfer in a table (actually, a worksheet, because you are exporting to Excel) named OrderSummary, as shown in Figure 8.6. (Note that you need to supply the name "OrderSummary" by typing it in the appropriate place on the screen.) Next, you want to perform a transformation on the data to make sure it is in the format you want. Click on the ellipsis (…) button to bring up the Column Mappings and Transformations dialog box shown in Figure 8.7.

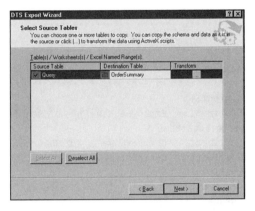

Figure 8.6 Specify the worksheet name and column information for the exported data.

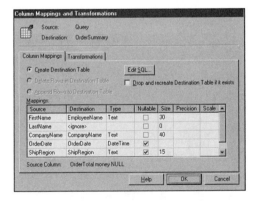

Figure 8.7 Edit the column mappings for the exported table as shown here.

You could use the information on this tab to change the destination column names and data types. You could also use these options to selectively exclude certain columns from the transfer, but you already accomplished that with the query. Because you want to combine the employee First Name and Last Name columns, however, edit the column mappings as shown in Figure 8.7. Then you need to edit the transformation script to accomplish this transformation. Select the Transformations tab to edit the transformation script (see Figure 8.8).

Select the option Transform Information As It Is Copied to the Destination so you can edit the transformation script. The following is the full text of the transformation script:

```
'*********************************************************************
'  Visual Basic Transformation Script
'  Copy each source column to the
'  destination column
'*********************************************************************
Function Transform()
        DTSDestination("Employee Name") = DTSSource("FirstName") & "
➡" & DTSSource("LastName")
        DTSDestination("CompanyName") = DTSSource("CompanyName")
        DTSDestination("OrderDate") = DTSSource("OrderDate")
        DTSDestination("ShipRegion") = DTSSource("ShipRegion")
        DTSDestination("OrderTotal") = DTSSource("OrderTotal")
        Transform = 1
End Function
```

When you finish entering the script, click OK and then Next to continue with the wizard.

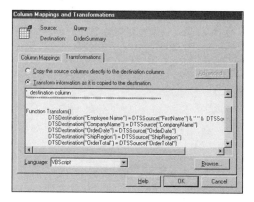

Figure 8.8   From the Transformations tab, you can specify a transformation script. Use the transformation script given in the text.

6. *Run and save the package.* You are finally ready to execute the script. By default, the Run Immediately option is selected. Because you also want to save the transfer package, select the Save Package on SQL Server option, as shown in Figure 8.9. Then click Next to finish the wizard. The screen shown in Figure 8.10 appears.

Enter the requested information about the package, and then specify which SQL Server you want the package to be saved on. Optionally, you can specify a password to prevent others from opening and modifying the package. Click Next, and a summary screen appears. Click Finish, and the package runs. SQL Server then displays a status window to tell you whether the transfer was successful, as shown in Figure 8.11.

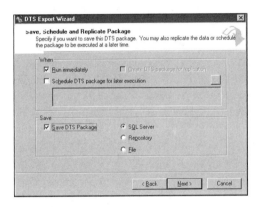

Figure 8.9   At the end of the wizard, you will be prompted to run and/or save the DTS package.

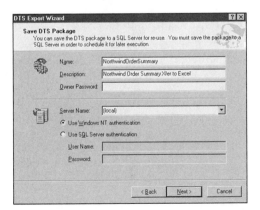

Figure 8.10   You can save the DTS package in a number of different locations. Here you specify where you want to save the package.

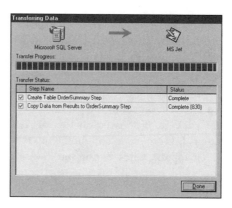

Figure 8.11   When the DTS package is running, this status window is displayed.

DTS Packages

Although the DTS Import and Export wizards are useful, they have their limitations. One of the biggest limitations imposed by the wizards is the inability to transfer between different schemas. For example, if you have a flat file that came from a mainframe, it probably contains denormalized data. If you want to normalize the data into multiple tables, the wizards fall short. The wizards are useful for defining transfers from one or more source tables to one or more destination tables, but they require a one-to-one mapping between a source table and a destination table.

That limitation is actually by design: The DTS data "pump" is designed to transfer only from one table to another. However, you can create a DTS package that not only transfers data, but also executes a series of SQL scripts to perform more advanced transformations on that data, such as normalization. DTS packages can also execute scripts and command-line programs, send mail, transfer database objects, and perform bulk data inserts using the OLEDB bulk copy library. Steps can occur in parallel for optimum performance, and they can be linked together to execute in a certain order.

The next section outlines the different concepts you will need to understand to create DTS packages and introduces you to the DTS package designer. The section after that walks you through the steps required to create a package by using the package designer.

Using the Package Designer

To open the package designer, connect to a SQL Server through Enterprise Manager. Right-click on the Data Transformation Packages folder and select New Package. Alternately, you can open an existing package for editing. Figure 8.12 shows the package designer window.

The package designer window consists of three main parts:

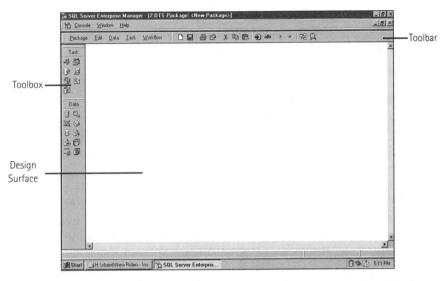

Figure 8.12 The main package designer window, where you can create and edit DTS packages.

- *Toolbar.* The toolbar contains options for saving and viewing the package; commands for starting and stopping the package; and commands for creating new data transfers and defining links (or a "precedence") between package components.

- *Toolbox.* The toolbox contains all the components you can add to a package. It is divided into two areas. The "Data" area lists the connections (both OLE-DB and ODBC) you can add to the package. The "Tasks" area lists the tasks you can add to the package.

- *Design surface.* The design surface is where the real action takes place. You build a package by dragging connections and tasks from the toolbox to the work surface and then connecting them with data transfers and links. The design surface is a graphical representation of the package.

To create a package, follow these basic steps:

1. *Drag two or more connections from the toolbox to the design surface.* When you drop the connection on the design surface, the package designer prompts you to fill out a property sheet that defines the name of the connection and other properties of the connection, such as a username and password for a database connection. The property sheet looks very similar to the first few screens of the import and export wizards.

2. *Define required data transfers between connections.* After you have placed the required connections on the design surface, you create data transfers between the connections. For instance, you might create a transfer between a connection to a text file and a connection to a database. To define a transfer, first select the source connection for the transfer. Then hold down the Ctrl key and select the destination connection for the transfer. Next, click on the Transform Data button on the toolbar. This draws a transfer line between the connections. Finally, double-click on the transfer line to edit the properties for the data transfer.

3. *Drag any required tasks from the toolbox to the design surface.* After defining the data transfers for the package, you must drag any required tasks from the toolbox to the design surface. For example, you could add a SQL task that executes a query to process the transferred data. Double-click on the tasks to edit their properties.

4. *Define precedence between tasks and transfers in the package.* Finally, you define precedences (order of execution) between a data transfer and a task or between tasks. For instance, you might want a SQL task to execute after a transfer has taken place. To define a precedence between two objects on the design surface, first select the object that is to occur first. Then hold down the Ctrl key and select the object that is to occur after the first object executes. Next, select one of the precedence options from the workflow menu on the toolbar. The package designer draws an arrow from the task or transfer to be completed first to the next task or transfer to be executed. You can choose from three types of precedences:

   - *On Success.* The next task or transfer occurs only if the first is successful.

   - *On Failure.* The next task or transfer occurs only if the first is unsuccessful.

   - *On Completion.* The next task or transfer occurs after the first regardless of whether the first is successful or unsuccessful.

5. *Save and/or run the package.* After you have defined the package, you can save or run the package by using the appropriate commands on the toolbar.

In the simplest case, you would place two connections on the work surface, define a data transfer, and be done. The next section demonstrates the features of the package designer by example. However, not every feature is touched upon. See the SQL Server Books Online for more information about the properties available for tasks and transfers.

Sample Transfer

This example demonstrates a relatively simple transfer package that normalizes data into two tables from a text file containing denormalized data. The following text file contains a list of employees and the amount of sales they made per month:

Making Some Assumptions

This example works on the assumptions that the text file exists and the required tables have been created in the Northwind sample database.

```
"David Noel","January",124996
"David Noel","February",175000
"David Noel","March",204050
"Jon Press","January",117000
"Jon Press ","February",305120
"Jon Press ","March",178990
```

This information will be stored in these two tables:

```
CREATE TABLE Employee (
    EmployeeID      int           IDENTITY(1,1) PRIMARY KEY,
    EmployeeName    varchar(30) NOT NULL
)
CREATE TABLE EmployeeSalesSummary (
    EmployeeID    int           NOT NULL REFERENCES Employee,
    SalesMonth    varchar(10) NOT NULL,
    SalesAmount   money,
    PRIMARY KEY (EmployeeID, SalesMonth)
)
```

To define the package, perform the following steps:

1. *Open the package designer from Enterprise Manager.* A blank package designer window appears (refer to Figure 8.12).

2. *Create a connection for the source text file.* Drag the Text File (Source) connection type from the toolbar to the design surface. In the dialog box that appears, enter the path and format information for the text file. Your screen should then look something like that in Figure 8.13.

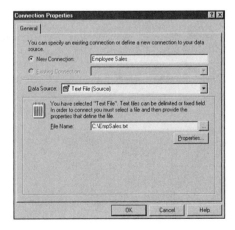

Figure 8.13 When you are creating a text file connection, this screen appears. Here you can specify the path and format for the text file.

3. *Create a connection for the destination database.* Drag the Microsoft SQL Server 7.0 Only (OLE DB Provider) connection type from the toolbar to the design surface. In the dialog box that appears, name the connection and point it to the Northwind database. Your screen should then look similar to that in Figure 8.14.

4. *Define a transfer between the connections.* Select the text file and database connection, and then click the Transform Data button on the toolbar. A black arrow appears, stretching from the text file to the database (see Figure 8.15).

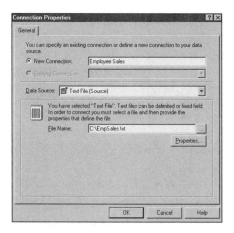

Figure 8.14   When you are creating an OLE-DB connection, this screen appears. Here you can specify the properties for the connection.

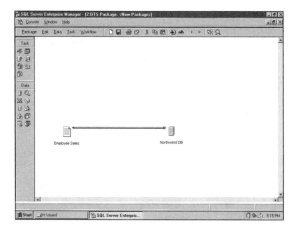

Figure 8.15   If you are following along with the example, your DTS package will look like the one shown here.

Double-click on the black arrow to define the transfer. The Data Transformation Properties property sheet appears. Enter a description for the transformation, as shown in Figure 8.16. Then choose the Destination tab.

On the Destination tab, click on the Create New... button and enter the following SQL statement:

```
CREATE TABLE OrderDenormalized  (
    EmployeeName    varchar (255) NOT NULL,
    SalesMonth        varchar (255) NOT NULL,
    SalesTotal         money NULL
)
```

Click OK to save the table definition. The property sheet should then look like that in Figure 8.17.

Figure 8.16   This screen appears when you double-click on a data transfer arrow in the DTS package designer. Here you can define the properties for the transfer.

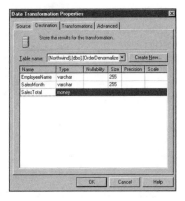

Figure 8.17   On the Destination tab, you can define where the transferred data will reside.

You can look at the Transformations tab, but because you are simply copying the text data to the database without performing any column transforms, you do not need to define a transformation script. Click OK to save the changes you made to the transformation.

This transformation simply copies the text file to a temporary table in the database. Next, you must normalize the data in that temporary table and store the normalized data in the final tables.

5. *Create a SQL task to normalize the data.* Drag the Execute SQL Task task type to the work surface, and then double-click on the resulting SQL task to edit its properties. Name the task "Normalize Data" and enter the following SQL Statement in the SQL Statement text box:

```
BEGIN TRANSACTION

INSERT Employee (EmployeeName)
SELECT DISTINCT EmployeeName
FROM OrderDenormalized

INSERT EmployeeSalesSummary (EmployeeID, SalesMonth, SalesAmount)
SELECT EmployeeID, SalesMonth, SalesTotal
FROM OrderDenormalized JOIN
      Employee ON Employee.EmployeeName LIKE
➥OrderDenormalized.EmployeeName

COMMIT
```

The property sheet should then look like that in Figure 8.18. Click OK to save your changes.

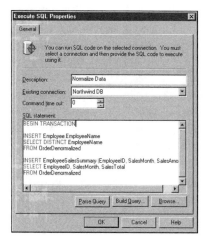

Figure 8.18   You edit the properties for a SQL Task using this window. The query shown here will normalize the data loaded from the example's text file.

6. *Create a precedence between the transfer and the SQL task.* Select the destination connection (the connection to the SQL Server database), press and hold down the Ctrl key, and select the SQL task. From the workflow menu, select the On Success Precedence option. This means that the SQL task will not execute unless the data transfer succeeds. The package is now complete, and it should look something like the one shown in Figure 8.19.

7. *Save and run the package.* On the toolbar, select the Save button. The Save DTS Package dialog box appears (see Figure 8.20). Enter the name of the package and choose to save the package to a SQL Server. Then run the package by clicking on the Run button on the toolbar.

This package is by no means a robust transfer. For instance, it does not clear the OrderDenormalized table before importing data, nor does it check for duplicate employees when populating that table. However, it demonstrates all the basic skills you need to create a DTS package of your own.

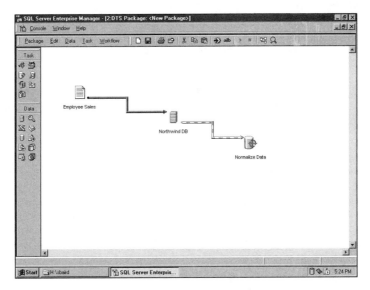

Figure 8.19 If you have been following along with the example, your final DTS package should look something like the one shown here.

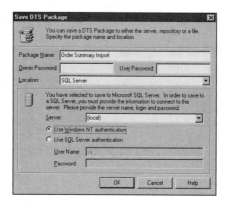

Figure 8.20   The Save DTS Package dialog box.

Conclusions

In this chapter, you studied the multiple data transfer methods supported by SQL Server 7.0. Whether you need to import data into SQL Server, export data from SQL Server, or transfer data between different data sources, SQL Server has a data transfer option that will work for you. Now that Microsoft has added the Data Transformation Services (DTS) to SQL Server, writing robust data transfers and transformations is much easier. This should help Microsoft realize its goal of making SQL Server 7.0 a major contender in the data warehousing market.

Replication

John Lynn

Easy replication of information has always been an intriguing capability among system administrators as a means of providing essentials such as backups for disaster recovery and distributed information. Replication systems for databases have particularly taken off in recent years as people discover new ways of using automated copies of all sorts of data. Everything from electronic mail systems and document management to data warehouse and decision support systems readily benefit from a good replication scheme. Over the years, replication has become available in vendor products ranging from simple desktop replication (like what we see now in Microsoft Access 97) to high-capacity multisite hot backup systems.

In most database server systems, replication was packaged as a separate, extra-cost option; Microsoft SQL Server started including replication as part of the product with release 6.0, and most Relational Database Management System (RDBMS) vendors have seen fit to follow suit.

When SQL Server database replication was introduced in SQL Server 6.0 and enhanced in release 6.5, replication was defined in terms of publishing, distributing, and subscribing; this paradigm continues in SQL Server 7. Before delving into the enhancements of SQL Server 7 replication, review the simple model used by SQL Server 6.5:

1. A *publication* consists of one or more *articles*.

2. Articles are simply database tables with SQL SELECT logic optionally applied to select a subset of rows and columns to publish.

3. When a destination server agrees to *subscribe* to a publication, an initial *synchronization step* ensures that the destination database matches the publication's schema column and data types and that the data is in sync to start out with.

4. After the initial synchronization step, changes that are made to table rows and columns that are part of a publication are detected and saved in a *distribution database* to be applied to the destination subscriber.

5. After a set number of transactions or at a set time schedule, the changes are read from the distribution database, and commands are executed to cause the destination (subscriber) to be brought up-to-date with the source.

Armed with this understanding of how things were in SQL Server 6.5, you're ready to see how SQL Server 7 builds upon this design. The main topics to be covered in this chapter include the following:

- Top features
- Setup and configuration
- Replication agents
- Snapshot replication
- Transactional replication
- The Immediate Updating Subscribers option of snapshot and transactional replication
- Merge replication
- Replication and the new SQL Server security roles
- Subscribing

Microsoft SQL Server Replication Is Not Asbestos

For the most part, SQL Server 6.5 replication was a pain to work with, especially as the number of transactions to be replicated grew. It would get fussy and unstable and sometimes stop working altogether without warning, prompting manual intervention and creative detective work to get things moving again.

In addition, the replication model used by SQL Server 6.5 did not easily serve all business needs. The goal of SQL Server 6.5 replication was that of transactional consistency: that changes made to tables in a publication would eventually be put into place at the subscriber. The subscriber was definitely at the receiving end. The situation got complicated when the people using the subscriber wanted to update their pieces of the publication and have the changes reflected back to the source, which is a perfectly reasonable and desirable thing to want.

In this chapter, you'll see how SQL Server 7 addresses this and many other common business needs. Replication in SQL Server 7 promises to be much more stable, easy to set up and use, and easier to troubleshoot.

- Monitoring replication
- Advanced replication topics

First, take a minute to examine some new features of SQL Server 7 replication.

Top Features

Although the list of new features introduced by SQL Server 7 replication is long, several features really stand out:

- Wizards
- New replication types
- Update replication
- Anonymous subscribers
- Publishing the Execution of Transact-SQL stored procedures
- Scripting the replication topology
- New SQL Server agents for replication tasks
- Better support for heterogeneous replication
- Replication ActiveX controls

The following subsections introduce these features. Each will be covered in greater detail later in the chapter.

Wizards Make It Easier

A common theme throughout all facets of administering replication with SQL Server 7 is the presence of the step-by-step wizard interface to reduce even the most complex setup tasks to a manageable level. This will be apparent throughout this chapter.

The outcome of these wizards is the execution of stored procedures that do the actual work of creating the replication, so it's possible to manage replication without using the wizards. In addition, because replication setup is now completely scriptable, scripts can be generated automatically from an existing configuration. This will be covered in the section "Scripting the Replication Topology."

New Replication Types

SQL Server 7 replication offers 3 types of replication, each designed to solve a particular set of challenges:

- Snapshot
- Transactional
- Merge

Snapshot replication performs a complete refresh of the destination at scheduled intervals. Snapshot replication was available in SQL Server 6.5 as a "Scheduled Table Refresh," a sort of repeating automatic synchronization.

Transactional replication detects changes made at the source and applies the same changes in the same order at the destination. SQL Server 6.5 also provided this replication type.

Merge replication intelligently analyzes changes made at both the source and destination and applies the changes to whichever target is appropriate. It uses a conflict algorithm provided by SQL Server 7, but if you prefer, you can tailor your own conflict-detection scheme with either stored procedures or COM components.

Each of these replication types is discussed in greater detail later in the chapter.

Update Replication

It sounds like a new type of replication, but update replication refers to the concept of enabling subscribers to modify data and have their modifications applied at the publishing server, where they are in turn sent to all other subscribers. While some shops have rigged homemade solutions in the past to get the same effect, update replication now comes in the box.

All three replication types support update replication:

- Snapshot and transactional replication optionally support update replication by using a method called *Immediate Updating Subscribers*.

  This option allows subscriber tables to be updated. The replication uses the Two-Phase Commit (2PC) protocol to ensure that the update at the subscriber end is applied to both the subscriber and the publisher, in an all-or-nothing transaction. If the transaction succeeds, the record has been updated in both places and will be part of the next replication to all other subscribers of the affected publication. Note that this option generally requires good communication links between the subscriber and publisher because an update is handled *synchronously* in this case.

- Merge replication is a new type of replication that is designed to enable updates by subscribers by default, even if there is a large number of occasionally connected subscribers. Each time a replication takes place, an exchange occurs between the publisher and the subscriber; updates that have occurred since the last replication are loaded down to the subscriber and up to the publisher. When both the publisher and the subscriber have updated the same column in the same record (a *field*), a conflict occurs. The conflict resolver is then called to settle the conflict, and either the updated field from the subscriber is applied to the publisher, or the updated field from the publisher is applied to the subscriber.

  The default resolver uses a priority-based scheme, but it can be overridden with a custom resolver that more closely matches specialized needs.

As you learn about each replication type, look at the manner in which update replication is accomplished for that type.

Anonymous Subscribers

A routine part of SQL Server replication setup is enabling subscribers so that the subscriber is able to start using a publication. Administration can become a burden when the number of subscribers climbs into the double or triple digits, which is certainly feasible with SQL Server 7 desktop edition users and Internet subscribers. Enabling a publication to allow anonymous subscribers is an easy solution to this problem. Anonymous subscribers are covered in depth in the section "Anonymous Subscriptions," later in this chapter.

Publishing the Execution of Transact-SQL Stored Procedures

A significant new capability of replication is the capability to replicate the *execution* of Transact-SQL stored procedures. If you include a stored procedure as an article of a Transactional publication, the execution of that stored procedure will be replicated, not the changes made by the execution of the stored procedure. If the stored procedure causes 100,000 records in a published table to be updated, the 100,000 updates are not what's replicated; only the executed procedure is replicated after the procedure finishes successfully.

Scripting the Replication Topology

Once replication is set up on one server, it is often desirable to set up additional servers in the same way. In the past, there was no way to perform this setup without taking copious notes as you clicked your way through the setup using the graphical interface of Enterprise Manager. SQL Server 7 provides welcome relief from this drudgery with its capability to script replication topologies (to capture an existing replication setup as Transact-SQL scripts). The scripts can be used as cookie-cutter templates to set up additional servers or to restore a replication configuration as part of a business disaster recovery.

Exploiting New SQL Server Agents for Replication Tasks

Past versions of SQL Server used the SQL Executive task scheduler to manage all the job executions that carried out replication tasks. The SQL Executive performed everything from the initial synchronization to scheduled refreshes. Unfortunately, it served as a single point of failure that could cause many reliability problems. SQL Server 7 uses discrete components known as *agents* for each part of replication. Each step of replication is assigned its own agent, and each agent keeps a history of actions performed. Overall, the separation of tasks into specialized agents provides for better replication monitoring, troubleshooting, and performance. The different types of agents are mentioned throughout this chapter.

Better Support for Heterogeneous Replication

SQL Server 6.5 introduced the idea of replicating to non–SQL Server subscribers, such as Microsoft Access, but it never seemed to catch on because setup and operation of heterogeneous replication in SQL Server 6.5 was tricky and problematic. Because of the OLE DB support that's built into SQL Server 7, heterogeneous replication is as much a usable option as is replication to other SQL Server databases, and this is reflected in the wizards used to configure publishers and subscribers. SQL Server 7 also introduces the capability to publish from heterogeneous sources to SQL Server by interfacing with the Data Transformation Services (DTS).

Replication ActiveX Controls

SQL Server 7 packages several key elements from replication into ActiveX controls that you can use to enable your own applications to perform replication tasks. You can, for example, start a replication update to pull data to a sales force automation package written in Visual Basic, without having to interface with the publishing server in the traditional ways (using SQL-DMO objects, for example). The ActiveX controls actually externalize the functionality that SQL Server components use, enabling them to perform replication tasks themselves.

Setup and Configuration

Before a server can be used to publish database articles, it must be configured as a *publisher*. Each publisher also needs a *distributor*, a server where replicated data is temporarily stored and used by replication agents. The place to store this data is called the *distribution database*. The server with the distribution database is considered the distributor.

In most cases, the publisher is located on the same server as the distributor, but it doesn't have to be. In fact, sometimes you wouldn't want to use the same server for both publishing and distribution, especially if many publications are to be managed. The task of collecting and tracking transactions may have a negative effect on replication performance; in such cases, it makes sense to specify a *remote distributor,* using the Configure Publishing and Replication Wizard.

You can tell at a glance whether a server has been set up for replication just by looking at the unexpanded tree under the server in Enterprise Manager (see Figure 9.1). When you enable replication, or more precisely, when you enable a server to be a replication distributor, the Replication Monitor icon appears in the console tree.

You can configure a server by using the Configure Publishing and Distribution Wizard as described in the next section.

Figure 9.1   Notice that this server does not have the Replication Monitor icon, which means this server has not been configured as a distributor for replication.

The Configure Publishing and Distribution Wizard

This wizard is used to configure a server as a Publisher or as a distributor to use with the publisher. If one server is to be both the distributor and the publisher, the wizard also creates a distribution database on the server.

To use the wizard, follow these steps:

1. Click the taskpad sequence Replicate Data and then Configure Replication; or open the Tools pull-down menu and select Wizards.

2. From there, expand the Replication tree to display all the replication wizards and select Configure Publishing and Distribution Wizard.

The wizard creates a distribution database and sets some preliminary conditions:

- Enable publishing from the server
- Allow other publishers to use the server as a distributor
- Enable subscriptions from specific servers

The wizard suggests very safe defaults, such as using the same server for both publishing and distributing and allowing the server to subscribe to its own publications. Most steps in the sequence enable you to access detailed dialog boxes containing options for customizing parameters. As is typical of the wizard interface style, all selections and settings are displayed for your review. Look them over carefully before you click the Finish button.

The Enterprise Manager interface takes on a few additional entries after you use the Configure Publishing and Distribution Wizard. For one, the Replication Monitor becomes available in the Enterprise Manager tree, displaying its list of publishers, agents, and alerts. In addition, the new distribution database appears in the Databases section (see Figure 9.2).

After you configure the publisher, you must create publications of the type needed to solve the business problem at hand and then subscribe to these publications. Before you investigate the various types of replication in detail, however, read the next section, which describes the general steps for creating any type of publication.

Setup Steps Common to All Types of Replication

Creating a publication sounds complex, and in fact, it is. But before you go off looking for the three-day Microsoft class on SQL Server replication configuration, take a look at the wizards waiting to help you. Microsoft transformed a complex set of activities into a pleasant step-by-step interaction with some wizards, making replication setup a relatively painless task.

You use the Create Publication Wizard to create publications of all types:

1. Open the Tools menu, select Replication, and choose Create and Manage Publications. In the dialog box that appears, select the database to be published from (see Figure 9.3).

2. Click the Create Publication… button to start the Create Publication Wizard.

3. If the database you're publishing from already contains publications, the wizard offers to use one of those as a template for the publication being created (to automatically answer the questions that follow).

    If this is the first publication in the database, the wizard asks you to select the publication type. Select Snapshot, Transactional, or Merge Publication.

4. Specify the type of subscribers that will subscribe to the publication (indicate whether there will be only SQL Server subscribers or possibly some non-SQL Server subscribers).

5. Select articles to add to the publication by selecting tables, and for Transactional and Snapshot publications, stored procedures.

Revealing the Distribution Database

If the distribution database is not listed, right-click on the server in Enterprise Manager and select Edit SQL Server Registration…. In the dialog box that appears, make sure that Show System Databases and System Objects is checked.

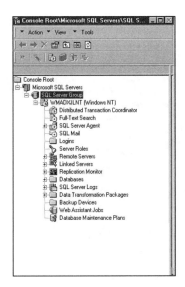

Figure 9.2 The Replication Monitor icon indicates that the server is configured for replication and is being used as a distributor.

6. You'll be asked to choose a publication name and description.

   Then you can either accept a rather large number of defaults, or you can refuse the defaults and enter a kind of extended dialog with the wizard, in which each option is presented in turn. For the purpose of this exercise, accept the defaults. Note that all the default properties appear in the scrollable window (see Figure 9.4), where you can easily select them for a handy copy/paste operation to document the properties of this publication.

7. In the last wizard screen, click the Finish button to create the publication.

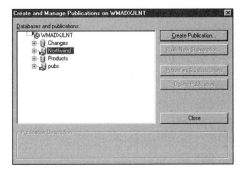

Figure 9.3 In the Create and Manage Publications dialog box, select a database.

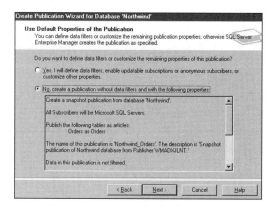

Figure 9.4 Leaving the "No" radio button checked to answer the question, "Do you want to customize this publication further?" enables you to accept defaults for many properties of the publication.

To review and change a publication that's already been created, access the Enterprise Manager console tree, select the desired database, expand the tree, and select the Publications node.

Under Publications, select the desired publication, and then right-click and select Properties. Figure 9.5 shows the properties of a publication called Northwind_Employees.

The tabs in this dialog box not only summarize all the attributes of the publication, but they contain options that enable you to control and change such attributes as the following:

- Articles included in the publication (you can add more if needed).

- Agent status for the SQL agents involved in the publication.

- Subscribers to the publication.

- Replication scripts for the publication.

Note that making changes in the publication Properties dialog box may require you to resynchronize or reinitialize the publication. In addition, you cannot make structural changes to the publication that remove columns or that filter rows if any subscriptions are already using the publication. The next section describes the agents that perform all the various tasks of replication.

Where's My Publication?

You may have to right-click and select Refresh if you just created a publication but the Publications node does not show up under the database.

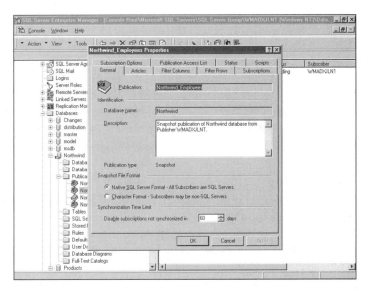

Figure 9.5 The publication Properties dialog box shows all the properties of a publication in an easy-to-understand format.

Replication Agents

Four agents carry out all the tasks of SQL Server replication:

- The Snapshot Agent
- The Log Reader Agent
- The Distribution Agent
- The Merge Agent

These agents are specialized jobs of the new SQL Server Agent, which is described in full in Chapter 5, "The SQL Agent."

Each type of replication—snapshot, transactional, and merge—combines the efforts of one or more of these agents to actually carry out the replication. Each agent has a domain of specialization, as described in the following subsections.

Snapshot Agent

The Snapshot Agent prepares snapshots for initial synchronization or for snapshot replication. A snapshot is a point-in-time image of a publication's schema and data. Snapshots are used to initialize a publication so that the replication has a starting point where the destination is equal to the source. This initial sync step is performed for both transactional and merge replication. In snapshot replication, the total set of data is re-sent each time the replication is run, so the Snapshot Agent prepares a new snapshot for each replication cycle.

Log Reader Agent

The Log Reader Agent keeps an eye on published databases' transaction logs, looking for changes that affect published tables. As it finds transactions that affect these tables, the Log Reader Agent copies the transactions into the distribution database, where they'll be picked up later by the Distribution Agent to be applied to subscribers.

The Log Reader Agent checks the transaction log either periodically according to a schedule that was set when the publication was created or on an ongoing, continuous basis.

Distribution Agent

The Distribution Agent performs the actual movement of data: copying data and schemas for snapshot replication, applying transactional changes for transactional replications, and so on. The Distribution Agent executes on the distributor for push subscription and executes on the subscriber for pull subscriptions. Remember that the distributor is the designated server that houses the distribution database. The Distribution Agent looks at the distribution database for replication commands that are to be carried out.

Merge Agent

The Merge Agent, used exclusively in merge replication, has several jobs to do. For one, the Merge Agent is used to deliver the initial synchronizing snapshot when a merge publication is created. The Merge Agent merges updates and detects conflicts and also calls the resolver to work out conflicts that are detected when both the publisher and the subscriber update the same record. The Merge Agent executes on the distributor for push subscriptions and executes on the subscriber for pull subscriptions.

Now that you've covered the basic elements needed by all replication types, it's time to look at each type in detail.

Snapshot Replication

The simplest type of replication, snapshot replication, simply refreshes the subscriber on a scheduled basis. A refresh is the same as the initial synchronization that takes place with a new subscriber. Each time the snapshot replication runs, an exact copy of the publication's schema and data is created at the subscriber's databases. The complete set of schema and data to be applied at each subscriber is called a *synchronization set*. There is a synchronization set for each article in a snapshot publication. The synchronization set is created each time a snapshot publication executes, so that referential integrity between tables in the set is maintained.

The upcoming subsections further explore snapshot replication:

- Applications for Snapshot Replication
- How Snapshot Replication Works
- Snapshot Replication Setup

This same basic type of coverage—and in the same basic format—is offered for each of the replication types. Being armed with specific knowledge about each replication type in detail enables you to better evaluate the solution available to any given replication scenario.

Applications for Snapshot Replication

Because snapshot replication is a complete refresh each time, it can be used as part of a low-cost warm backup setup, perhaps configured to snapshot during periods of low network activity, such as overnight or weekends. It's also ideal for applications that need to be periodically refreshed (such as monthly totals in a decision support environment, data-driven Web sites, and other occasionally connected subscribers). With the advent of embedded SQL Server applications on the desktop and mobile units, it's attractive to imagine using snapshot replication to reload these units with updated application code at connection time.

Snapshot replication serves the well-connected subscriber as well. With the Immediate Updating Subscriber option, updates can be made at the publisher and the subscriber simultaneously, and then later, the new snapshot is delivered, updates and all. Snapshot replication generally requires less processing overhead on the publisher and distributor because it's not a transaction-based continuous update operation.

In addition, snapshot replication is a viable way of replicating databases that are routinely populated by using nonlogged bcp or select into, when transactions are not present to drive the replication.

Schema Changes Go Undetected

Changes to schema that vary from the original schema and that occur after the publication is created are, unfortunately, not replicated to the subscribers. So if you add a column to a published table, for example, the new column won't show up at the subscriber. A workaround is to create another publication containing the added column, and then subscribe to it.

Snapshot Replication: How It Works

Each snapshot publication is assigned two agents:

- Snapshot Agent
- Distribution Agent

The Snapshot Agent prepares files that are needed to replicate the publication's schema and data, and the Distribution Agent carries out the replicating tasks. The Snapshot Agent creates schema files that represent the design of the tables in the publication, as well as data files that hold the actual records from the published articles.

The schema files are the SQL Data Definition Language (DDL) commands required to create the table in the destination database. The data files are created either in bcp format (.bcp files, see Chapter 8) if the subscriber is a SQL Server database, or in text format (.txt files) for subscribers using other database systems such as Oracle or Microsoft Access. If there is an index on any of the articles, an index file (.idx) is also created, which holds the command required to re-create the index.

The schema files and the data files are referred to as the *synchronization set* for each article in the publication. You can find these files in the directory: `Mssql7\Repldata\` `unc\`*ServerName*`_`*DatabaseName*`_`*PublicationName*`\`*DateTimeStamp*`\`, where *ServerName* is the SQL Server machine name, *DatabaseName* is the database where the publication is located, *PublicationName* is the name of the publication, and *DateTimeStamp* is a 14-digit representation of the date and time in the format YYYYMMDDHHMMSS (see Figure 9.6).

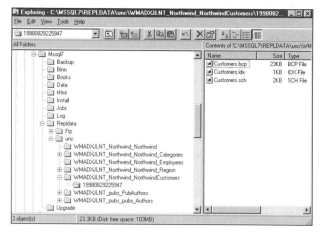

Figure 9.6 The format of the directories created by the Snapshot Agent to hold synchronization sets; notice the naming convention that SQL Server uses when creating these directories.

After creating the synchronization sets, the Snapshot Agent notes where the synchronization sets are located and records that information in a table called MSrepl_Commands located in the distribution database. When a subscriber comes along to pull down the publication, or when the publication is pushed to a subscriber, the Distribution Agent looks at this table to find the schema, data, and commands needed to execute a snapshot successfully.

Snapshot Replication Setup

Setting up a snapshot replication is simple. Just follow the steps in the Create Publication Wizard, as outlined in the section "Setup Steps Common to All Types of Replication" (earlier in this chapter).

You must decide whether to allow Immediate Updating Subscribers when you're setting up the publication. There are two restrictions on using Immediate Updating Subscribers:

1. Only SQL Server 7 subscribers can be Immediate Updating Subscribers.

2. Subscribers should not update timestamp columns because doing so would interfere with the mechanism that detects conflicts between the subscriber and publisher.

The schedule that controls when the Snapshot Agent creates the synchronization set is usually set by default in the Create Publication Wizard; however, the schedule can be changed. To edit the schedule after the publication is in place, do the following:

1. In Enterprise Manager, choose Replication Monitor and select Agents.

2. Click on Snapshot Agents. A set of publications for which the Snapshot Agent is responsible appears in the right pane.

3. Right-click on the desired publication and select Agent Properties from the context menu.

4. In the Job Properties dialog box that appears, select the Schedules tab.

5. Edit the schedule as desired. Figure 9.7 shows all screens used in the sequence, with a schedule that can be edited.

The Directory Naming Convention

The UNC directory is used for LAN-connected, WAN-connected, or otherwise NetBIOS-connected subscribers. Internet subscribers reach the distributor strictly via FTP connection, so the ftp directory is used for those subscribers instead.

Internet-configured publications are described later in this chapter, in the section "Advanced Replication Topics."

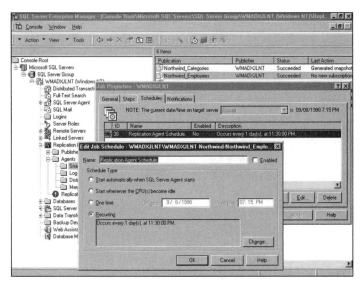

Figure 9.7   You have a great deal of flexibility when changing an agent's schedule.

Note that the schedules for both the Snapshot Agent and the Distribution Agent can be tailored. The Snapshot Agent's schedule refers to when the synchronization set is created and refreshed, not when the publication actually is sent out. The Distribution Agent's schedule becomes important only when someone subscribes to the publication, because the type of subscription determines when the Distribution Agent executes.

The Distribution Agent assigned to the publication starts at the scheduled time and reads the commands the Snapshot Agent created. The Distribution Agent then connects to the subscriber and moves the data and schema commands to the subscriber.

Because these are snapshot publications, a `DROP` command is executed first, before the tables are re-created on the subscriber.

Transactional Replication

This is the "classic" style of replication introduced in SQL Server 6.0 and enhanced in SQL Server 6.5. Transactional replication is log-based; commands affecting published tables are saved and then executed at the subscriber by the Distribution Agent at replication time, either according to a schedule or after a number of transactions have occurred.

Applications for Transactional Replication

Transactional replication is an effective means of getting near real-time updates to subscribers in a well-connected environment; it's been designed to apply updates to subscribers within a minute or so after they occur in the source database, with guaranteed consistency. Transactional replication is also useful in the occasionally connected environment because only the changes to published tables are replicated to the subscribers (instead of the complete refresh that's sent with Snapshot replication), which means reduced network traffic. If 160 rows were inserted in a two-gigabyte published table today, 160 `INSERT` commands would be replicated and executed at the subscriber when the replication takes place.

Transactional Replication: How It Works

The following agents handle each transactional publication:

- Snapshot Agent
- Log Reader Agent
- Distribution Agent

When a transaction publication is created, the Snapshot Agent performs its task of creating a synchronization set (exactly the same as it does in snapshot replication). This is used to initialize new subscribers to a state consistent with the publisher before the incremental changes can be sent out.

Transaction-based replication works by detecting changes in published tables and forwarding those changes to subscribers in the form of SQL transactions (insert, update, and delete statements).

Transactional replication uses the Log Reader Agent in addition to the Snapshot Agent. The Log Reader Agent is responsible for checking the transaction log of the database where the published table resides. This is the very same transaction log that's used in the general processing of database changes that have nothing to do with replication.

The Log Reader Agent watches the transaction log, looking for insert, update, or delete statements that affect tables marked for replication. The Log Reader Agent copies any such statements into the distribution database, where they remain until the Distribution Agent applies them to the subscriber database in exactly the same sequence in which they were executed at the source database.

The Distribution Agent runs on the publisher (for push subscriptions) and the subscriber (for pull subscriptions).

The Distribution Agent can be run either on a fixed schedule or continuously.

Transactional Replication Setup

Follow the steps in the section "Setup Steps Common to All Types of Replication," by using the Create Publication Wizard. One item of interest for transactional publications is that the wizard offers to publish the execution of stored procedures as part of the publication's articles. In the Specify Articles step, you can select a check box to include stored procedures in the article. This causes a dialog box to appear, in which you can tailor the replication of the execution of the stored procedure (see Figure 9.8).

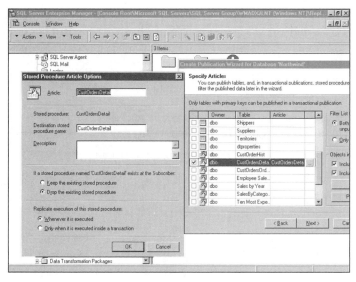

Figure 9.8   Replicating the execution of a stored procedure in a transactional publication is just as easy as adding tables to the publication. (Notice the pencil and pad icon that represents stored procedures.)

The Immediate Updating Subscribers Option of Snapshot and Transactional Replication

SQL Server 7 introduces a way to enable subscribers of snapshot and transactional publications to update the very articles that come to them by way of replication: an option called Immediate Updating Subscribers. This updating occurs at the subscriber end, so there's no need to connect over the WAN to the central site when a business branch desires to make a change to replicated data.

Records that are updated at the subscriber end in a publication that has Immediate Updating Subscribers enabled are also updated at the source using a Two-Phase Commit (2PC) transaction that occurs completely behind the scenes and is managed by the Microsoft Distributed Transaction Coordinator (MSDTC). The update is guaranteed to either succeed at both the subscriber and the publisher or fail altogether.

For snapshot replication, when the next snapshot is replicated to all the subscribers, the updated record is included in the snapshot. For transactional replication, the record updated by the subscriber is identified as a replicated transaction to be distributed to all the subscribers of the affected publication, with the exception of the subscriber doing the updating. SQL Server uses a loopback mechanism to identify the server making the update so that it can be excluded from receiving the transaction again.

There is one potential problem with Immediate Updating Subscribers: trying to update or delete a record that no longer exists at the publisher. Triggers at the publisher detect this and cause the transaction to fail. This situation is handled elegantly, however, by merge replication, which is described in the next section.

Merge Replication

The newest addition to the set of replication types in SQL Server 7 is merge replication. Borrowing concepts from JET database replication introduced with Access 95 and enhanced with JET 3.5 and Access 97, merge replication works to resolve conflicts among updates to the same record by both the publisher and one or more subscribers so that they end up with the same value.

When the same record is updated at both the publisher and subscriber table, either the publisher's record is updated at the subscriber, or the subscriber's record is updated at the publisher, depending on how the conflict was resolved. Only the last state of a changed record is considered at replication time; even if a particular column in a particular record was changed 100 times between replications, only the last value is involved in the merge.

Information about resolved conflicts is kept so that the conflict history can be reviewed later. SQL Server 7 includes a simple conflict resolution algorithm, but you can augment or replace this with your own resolver.

Applications for Merge Replication

Merge replication offers a great deal of autonomy to subscribers. Because updates flow in both directions at merge time, the benefit of updating subscribers is realized without the strict atomicity of a transaction-based subscriber update (which is required by the Immediate Updating Subscriber option of snapshot or transactional replication).

Another difference from the Immediate Updating Subscriber method is that with merge replication, all changes are somewhat *negotiable*. In cases in which a conflict would normally cause a rollback, a resolver is called instead to mediate. This can make administrating distributed updatable replicas an easy task, because everything is automated.

The conflicts you've been reading about are, by default, column-based. A *conflict* occurs when the data in the same column and the same row is updated in two (or more) different tables. This means that updating *other* columns in the same row in two different places does *not* cause a conflict; instead the information is simply *merged* together.

For example, a large travel agency with many office locations likes to keep customer profiles online so the customer's travel and hotel preferences are readily available. Suppose a business traveler far from home walks into a local branch to make a reservation, and she changes her airplane seating preference from "aisle" to "window" after thinking about the boring flight earlier that day. The branch office updates and saves the customer's record. At the same time, the traveler's administrative assistant back home speaks to the local travel agency branch office to update the traveler's email address, and that change is also applied and saved. The Merge Agent runs at each location, and every branch ends up with an updated record that includes both the new seating preference and the new email address. The two updates were not considered to be a conflict, because they weren't updating the same record/column (field). Therefore, the result is a merge.

Note that this is the default behavior of a merge replication; you can turn column-based conflict off so that anytime two servers update more than one column in a row, it is considered a conflict.

Merge Replication: How It Works

The Merge Agent takes the initial snapshot prepared by the Snapshot Agent, applies it to subscribers, and then applies incremental changes to either the source or the destination, based on the resolution of conflicts when both source and destination records are updated. To help resolve conflicts, several schema changes are made to each table as it is prepared to participate in a merge publication:

1. Each row must be assigned a globally unique value by adding or using a new column of the SQL type uniqueidentifier. If the row already has a uniqueidentifier column with the ROWGUIDCOL attribute, it's used to uniquely identify the record among all networked computers in the world (see the upcoming sidebar "Unique Records in the Universe"). If SQL Server adds a column to contain the globally unique column, it names the column rowguid.

2. *Tracking triggers* are added to detect changes to each row, column, or both row and column of the table that's being added to a merge publication. These Transact-SQL triggers capture the changes being made and record the change in merge tables, which are also added when the publication is created.

Figure 9.9 shows the tables that are added to a database after a merge publication is created. In this example, a publication was created in the SQL Server pubs sample database, and a single article was created that includes only the authors table.

After the Merge Agent resolves conflicts involving two rows in which the same column was updated by both publisher and subscriber, one of the following results takes place:

- The winning rows are saved in the actual table (on either the publisher or the subscriber).

- The losing rows at the publisher are saved in a table called Conflict_*<TableName>*, where *<Table_Name>* is the actual table name, for example, conflict_authors.

- Any rows that were deleted are saved in a table called Msmerge_delete_conflicts at the publisher.

- Any inserted rows are inserted in both the source and destination.

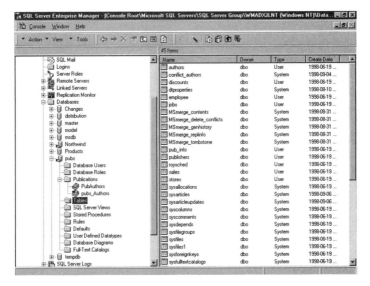

Figure 9.9 Tables with the names MSxxxx that are added to the pubs database after defining a merge publication are used for the various tracking activities of merge replication.

Unique Records in the Universe

Armed with the new uniqueidentifier data type and the column attribute ROWGUIDCOL, you're set to create as many globally unique values in a table as desired:

```
CREATE TABLE GUID_bucket
(guid uniqueidentifier ROWGUIDCOL,
ITEM int)
```

To add some records to this little GUID_bucket, execute the following INSERT several times. Note the use of the NEWID() function to generate the value for the guid column:

```
insert into GUID_bucket values(newid(), 100)
select * from guid_bucket
guid                                    ITEM
--------------------------------------  ----------
06FD8E8E-3E82-11D2-A68A-788540000000    100
06FD8E8F-3E82-11D2-A68A-788540000000    100
06FD8E90-3E82-11D2-A68A-788540000000    100
```

The little column called guid in the preceding example is added to a table that's being prepared for merge replication.

Merge Replication Setup

Follow the steps in the section "Setup Steps Common to All Types of Replication," by using the Create Publication Wizard. The setup for a merge publication has no surprises; it's very similar to setting up any other type of publication.

When a merge publication is in place, you can view and change some attributes of the publication and even the individual articles by going to the publishing database in Enterprise Manager and selecting the Publications tree node. Right-click on the desired publication and select Properties. Then go to the Articles tab to see which articles were included in this publication. Select the build button (...) to the right of an article, and another tabbed dialog box shows the options for that particular article (see Figure 9.10). The three tabs contain the various options for creating and maintaining the article. Figure 9.10 shows the General tab, which offers options for overriding the default behavior that specifies what causes a conflict; you could check the radio button labeled Consider Changes Made to the Same Row As a Conflict, for instance, to cause an update to any column in two of the same rows to be considered a conflict that needs to be resolved.

You can also use the Resolver tab to specify a SQL-stored procedure to be called upon to handle conflict resolution. SQL Server will use your stored procedure to resolve conflicts that occur in updates to that particular article only. This stored procedure executes at the publisher. The parameters to the stored procedure include the following:

@tablename. Name of the table for which a conflict is being resolved.

@rowguid. uniqueidentifier that identifies the row having the conflict.

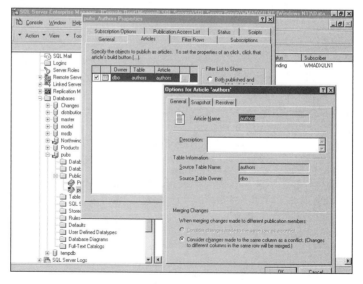

Figure 9.10   You can view the article options, install an overriding conflict resolver, specify what constitutes a conflict, and more.

@source. Name of the server from which a conflicting change is being propagated.

@source_db. Name of the database from which a conflicting change is being propagated.

@source_security_mode. Security mode for connecting to a source server.

@source_login. Login name used when connecting to the source server.

@source_password. Password used when connecting to the source server.

@dest. Name of the server to which changes are propagated.

@dest_db. Name of the database to which changes are propagated.

@dest_security_mode. Security mode for connecting to the destination server.

@dest_login. Login name to use in connecting to the destination server.

@dest_password. Password to use in connecting to the destination server.

Remember that, by default, a conflict indicates that the same field (row/column) is being updated at two servers. The resolver stored procedure should look at the record identified by @rowguid in the table at both servers, decide what to do, and then return a single row to be put into place at both servers.

You determine what happens to resolve the situation. For example, you might merge the columns from both records into one composite record, or add numeric columns together to overlay binary fields in logical operation, or whatever is desired.

The stored procedure is created either in the publisher database or in the master database that's marked as a system object so that it can be found.

If you have access to COM expertise, you can use an in-process DLL COM module that implements the `ICustomResolver` interface as a custom resolver. SQL Server 7 ships with an example of this in the directory Mssql7/Devtools/Samples/sqlrepl/resolver. To select a COM resolver, select the resolver from the list of registered resolvers that appears under Use This Custom Resolver (refer to Figure 9.10).

You have now covered all the replication types. In the following sections, you'll examine replication security issues and learn how to go about subscribing to publications, monitoring replication, and more.

Replication and the New SQL Server Security Roles

SQL Server 7 replication has several built-in SQL Server security roles. You must be a member of one of these roles in order to perform the specific activities of replication setup. Most of the tasks require the server role sysadmin, but some tasks are database-specific and can be performed with the db_owner role. Table 9.1 lists replication tasks and the corresponding role or roles required.

Table 9.1 **Required Roles for Replication Tasks**

Task	Role/Roles Required
Configuring distribution	sysadmin
Enabling databases for replication	sysadmin
Configuring publishing	sysadmin
Creating publications	sysadmin or db_owner
Creating push subscriptions	sysadmin or db_owner
Creating pull subscriptions	Any login in the publication's Publication Access List
Dropping subscriptions or creating login	sysadmin or db_owner
Monitoring replication	sysadmin
Updating default publication access list	sysadmin
Updating a custom publication access list	sysadmin or db_owner
Agent logging in to publisher	Login must be in the Publication Access List of the referenced publication
Agent logging in to distributor	Login must be in the Publication Access List of the referenced publication
Log Reader Agent logging in to publisher	db_owner
Agents logging in to subscriber	db_owner

SQL Server replication adds another component to security: the Publication Access List (PAL). This is similar to the Windows NT Access Control List (ACL).

When the server is first configured for replication, a default PAL is established, which is the default security mechanism that limits access to pull and updatable subscriptions. You can create a custom PAL to be specified to further control a particular publication.

To view and change the default PAL for a server, follow these steps:

1. Choose Tools, Replication and select Configure Publishing Subscribers and Distribution....

2. Select the Publication Access List tab to add and remove users.

To view and change the custom PAL for a publication, follow these steps:

1. In the database that contains the publication you want to control, right-click the desired publication and select Properties from the context menu.

2. Select the Publication Access List tab.

3. Click the radio button labeled Use the Following Custom Access Control List for This Publication.

4. The list of users will be initialized with the list from the server's default PAL. Add or remove users from this list as desired.

Note that an anonymous subscriber can connect to a publication without being checked against either PAL.

Subscribing

As in SQL Server 6.5, there are two types of subscriptions: push and pull. A publication can be both pushed to some subscribers and pulled from other subscribers.

One change from SQL Server 6.5 to 7.0 is that now subscribers are only supposed to receive publications, and not the individual articles of publications. As the SQL Server Books Online states, the user interface (Enterprise Manager) does not support subscribing to individual articles, although that action is still supported by SQL Server 7. Microsoft suggests that you migrate your subscriptions to the publication level, where each publication is composed of one or more articles.

Except in the case of publications that are enabled to accept anonymous subscribers, only enabled subscribers are permitted to subscribe. Subscribers are first added when the server is configured for publication. But you can enable additional subscribers later. To do so, follow these steps:

1. In Enterprise Manager, select the publishing server to add subscribers to.

2. Select Tools, Replication, Configure Publishing, Subscribers, and Distribution.

3. In the dialog box that appears, select the Subscribers tab and click New Subscriber....

4. Select SQL Server or another type of subscriber (see Figure 9.11).

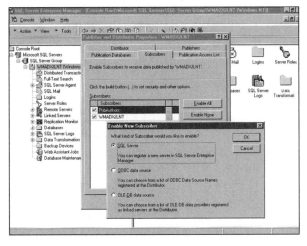

Figure 9.11   From this dialog box, you can add new SQL Server, ODBC, or OLE-DB-linked servers as subscribers.

5. Note that by using the build (…) button next to the subscriber's name on the Subscribers tab, you can access another dialog box to set several options regarding how to deal with that particular subscriber (options such as login attributes for replication agents connecting to the subscriber, default schedules, and so on).

Each type of subscriber has its own distinct advantages. Publications can be *pushed to* or *pulled from* subscribers. In addition, a publication can be configured to be pulled from known or anonymous subscribers. The next sections describe these concepts.

Push Subscriptions

A push subscription is created at the publisher and pushed to the subscribers (instead of leaving the publication available to be selected by a subscriber creating a pull subscription).

You create a push subscription by using the Push Subscription Wizard. To locate the wizard, right-click on the desired publication under the Publications node of a database name in SQL Enterprise Manager.

The value of push subscriptions is ease of administration: You can set up the publication and push it to the desired subscribers—even a large number of subscribers—all in one step. In fact, by using the new Replication Scripting facility in SQL Server 7, you can save the whole scenario in a script file to be used to create publications and their subscribers. All you need to re-create the configuration is an ISQL command line. Packaged software products that use replication might also want to use this feature in their install procedures.

Pushing a subscription is the easiest way to publish to heterogeneous data sources such as Oracle, Microsoft Access, and other ODBC destinations.

Pull Subscriptions

The subscriber initiates a pull subscription when the subscriber is ready to receive updates. Pull subscriptions are well-suited for large numbers of subscribers because the subscriber creates and administers the replication instead of the publisher. Subscribers using the Internet, for instance, would pull subscriptions from a publisher.

With pull subscriptions, the work of designing and creating publications can be done at the publisher ahead of time, before any subscribers need to use the publication. When a publication is created, a synchronization set is also created so that the publication is ready to initialize any new subscribers that come along.

A big advantage of using pull subscriptions is that the agents that perform the replication tasks run at the subscriber, not at the publisher. This removes the processing from the publisher and allows the subscriber to set the schedule (which is another reason to use pull subscriptions when the number of subscribers is large).

A subscriber creates a pull subscription by using the Pull Subscription Wizard. Only SQL Server subscribers are able to use this wizard because it's a component of SQL

Server Enterprise Manager. There is a way, however, to perform a pull subscription from a non-SQL Server subscriber by using the embedded Distribution control.

Anonymous Subscriptions

An anonymous subscriber is a pull subscription from a subscriber that has not been specifically enabled to receive publications from this publisher. You make the decision of whether to use anonymous subscribers when you first create the publication.

Anonymous subscribers are well-suited for publications that are available to be pulled from Internet subscribers because there could never be any way to know in advance all the subscribers that would need to be enabled.

When creating a publication by using the Create Publication Wizard, you have the opportunity to enable anonymous subscribers. You can't add or enable subscribers in that wizard, however; the only choice is whether or not to allow anonymous subscribers (see Figure 9.12). To add subscribers, you must use the Configure Publishing, Subscribers, and Distribution Wizard. In addition, you can modify existing publications to allow anonymous subscribers by using the publication's Properties dialog box.

Monitoring Replication

One of the biggest advantages that SQL Server 7 has over previous releases is that it makes it much easier to get a detailed status of exactly what is happening, what was happening, and even what will happen with regard to replication.

Much of this is due to the use of SQL Server Agent jobs to manage replication activities. As described in Chapter 5, "The SQL Agent," the SQL Server Agent is industrial strength as compared to the SQL Executive of previous releases. The SQL Server Agent is used as the basis upon which the replication agents are built.

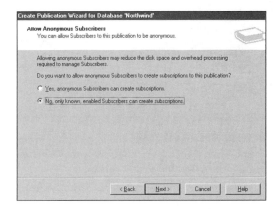

Figure 9.12   Subscribers are either anonymous or not, which must be specified at the time the publication is created; a publication can be made anonymous later via the publication's Properties dialog box.

There are several places to check on the progress and history of a publication, and preconfigured SQL Server Agent alerts let the server notify you when there is a problem.

Monitoring Replication Agents

In Enterprise Manager, the Replication Monitor is available if the server is enabled as a distributor and the current user is a member of the sysadmin fixed server role. By opening the Replication Monitor, you can view publishers, agents, and replication alerts.

Under Publishers, you'll find a list of publishers that use this server as a distributor, along with a list of all their publications. Select a publication here to see a list of all the agents responsible for carrying out the replication tasks for that publication—usually the Snapshot Agent is listed first, followed by the agents involved in the publication: Log Reader Agent, Distribution Agent, or Merge Agent, as shown in Figure 9.13.

If instead of Publishers you select Agents under Replication Monitor, the four agents of replication are displayed. Select one of the agents, and a list of the publications handled by that agent appears in the right pane of Enterprise Manager. Figure 9.14 shows all of this in one screen.

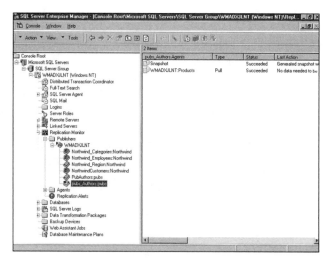

Figure 9.13 The right pane shows the agents responsible for carrying out the steps of the publication called pubs_Authors; the left pane shows the agents' current status for the selected publication.

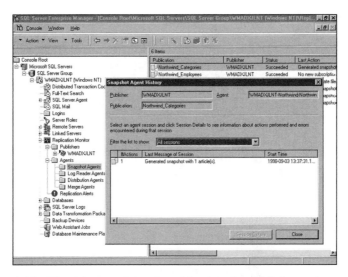

Figure 9.14   The right pane shows the publications for which the agent currently selected in the left pane is responsible.

Select a particular publication in the right pane, and right-click to reveal Agent History and Agent Properties. Use the Agent History option to show the summary results of every execution for that specific publication and, by using the Session Details button, every step of an execution for the particular agent servicing the particular publication. Figure 9.15 shows the steps of one particular execution of the Merge Agent for a publication called pub_Authors.

Another great place to get information about replication agents is under the SQL Server Agent node. Select the Jobs section of the console tree. The right pane displays a list of SQL Server Agent jobs, many of which are related to replication tasks. Those with a category name that starts with 'REPL' are replication jobs associated with the replication agents.

To refresh the jobs shown in the right pane, right-click on Jobs and select Refresh. Right-click on a selected job and select Job History for a detailed account of when the job ran, the results of the job, and optional details of the job showing every step. Figure 9.16 shows the job history for a Snapshot Agent.

Replication Alerts

SQL Server 7 provides a few alerts that can be used to route replication-related problems to the appropriate people so that manual intervention can be used to correct the problem. As described in Chapter 5, the alert facility provided by SQL Server Agent is a powerful component that you can use in many creative ways.

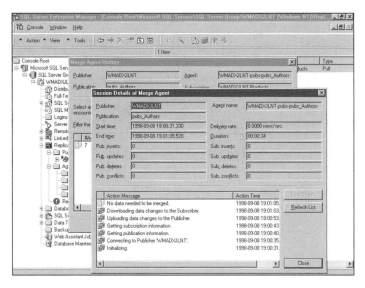

Figure 9.15   You can examine each step of one particular execution of the Merge Agent in this session detail window.

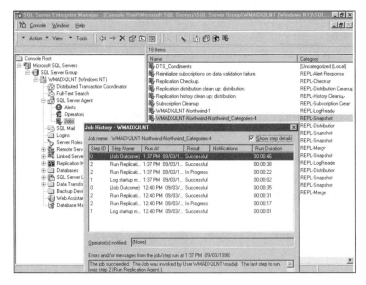

Figure 9.16   All replication agents appear under SQL Server Agent/Jobs. Select an agent to get a detailed job history.

The alerts that are preconfigured with SQL Server 7 include some of the more catastrophic error conditions. These alerts are SQL Server event alerts, which means that they are invoked upon occurrence of a particular error condition with a specific error code.

It's easy to add your own alerts to the Replication Alerts section of Replication Monitor. Just right-click on Replication Alerts and select New Alert. Fill out the dialog box that appears, describing your new alert. Select the error number you want the alert to react to and specify the actions of the alert.

Troubleshooting

It's not too difficult to spot a critical problem that affects a replication component. The agents that handle replication show problem status visually in Enterprise Manager (see Figure 9.17).

To locate the problem, look to the agents for answers. From the Replication Monitor, first locate any error indicators (the big white X in a red ball), and then expand the console tree.

Select Publishers to view a list of all publications handled by this distributor; failing publications are marked with the error indicator. Select a failing publication by clicking on it once. The right pane displays all the agents involved with the particular publication, and the failing agent is highlighted with the error indicator. In Figure 9.18, for instance, you can see that there is a problem with the Snapshot Agent for the publication Northwind_Region in the Northwind database.

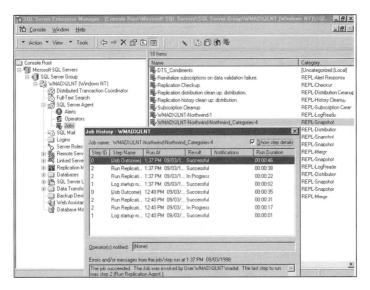

Figure 9.17   It's easy to spot trouble, as you can see in this visual display of an error reported in Enterprise Manager.

Right-click on the publication to access a context menu that conveniently has a selection at the top labeled Error Details. Click on that option to see what error caused the replication to fail.

You can also analyze failed replication jobs by looking at the SQL Server Agent's log (because the replication agents are job instances of SQL Server Agent). In SQL Server 7, the SQL Server Agent has its own log that is separate from the SQL Server error log. In Enterprise Manager, go to SQL Server Agent on the main console tree, right-click, and select Display Error Log… to analyze the current SQL Server Agent error log. The current log is located in the directory ..\Mssql7\Log\ and is named SQLAGENT.OUT; history files in the same directory are named SQLAGENT.<x>, where <x> is a number from 1 to 9, with 1 being the most recent and 9 the oldest. You can view these history files with any text editor.

To augment the information in the SQL Agent logs, right-click the SQL Server Agent and select Properties to display the SQL Server Agent properties dialog box. Then check the box labeled Include Execution Trace Messages in the Error Log section (see Figure 9.19).

Looking at all of the various logs is the best way to get a quick ballpark idea of what the problem is.

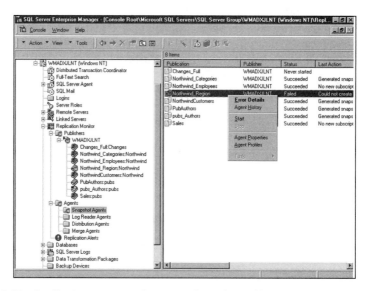

Figure 9.18 Replication Monitor takes you right to the problem area. Select Error Details from the context menu to see what error caused the replication to fail.

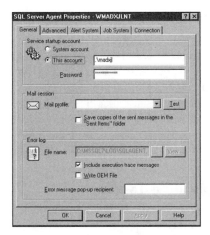

Figure 9.19 Use the Include Execution Trace Messages check box to include execution trace messages for SQL Server Agent.

Resolving Conflicts with Merge Replication

SQL Server 7 Books Online has some good advice for working with database tables that use IDENTITY property and need to be replicated by using merge replication. The advice is to use the NOT FOR REPLICATION attribute of the table's IDENTITY column and then use different IDENTITY ranges for publishers and subscribers if at all possible.

IDENTITY columns are table columns that are automatically populated with the next incremental value each time a record is inserted. There is no need to increment the identity, however, when the process doing the inserting turns out to be a Distribution or Merge Agent, which is what the NOT FOR REPLICATION attribute indicates. Check SQL Server 7 Books Online carefully for cautions about using IDENTITY columns with merge replication and for details about how to avoid conflicts.

When conflicts occur, they must be resolved by using either the default conflict resolver or one that you provide. See the section "Merge Replication Setup," earlier in this chapter, for more information on setting up a custom resolver.

Advanced Replication Topics

In this section, you'll examine features of SQL Server replication that aren't particularly advanced by themselves; rather, these features are advanced when compared to what's been available in past versions of SQL Server as far as exploiting the workings of replication are concerned. The goal of these features is to make the lives of database administrators easier by providing the facilities to solve more problems.

Configuring Replications for the Internet

Making a snapshot, transaction, or merge publication available to subscribers connecting over the Internet or a corporate intranet is as simple as marking a check box in a publication's Properties dialog box when you're creating the publication. Both push and pull subscriptions can be enabled to use the Internet in this way.

For a snapshot publication, the subscriber connects to an FTP server at the publisher to retrieve the synchronization sets that initialize the publication. After that, the Merge Agent or Distribution Agent connects over the Internet to deliver updates at replication time.

Scripting the Replication Topology

After you have configured replication, it is often convenient to save the configuration so that everything can be easily set up again if a disaster strikes. The best way to do this is to script the replication topology and save the scripts. To create scripts, follow these steps:

1. In Enterprise Manager, select a server.

2. Choose Tools, Replication and select Generate Replication Scripts.

3. The General tab of the dialog box that appears offers two check boxes: Distributor Properties and Publications in These Selected Databases.... To script this server's replication setup in its entirety, check both boxes (see Figure 9.20).

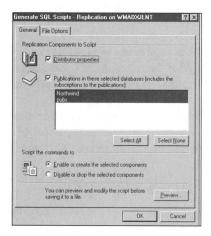

Figure 9.20   To script a replication configuration, select the publications to script and check the Distributor Properties check box.

Pay particular attention to the options under Script the Commands To, which are used to script either the commands to create the publication or the commands to drop the items being scripted. In most cases, scripting the commands that create things is the appropriate choice, although there might be a reason to script in order to destroy a publication or disable a server for replication. In fact, in previous releases of Microsoft SQL Server, disabling and dismantling replication was not an easy feat to achieve without referencing the Microsoft Support Knowledge Base article that described how to do it.

Replication ActiveX Controls

Microsoft SQL Server 7 includes two ActiveX controls: the SQL Distribution control and the SQL Merge control. These controls can be used from any environment that's able to use ActiveX controls—such as Visual Basic, Microsoft Office, and so on.

Because they're not visual controls, scripting environments, such as Active Server Pages and Windows Scripting Host, can use the Replication controls, too.

In general, there are three methods available in each control:

- The Initialize method
- The Start method
- The Terminate method

Normally, only Initialize and Start are needed, so this makes a very clean interface for a complex capability.

To use the controls, set all the required parameters by setting properties of an instance of the control in your application, and then call `Initialize`. If no errors result, call `Start`, and the agent will start, connect, and perform replication.

The control raises one event, the Status event, which periodically fires to report replication completion status. To receive the event, your application must declare the instance of the Replication ActiveX control by using the `WithEvents` attribute.

Several properties can be set in order to connect to publishers and subscribers using specific network protocols and specific security. When using these controls, an application has total control over how replication instances are handled.

A sample Visual Basic application ships with SQL Server 7. That application is located in the directory \Mssql7\Devtools\Samples\ Sqlrepl\Replctrl\Vb.

An ideal use for the SQL Distribution control is to serve as a distributor in an application that needs to act like a pull subscriber. Usually, the subscription must be pushed when publishing from SQL Server 7 to heterogeneous data sources such as Microsoft Access, because a Microsoft Access database doesn't have the "smarts" to perform a pull operation. The SQL Distribution control can provide these "smarts," eliminating the administrative work needed to create push subscriptions to these heterogeneous desktop databases.

Replication to and from Heterogeneous Data Sources

Microsoft SQL Server 6.5 replication introduced the capability to publish to heterogeneous data sources such as Oracle, Microsoft Access, and other ODBC destinations. This was accomplished by using a push subscription and ODBC to push to these data sources. It was an interesting novelty that never gained much popularity. In SQL Server 7, this feature has been enhanced greatly, enabling you to do the following:

- Publish to ODBC/OLE DB data sources
- Use Data Transformation Services (DTS) packages as a source of replication
- Use other data sources as the publishing source

The next sections examine each of these capabilities.

Publish to ODBC/OLE DB Data Sources

Publishing to heterogeneous data sources is a significant capability that greatly extends the range of subscribers in a multivendor shop having databases such as Microsoft Access, Oracle, and even DRDA sources (including AS/400 and DB2 Universal Database). As long as you use the ODBC drivers specifically provided by Microsoft for this support, replicating to these destinations is fully supported and encouraged in SQL Server 7.

Publishing to heterogeneous data sources is typically accomplished via a push subscription, unless the destination is an application that initiates a pull subscription using the SQL Distribution control.

The following steps outline the process for publishing to heterogeneous subscribers:

1. Create an ODBC data source by using the Control Panel at the publishing source. When creating the ODBC data source, make it a System DSN.

2. Create a new subscriber to push the subscription to. Choose Tools, Replication, and then select Configuring Publishing, Subscribers, and Distribution. Select the Subscribers tab and click on the New Subscriber... button. A set of selections appears, one of which is ODBC Data Source (see Figure 9.21). Select the data source you just added.

3. Create a publication by using the Create Publication Wizard and enable the publication to replicate to non-SQL Server subscribers (see Figure 9.22). This ensures that the initializing sync set used in the initial snapshot will be in a format that can be used by non-SQL Server subscribers (usually character-mode format).

4. Push the new publication to the ODBC subscriber. Select the published database, expand the Publications node, and select the publication to be pushed to the new ODBC subscriber you just created. Right-click the publication and select Push New Subscription to start up the Push Subscription Wizard.

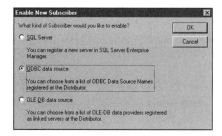

Figure 9.21   From the Publisher and Distributor Properties dialog box, select Subscribers to add an ODBC subscriber.

5. The wizard will ask you to select a subscriber from a list of enabled subscribers. Select the new ODBC data source subscriber and set the schedule for initial synchronization and replication.

Use Data Transformation Services (DTS) Packages As a Source of Replication

You can easily import data to SQL Server 7 from a variety of sources by using the new Data Transformation Services (DTS). This feature is described in greater detail in Chapter 8.

Imports created by using DTS can be used as a source of data in a snapshot publication. As an application of this capability, imagine running a nightly refresh of a SQL Server 7 data warehouse that's fed from an OS/390 DB2 system. Having this level of integration included in the box and ready to set up without a lot of development and maintenance is quite a premium.

To use a DTS package to perform a snapshot-style refresh, perform the following steps:

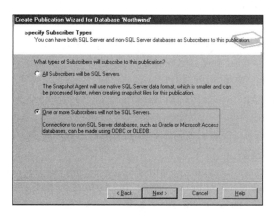

Figure 9.22   Enable non-SQL Server subscribers when you create the publication.

1. Start the DTS Import Wizard by choosing Tools, Data Transformation Services and selecting Import into SQL.

2. Go through the steps in DTS to select the data source, the SQL Server destination database where the snapshot will be loaded, the transformations to be applied, and so on.

3. At the step in the wizard that's titled "Save, Schedule, and Replicate Package," check off the options by filling in the check boxes as outlined here:

Option	Response
Run Immediately	Optional.
Create Replication Publication	Check it.
Save Package on SQL Server	Check it.
Schedule DTS Package for Later Execution If you check it, use the build button (...) to set the schedule.	Optional.

4. Save the DTS package with a useful name and description.

5. Complete the wizard by clicking Finish. The package will then run if you checked Run Immediately.

Use Other Data Sources As the Publishing Source

SQL Server 7 offers something completely new that's bound to attract the attention of other vendors seeking to integrate into the Microsoft SQL Server 7 replication environment: the ability to create publications and use the distribution capabilities of SQL Server 7 from another database system. This new capability is made possible by two services from SQL Server 7:

- *SQL-DMO (Distributed Management Objects),* which performs the administrative chores of setting up the publisher, publication, and subscribers.

- *The new Replication Distributor Interface,* which stores replications in a SQL Server 7 distribution database where they are picked up and distributed for replication.

The following steps outline the process for using other data sources:

1. Create a Visual Basic program to use SQL-DMO to perform the administrative work of setting up a publication.

2. Use the Replication Distribution Interface, a COM interface, to insert replicated transactions into the distribution database.

SQL Server Books Online has examples for both of these tasks; the Replication Distribution Interface example is in C++.

Both of these are nontrivial projects that really are not suitable for most database administrators to tackle, but hopefully some interesting products on the horizon will dovetail into the SQL Server replication environment.

Conclusions

Microsoft has stated that they want to take a leadership role in database replication, and this is certainly reflected in SQL Server 7, both now and in plans for future releases. The next release of SQL Server 7, for example, will be able to interface with the Microsoft Message Queue Manager so that replication can continue even when servers are not attached. Replicated transactions will simply be queued until they can be delivered.

With a solid replication technology in place both now and in the future, system administrators are released from the juggling act of performing manual data duplication and are free to spend time in other ways.

10

Achieving High Availability

Chris Miller and
Sean Baird

SQL SERVER PROVIDES CAPABILITIES TO SUPPORT high-availability operations in the enterprise. That means that if SQL Server is set up on the right hardware and the software is configured correctly, SQL Server can provide data services in a reliable manner.

In this book, high availability refers to a set of different technologies that can reduce the risk and costs associated with downtime related to hardware failure, operating system failure, or a failure in SQL Server. As with many other topics discussed in this book, such as security and backup, a strong emphasis is placed on cost and the benefits of different solutions, so you can pick the best solution for your case. To coin a phrase, don't buy a twenty-dollar lock to protect a ten-dollar horse.

Here's what you'll find in this chapter:

- Redundant Hardware
- Warm Spares
- Clustering

Redundant Hardware

One of the most recent technologies to extend from the mainframe world to the Windows NT world is the notion of redundant hardware. Finally, servers are available that have redundant power supplies, redundant processors, redundant processor power supplies, and redundant drive technology. Combined with a good UPS and careful environmental management, these technologies can go a long way toward helping you achieve the goal of eliminating hardware-caused downtime. In this section, you'll learn about the types of redundant hardware that can be employed and the advantages of each:

- Power management
- Disks and disk arrays
- System board technologies
- Fault-tolerant hardware
- Monitoring

Power Management

Power management is one of the fundamental hardware solutions for failure. In some areas, thunderstorms, floods, and ice storms can play havoc with the power coming into a building. But power outages can be caused by many problems that aren't weather related, such as power company equipment failure. These things happen all the time. Luckily, there are a few technologies you can use to make your server more tolerant of power discrepancies.

The most obvious is the UPS system. An Uninterruptible Power Supply detects power outages and turns on backup power, usually from a battery. More advanced models also detect brownout conditions, in which power drops below a level that will keep everything running. In addition, most models will filter out power spikes for total power protection.

Most new servers offer an option for a redundant power supply. This option provides two distinct features. First, each power supply can be plugged in to a different circuit and a different UPS, so if the circuit blows, the UPS dies, or one power supply dies, the other power supply will take over. The power supply is one of the most common components to fail because it incurs a lot of heat and usually houses the fans, which are also prone to breaking more quickly than other parts.

If your server is in a server room that has a room-based UPS, make sure you're on the list of persons to be notified of maintenance and that the server operators know how to take the server down in the event of an extended outage.

Disks and Disk Arrays

When a disk drive fails, it can have an enormous effect on the operation of a computer. Even with the highly reliable drives available today, the chances of having a failure increase because so many drives are out there. However, several technologies are available to reduce these risks.

RAID systems are common features in today's servers. They are great for providing performance benefits, increased capacity, and redundancy in one package. RAID comes in two flavors. Windows NT Server ships with a built-in software RAID system that provides some of the fault-tolerance features but not all the performance benefits of a good RAID system. The Windows NT disk striping technology provides redundancy, but it doesn't have the hardware acceleration that hardware RAID systems offer.

Hardware RAID is a great technology. RAID levels were discussed in an earlier chapter (Chapter 4). The main thing to watch for when implementing a RAID system is that the Windows NT drivers and the controller firmware are up-to-date. The controller firmware is the programming on the card that controls the interaction between the controller and the disks. Just like any other piece of software, it has glitches that have been discovered since it was shipped. Check your vendor's Web site periodically to look for new drivers.

Most hardware RAID systems have the additional advantage of hosting hot-swappable disk drives. If a drive fails, it can be replaced without taking the server down. When the drive is replaced, the RAID controller will immediately begin restructuring the new drive. Many configurations also allow a spare drive to be kept plugged in at all times so that if a drive fails, the controller can immediately begin reconstructing the data onto the new drive. At any rate, it's a good idea to keep spare drives on hand or to have a guaranteed schedule from the server vendor on the supply of replacement parts.

High-end disk technologies allow for advanced fault-tolerance features. EMC Corporation specializes in high-end fault-tolerance technologies for storing data from any source. These technologies combine to form a large data subsystem that can even back itself up with no intervention from Windows NT.

System Board Technologies

One of the most interesting technologies that has come about recently is the advent of hot-swap PCI. If a PCI-based peripheral breaks, a new one can be placed in the server without taking the server down.

Disk array controllers are available as hot-swap PCI peripherals. That means that you can put redundant controller cards into a server, and if the controller card fails, it fails over to the backup card. If it's a hot-swap PCI card, you can open the server, take out the burned-out controller, and replace it without taking the server down.

A technology that's been around for a while that's coming down into a commodity price range is ECC memory. Electronically correctable memory is kind of like RAID for memory. It detects and corrects errors before they affect service. ECC memory is available on most servers.

Warning: Read the Operator's Manual

Read your server operator's manual carefully before you attempt to open the case while the server is running. Failure to do so could cause damage to components or to software. Many cases have built-in power cutoff systems that will shut the server power off *without shutting down Windows NT* if the case is opened while the power is on.

Fault-Tolerant Hardware

Fault-tolerant hardware includes systems that lie at a level below clustering, which is covered later in this chapter. Fault-tolerant hardware solutions use specialized hardware and drivers that enable you to take advantage of all the benefits of clustering without having to buy special software. One example of a solution is Marathon Technologies Endurance 4000, a combination hardware/software solution that enables a set of machines to act as a cluster without any other special software. The Endurance 4000 specifically uses up to four commodity servers (such as Compaq, HP, or Dell servers) interconnected with special Marathon Interconnect (MIC) cards. This solution has two very unique advantages. First, it isn't bound to a single vendor for the server; the servers can come from anywhere. Second, the system works in such a way that the two parts of the cluster can be separated geographically to reduce the chance of downtime due to a natural disaster.

Monitoring

An essential part of any redundant system is monitoring. In a system with two power supplies, if one power supply goes out, there is no backup for the system. While this may sound trivial, the chances that both will fail close to the same time are fairly high. Keep in mind that both power supplies are running all the time, so if one fan goes out, the other fan may not be far behind. In addition, if the outage was caused by a voltage fluctuation, the working power supply may be hanging on only by a thread. Also, if there are two power supplies and one dies, all the power has to come from the other power supply, possibly adding to the strain and heat buildup on it.

In any case, server manufacturers provide monitoring software so you can tell whether one of the power supplies goes out and needs to be replaced. Keep in mind also that the monitoring software has to run at a very low level in order to return the necessary data. Therefore, you need to keep the software up-to-date and test it before deploying it widely.

Another essential point is to buy good components. Stories in the press tell about components that are supposed to be redundant but aren't. If possible, test the hot-swappable components, or devise a means of forcing a disk drive to fail, and then see whether the whole system crashes or whether it can continue to operate in a degraded capacity.

Before putting a new server into production, load it up with data and back up the data to tape. Then try out the redundant components according to the manufacturer's directions. Power supplies usually have a switch on the back that will disengage the power supply, as well as a mechanism for physically removing it from the server. With the server powered up but sitting at the "It is now safe to turn off your computer" prompt, flip the switch and cut the power supply. If the server keeps running, you'll know everything is actually working right.

Warm Spares

Warm spares are in no way a new feature for SQL Server 7. It is a technique that's been tried and used by many installations before the advent of clustering, and it has some benefits over clustering.

A warm spare system relies on two completely separate servers with similar disk capacities but not necessarily similar speed characteristics. A warm spare system has a primary server and a secondary server. The primary server is the active server. It's the one on which all the queries and inserts are performed. The secondary server (the warm spare) contains copies of the databases on the primary server, which are refreshed from a transaction log backup on a schedule, usually every 10 to 15 minutes. Unlike with clustering, a warm spare will not provide up-to-the-transaction disaster recovery; it is only as good as the last transaction log or differential backup that was applied. See Figure 10.1 for an example.

The advantages of using a warm spare over clustering are reduced complexity, generally less-expensive hardware, distance, and data availability. The reduction in complexity is achieved because the whole system relies on a simple set of scheduled tasks that handle the synchronization. They are very easy to implement and are probably already halfway implemented by your backup schedule. Data availability means that if a table is accidentally dropped or records are accidentally deleted, the warm spare will have a backup copy of the data until the transaction log backup that contains the deleted data is loaded. Simply pause the transaction log copy process, copy the data from the standby server, and restart the transaction log copies.

The cost of hardware and software for a clustering solution is about the same as that for a good warm spare setup. While a warm spare setup requires two independent servers, it doesn't require the state-of-the-art hardware and more expensive enterprise editions of SQL Server and Windows NT in order to operate.

Ensuring Redundancy

I've heard a few stories from my clients about how they purchased systems with built-in RAID controller software, only to find that the system still went down when one of the on-drive controllers failed. Only one drive was bad, but the server went down anyway instead of becoming degraded and allowing the other drives to pick up the slack. The advice I have on this subject is to carefully monitor the manufacturers and components in all the servers, and make sure you deal with reputable vendors and dealers who have been given decent reviews in the press. Also, keep up with those driver and firmware revisions from your vendor.

Where Does Clustering Fit In?

Clustering is defined for Windows NT as a set of two servers with independent system volumes and a data volume that is shared. The system volume includes the Windows NT operating system and the paging file. This implies that the two servers are reasonably identical, and that each server has its own system volume in addition to a large RAID array.

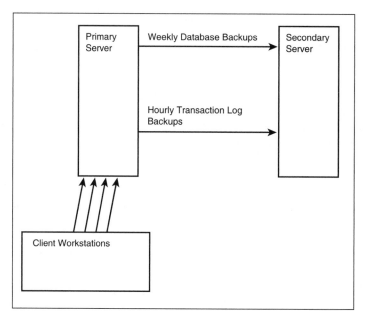

Figure 10.1   A warm spare system; notice that only one server processes requests at a time.

The other feature of a warm spare is that the two servers don't necessarily need to be in the same room, the same state, or even the same continent (distance). A cluster requires that all the parts of the cluster be connected by a dedicated cable, which may be practical for a campus solution but is not practical for a long-haul public data network connection. To refer to an example in Chapter 6, "Backup and Recovery," if a jumbo jet crashes into the building, the whole cluster will be in little pieces. If the other part of the warm spare is in a different building, the likelihood is smaller that both the servers would be disrupted in the event of a disaster, such as a falling aircraft. There's also no reason that a cluster couldn't be used as the primary server in a warm spare arrangement, which would provide more redundancy to the cluster.

The way a warm spare system works is that it takes advantage of the WITH NORECOVERY option of the RESTORE command. The following steps outline the process:

1. Perform a full database backup on the primary server. Copy the backup to the secondary server, and then copy the backup to tape.

2. Load the database backup on the secondary server using the NORECOVERY option.

3. Periodically (every 10 minutes to 2 hours), perform a transaction log backup on the primary server. Copy the transaction log to the secondary server and load it with the NORECOVERY option. Also, copy the transaction log backups to tape.

4. Go back to step 1 on a scheduled basis. If you're performing full database back-ups nightly, you should go back to step 1 every night and load the full backup onto the secondary server. If you're performing full database backups weekly, you should load the database weekly.

This process provides a two-level recovery scheme. First, the whole database up to the last transaction log is kept live on the secondary server. Also, each backup is copied to tape with Windows NT backup software. This provides a good level of redundancy. To activate the secondary server in a warm spare:

1. Take the primary server off the network.

2. Perform recovery on the secondary server's databases using the RESTORE DATABASE <*database name*> WITH RECOVERY.

3. Repoint the clients to the new server. This can be accomplished via a WINS alias, via a DNS secondary entry, or by changing the name of the server.

Step 3 is a little vague, so take a minute to look at it more closely. Basically, you need to make all the clients aware of the new server. There are a lot of different ways to do this. Ideally, you could go around to every client and reconfigure its database connection, or you could get software that would automatically start looking for the second server if the first wasn't available. Because very few pieces of software provide automatic failover, you'll probably end up changing the client addresses.

If you don't want to change the client addresses because they are too geographically disperse or too numerous, the other option is to change the server. If the clients are using TCP/IP Sockets to get to the server, you can change the DNS entry for the pri-mary server to point to the secondary server's address. If you are not using DNS but are using WINS instead, you'll use a similar process. However, you should consult a good book on WINS and Windows NT for details because it's a fairly involved process. The easy way out is to rename the server and reboot it.

That's really all there is to using a warm spare solution. It's not quite a real-time solution to a backup problem, and you may lose data, but at least you can get every-thing back up and running in short order.

Clustering

The other major option for achieving high availability is to use a server *cluster*. A clus-ter is a group of machines that appears to the outside world as a single machine. The primary benefits of clustering are fault tolerance and load balancing. The primary drawbacks are complexity and cost. In terms of achieving high availability, you'll focus on the fault-tolerant aspects of a cluster.

This last half of the chapter focuses on the practical information concerning clus-tering that you will need in order to accomplish these things:

■ Understand clustering technology, especially as implemented with Microsoft Cluster Server.

- Make a decision regarding the use of clustering technology.

- Understand the requirements of setting up SQL Server in a clustered environment.

Although a variety of clustering solutions exist for PC servers, this chapter focuses on Microsoft Cluster Server (MSCS). Cluster Server is designed to work with most standard hardware configurations, albeit with a more restricted set of hardware than a standard NT installation. In addition, SQL Server 7.0 has been designed to work best with the Microsoft clustering "hooks" built into the NT Server/Enterprise edition (NTS/E) product.

Clustering Theory

Clustering technology has been around for a number of years, and it has been designed to address the needs of larger enterprise-wide server systems. Specifically, these requirements include the following:

- Significantly reducing or eliminating server downtime for mission-critical systems

- Providing the best performance for extremely heavy server loads stemming from large numbers of concurrent users

- Improving the manageability of the numerous servers providing critical services

To get an idea of how these three requirements are met, take a look at how a cluster works. This section deals purely with clustering theory; you will see how SQL Server integrates with a cluster in the next section.

You already know that a server cluster consists of two or more physical machines, which are known as the *nodes* of the cluster. In an MSCS setup, each node has its own system disk that contains the base NTS/E operating system and the MSCS services. Each node is connected to a shared SCSI disk that contains application and data files. In addition, each node is networked to a common backbone, and another network card in each node connects that node to the common network.

The cluster provides a number of *resources,* such as disk space, applications (such as SQL Server), and printers, to name a few. The cluster then presents a "virtual machine" to the clients accessing these resources. In other words, the cluster is transparent to clients, and each client thinks it is connected to a single server.

Even Shared Disks Can Fail

Because the shared SCSI disk of an MSCS cluster is potentially a single point of failure for the cluster, a fault-tolerant disk solution such as RAID 0 (disk mirroring), RAID 5 (disk striping with parity), or RAID 10 (mirrored striped sets with parity) is recommended.

Each node "owns" a set of resources and is primarily responsible for serving up those resources. MSCS uses an *active/active* clustering scheme. This means that all nodes of the cluster can provide different resources. Compare this to an *active/passive* scheme, in which one node handles all resource requests, and the other remains idle while waiting.

Now that you understand the basics of how a cluster works, take a look at how these features fulfill the three primary needs of a large system: high availability, high scalability, and improved management.

Clustering provides fault tolerance and high availability by monitoring the state of all machines in the cluster by way of a *heartbeat*, a signal routinely monitored by the cluster to determine the status of a node. MSCS provides fault tolerance in two ways. First, MSCS monitors the status of cluster resources; if a resource fails, MSCS attempts to recover by restarting that resource on the owning node. If that attempt fails, MSCS transfers ownership of that resource to another node. Second, if a node fails, MSCS transfers all resources owned by that node to another node.

This feature is known as *failover*. A failover is not necessarily transparent to a client that is connected to the cluster. Because a failover can take as much as a minute, clients might experience a brief downtime when a node or resource fails. Even though there is a brief downtime, the advantage of using a cluster is that the failover occurs automatically without the need for an administrator's intervention.

For example, SQL Server applications that use a persistent connection (*stateful* clients) to the server will fail when they try to access the SQL Server resource during a failover. You may even need to restart the client application to reconnect to the server. These clients must be modified to automatically retry the connection in order to take full advantage of the cluster. On the other hand, applications that do not maintain a persistent connection (*stateless* clients) will be affected by a failover only if they attempt to connect to the database during the brief period of unavailability.

Another function of a cluster is to provide improved scalability for high-usage systems. Because MSCS uses an active/active clustering scheme, it is possible to manually load-balance a cluster by assigning each node different resources. For example, if a cluster provides both SQL Server and file sharing resources, one node can primarily

MSCS Is Limited to Two Nodes

At the time of this writing, MSCS supports only two-node clusters. Microsoft plans to add support for additional nodes in future releases of this product.

Clients Don't Need to Know About a Failover

One way to prevent clients from noticing a failover is to use another feature of NTS/E: Microsoft Message Queue (MSMQ). MSMQ provides guaranteed delivery of data, even if a server is unavailable. Clients can be written that submit transactions to a queue; in the event of a failover, the queue retains the transactions and delivers them to the surviving node as soon as it restarts the failed resource.

provide database resources while the other provides file services. After the initial release of MSCS, Microsoft provided automatic load-balancing capabilities for TCP/IP resources. Future releases of MSCS might provide automatic load balancing for other types of resources as well. As you will see in the next section, it is possible to manually load-balance SQL Server by creating two logical servers—one for each node.

The other advantage of clustering (as opposed to maintaining a fleet of standby servers) is that each node in the cluster can be administered as a unit (for more efficient manageability). MSCS provides an administration tool that can be used to manage the cluster and all nodes from a central location. In addition, cluster-aware applications like SQL Server 7.0/Enterprise Edition contain centralized management tools.

Deciding Whether Clustering Is Right for Your Business

Clustering is admittedly a very cool technology; however, good enterprise administrators do not implement new technologies for technology's sake. As with any technology, it helps if you perform a cost/benefit analysis before you decide whether to use clustering. To help you make this decision, look at some of the pros and cons of implementing MSCS for SQL Server.

Given the material in the previous section, the pros should be fairly obvious:

■ *Decreased long-term administration costs due to the high reliability of service provided by a cluster.* Because of the high availability provided by a cluster, you should see a reduced amount of time spent fixing server outages (and fewer late-night emergency calls).

■ *Decreased administration costs because of easier management tools.* Whereas servers that provide different resources (as in a warm spare situation) must be individually managed, a cluster can be centrally managed.

■ *Improved performance of applications that use a clustered back-end.* Although this is not guaranteed, careful load balancing between nodes can improve the performance, especially if your server provides non-SQL Server resources.

However, implementing a cluster has its drawbacks:

■ *Increased short-term administration costs.* Setting up a cluster can be a complicated task, so you should expect some extra work or required outsourcing up front.

■ *Additional training costs.* The people administering the cluster may need training before they can effectively manage the cluster.

Failover Versus Failback

MSCS also supports *failback,* in which a resource returns to its original owner when a node returns to service.

Future releases of MSCS may also provide a transparent failover, in which clients are totally unaware that any failure has taken place.

- *Increased software costs.* MSCS clustering requires the Enterprise Editions of NT and SQL Server, which cost more than their nonenterprise counterparts. In addition, Microsoft's licensing requirements require that you have a license for each operating system and application for each node in a cluster. Other non-MSCS solutions tend to be expensive as well.

- *Additional hardware costs.* Although MSCS is designed to run on standard equipment (with a few constraints on the technology you can choose), you can expect to pay more for the hardware used in a cluster. A notable example of where you will spend more money is in the shared external SCSI disk and fault-tolerant SCSI controller. Non-MSCS clustering technologies may require proprietary (and often expensive) hardware.

- *Additional software maintenance costs.* Different service packs are required for clustered servers and applications, and they may be more difficult to install.

- *The shared drive array of a cluster, even if it's fault-tolerant,* can still be a single point of failure if a hardware problem crops up in the power supply or SCSI bus.

- *Clusters do not address problems resulting from database corruption,* so clusters cannot replace regularly scheduled backups.

- *Clusters do not typically address the problem of physically distributing servers in the case of a natural disaster.*

When you are choosing between a clustered and a nonclustered solution, you need to seriously consider the following:

- *Do I really need the nearly perfect uptime provided by a cluster?* In other words, consider whether providing redundant hardware and performing scheduled maintenance is sufficient for most systems. Clusters shine when it comes to providing the uptime needed by banking systems, credit card processing, and other systems in which any downtime—even the downtime needed for regular maintenance—is unacceptable.

- *Do I need the ability to perform load balancing for cluster resources?* If the services provided by a cluster are subject to spikes in activity, you can offset the performance problems caused by such spikes by balancing the workload between nodes. (Of course, this won't be totally convenient until more PC clustering solutions provide automatic load balancing, but the technology is evolving to support that need.)

And remember, clustering is not a replacement for other good server administration practices, such as performing regular backups and ensuring the availability of offsite copies of mission-critical data.

Have you decided to use clustering? If so, read on. The next section covers the basics of using SQL Server 7.0 in a clustered environment.

SQL Server on a Cluster Server

SQL Server is an excellent candidate for a clustered solution. This section covers the general steps you must take to implement SQL Server on a cluster. Because Microsoft's clustering technology and SQL Server's support for this technology are constantly changing, and because implementing a cluster is a technically challenging task, refer to the SQL Server and Windows NT documentation for specific information on implementing SQL Server in a clustered situation.

To implement SQL Server on a two-node cluster, follow these steps:

1. Acquire the hardware needed for the cluster. Be sure to verify that the hardware you purchase is on the MSCS hardware compatibility list, which differs from both the NT Server and the NT Server/E lists. The basic requirements are two servers with the following configuration:

   ■ Pentium 90 processor or faster.

   ■ At least 64MB of RAM and 500MB of disk space.

   ■ SCSI disk controller that uses the PCI bus. If your system partitions on each node will use SCSI disks, this controller will have to support more than one SCSI channel. The shared SCSI disk must reside on a different SCSI channel than do the system disks. If you will be using IDE-type drives for the system disks, you will need IDE controllers as well.

   ■ Two network cards per node. One network card will be used for the cluster backbone; the other will be used for access to the external network. The networks must use the TCP/IP protocol.

   ■ The nodes can be of different hardware configurations, but both must be of the same platform (Intel or Alpha).

2. Install Windows NT Server/Enterprise Edition on the system drive of both nodes. Remember that you will need a licensed copy of NTS/E for each node.

3. Set up the NT cluster as outlined in the NTS/E documentation.

4. Install SQL Server/Enterprise Edition on the shared SCSI disk, making sure that all data files reside on this disk as well. SQL/E is cluster-aware, but be sure you carefully follow the instructions for installing the software. Also, remember that you will need two separate SQL licenses, one for each node.

Using a SCSI Shared Disk

Be sure to terminate the SCSI chain externally. Otherwise, the SCSI chain may not be terminated if a node loses power.

Installation Tip

Pause the other node of the cluster while you install SQL/E. This ensures that if the installation fails, the cluster will not attempt to failover the incomplete installation of SQL Server.

5. At this point, the cluster should be ready to use. For load-balancing purposes, you can define two different virtual SQL Servers and assign each to a node on the cluster.

The next release of SQL Server after 7.0 is slated to have automatic load balancing between nodes of a cluster. Until then, you can manually balance the load by creating a virtual SQL Server on each node. Each node has a copy of its own system databases and user databases, and each node acts as a failover backup for the other. Clients connect to the servers through different NetBIOS names, which the cluster redirects in the event of a failure. Virtual servers can also be used to distribute very large databases, and distributed transactions can keep each portion of the database consistent as needed.

Conclusions

This chapter covered three technologies for ensuring high availability. Redundant hardware, the first option, uses proven technology to provide a high level of availability. For that next extra step, you can also choose to build a warm spare setup, which will provide a minimal data loss/high availability solution. For as close-to-perfect recall as is available, use a cluster server, which provides quick and automatic failover in the case of a hardware or software failure.

The best solution for high availability is probably a combination of the three technologies. Use a cluster as the primary server in a warm spare setup. This is expensive, but it provides the high availability, the quick and automatic failover of a cluster, and the ability to physically separate two copies of the data (storing one in another building) to prevent loss due to natural disasters. By combining these technologies with the redundant hardware that's already built in to most servers, you attain a lot of insurance against data loss.

11

Performance Tuning and Optimization

Sean Baird

O NE OF THE HOTTEST TOPICS IN the SQL Server world for some time has been the question of "How do we get it to go faster?" Many companies have implemented an information system with SQL Server on the back end, only to find that they are unhappy with its performance. On the other hand, many other companies have been very pleased with the product's performance. So what's the difference between the two? Did the second set of companies hire high-priced consultants to change a few settings on their servers to eke the most performance from them?

The answer is usually "no." Basically, by luck or by education, these companies made design decisions that yielded the best performance.

Notice that phrase "design decisions." Performance Tuning and Optimization (PT&O) is somewhat of a misnomer because most performance problems with a SQL Server are not solved by tuning or optimizing the server itself. Rather, the biggest performance improvements are often accomplished by correcting problems in the database or application design or by optimizing queries sent to the server by an application.

Most often, the server is set up correctly or in such a way that server performance bottlenecks are minimal. Clients are often surprised and disappointed when, after a quick look at their server, a consultant points out several deficiencies in their database or application. After all, they usually have invested a lot of time and energy in that particular design.

The purpose of this chapter is twofold. First, it provides the information you need to make good design decisions so that your applications perform well from day one. Second, it serves as a troubleshooting guide for fixing performance problems in your existing applications. This chapter addresses the most common and effective optimization strategies, as well as examples of common problems—in the hopes that you can avoid them.

The following main topics are covered:

- How to Best Use This Chapter
- PT&O Theory
- Tools for Monitoring SQL Server and Windows NT
- Tracking Down a Performance Problem
- Application Optimization Strategies
- Server Optimization Strategies

How to Best Use This Chapter

If you are relatively new to the concept of performance tuning, try reading the chapter straight through. It begins with an overview of PT&O concepts, followed by an introduction to the tools used to diagnose performance problems. Following that are some specific troubleshooting and optimization strategies.

Reading the chapter straight through is also a good approach to take if you are starting to build a new application and want an overview of the performance issues surrounding client/server applications. Pay special attention to the section "Application Optimization Strategies."

If, however, you already feel comfortable with PT&O concepts and want to start diagnosing a performance problem immediately, skip to the section "Tracking Down a Performance Problem." After you find the general problem area, skip to the specific section that addresses that problem for tips on how to correct it.

PT&O Theory

Before jumping into specific strategies for tuning, take a look at some of the issues surrounding PT&O. Understanding the problems you face will help you better apply the strategies presented later in the chapter.

What Are the Goals of Performance Tuning?

At first, asking about the goals of performance tuning may seem like a silly question. After all, isn't the main goal to improve performance? Definitely, but the factors that contribute to the performance of an application are not always understood. Typically, the performance of an application is measured by three benchmarks:

- *Response time.* How quickly does the system respond to queries? Sometimes more importantly, what is the user's *perceived* response time?

- *Throughput.* How many queries or transactions can the system handle in a given period of time?

- *Resource usage.* How much of the processor, memory, disk, and network does the application use while achieving a given response time and throughput?

Performance tuning aims to minimize response time and maximize throughput, all while using the server and network resources as efficiently as possible.

Note the mention of perceived response time in the list. If your users perceive the system to be slow, you'll probably receive complaints regardless of the actual performance of the system. For instance, if a query that fills a data grid in an application runs quickly but the grid itself takes a long time to fill, you still have a performance problem, at least according to the user.

When optimizing and tuning a system, be aware of this fundamental truth: Performance bottlenecks will *always* exist, and fixing one bottleneck will always uncover another. Before tackling a performance problem, be sure to weigh the costs of fixing the problem against the performance improvements to be gained. For example, spending several days on a project to reduce the runtime of a query by a few seconds is probably not an effective use of your time—unless, of course, that query is frequently executed. By the same token, it may not be worthwhile to spend even a few hours optimizing a query that is run very infrequently, even if the performance improvement is great.

What Can You Tune?

Now that you understand what you're trying to accomplish, it's important to know what you can control. Client/server applications tend to be significantly more complicated than, say, desktop database applications. Consider all of the following factors that can affect the performance of your client/server application:

- *Database design.* The logical and physical design of the database tables and indexes can have a significant impact on performance. See the section "Database and Index Design," later in this chapter.

- *Application design.* How the application program interacts with the database affects performance. Poorly designed applications can quickly bog down the database server. For more information on designing good OLTP and OLAP applications, see the section "Application Design."

- *Query design and optimization.* Even with a well-designed database and a well-behaved client application, a few poorly performing queries can kill performance. The section "Query Design and Optimization" offers more information on finding and optimizing slow queries.

- *Server hardware.* The hardware used on your database server does have an impact on the performance of a client/server application. See "Choosing the Right Hardware for Your Server."

- *Server configuration.* Some configuration settings in NT and SQL Server can affect the performance of an application. The section "SQL Server Configuration" addresses this issue. In addition, Microsoft has two different versions of SQL Server available that address larger and smaller applications. See the section "Choosing the Right Flavor of SQL Server" for more information on this topic.

These factors are listed in the order of how they typically impact performance for a database application. Of course, there are exceptions to every rule, but for most performance problems, the first three factors impact performance the most.

Note that this idea defies the prevalent view that tuning and optimization are solely the database administrator's job. In fact, creating an optimized client/server system is as much the responsibility of the software developers as it is of the DBAs.

The Three Types of Database Applications

As you're probably aware, not all database applications are created equal. Each application is different, but for the purposes of our discussion, an application can be classified as one of the following:

- Online Transaction Processing (OLTP) application

- Online Analytical Processing (OLAP) application

- Batch processing application

Each application type has its own special tuning and optimization needs. These needs are discussed later in the chapter, but it is helpful to know the characteristics of each type of application.

OLTP applications generally consist of applications that support a large number of concurrent users adding and updating information on a regular basis. Examples include order processing, helpdesk, and customer support applications. Users expect fast response times and high availability from the system. Queries to find information are often simple and predictable, such as looking up a customer record or finding a product's inventory information. The performance of an OLTP system is generally evaluated by how quickly the users can modify data and the number of users the application can support.

OLAP applications, also referred to as decision support systems (DSS) or data warehousing systems, are quite different from OLTP systems. OLAP systems are used primarily for reporting and ad hoc queries, such as answering questions such as "what were the sales in the Midwest region compared to other regions over the past five years?" OLAP queries often use aggregation (totals, averages, and so on) and return larger amounts of data than do OLTP queries. In addition, OLAP systems usually have a smaller number of concurrent users, and slower response times and lower availability are often acceptable. OLAP systems that provide ad hoc query support are also prone to some downtime, because poorly formed queries can reduce system performance and, in some extreme cases, cause the database server to become totally unresponsive. The performance of an OLAP system is generally evaluated by how quickly users can retrieve the information they need.

Batch processing applications are characterized by large imports or exports of data to or from the database, by the processing of large numbers of database records, or by both. Examples include bulk loads of data from a mainframe or other database and updates to calculated values in a database. Batch processing is usually not multiuser, because large portions of the database are often locked at a given time to preserve the database consistency. In addition, the processing frequently occurs during scheduled downtime or periods of low database activity. The performance of a batch application is generally evaluated by which one can process the largest amount of information in the shortest amount of time.

All three types of applications are candidates for PT&O, but the strategies used to improve performance are often quite different, as you will see later in the chapter. Except for smaller database systems, OLTP and OLAP functions are generally provided on different servers. Batch processing may take place for both OLTP and OLAP systems, though it is more common with OLAP.

Tools for Monitoring SQL Server and Windows NT

One of the most challenging problems you'll face when optimizing and tuning a database system is finding out exactly where the performance problem lies. Fortunately, the tools at your disposal have been greatly improved in SQL 7. This section introduces you to the two main tools you'll use to find application problems: the SQL Server Profiler and the Query Analyzer. In addition, this section shows you your main tool for diagnosing server bottlenecks: NT Performance Monitor.

This portion of the chapter is meant only to give you an introduction to these three monitoring tools and how they are used for performance tuning. For more in-depth instructions on their use, see the SQL Server Books Online and Windows NT documentation.

SQL Server Profiler

The SQL Server Profiler application has evolved over time, starting with SQL Eye, an unsupported trace application available in the days of SQL 4.21. Version 6.5 introduced a more polished version of this application in the form of SQL Trace. SQL 7 presents the most refined version yet. Not only does SQL Profiler allow you to view SQL query statements and execution times like its predecessors, but it gives you an insider's view into almost all of the activity taking place on a SQL Server (see Figure 11.1).

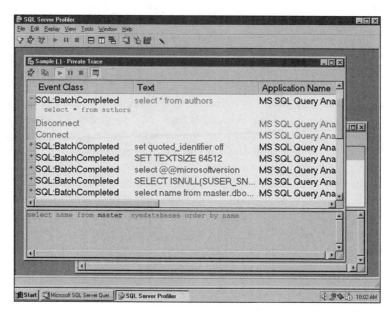

Figure 11.1   The SQL Server Profiler application is a useful tool for monitoring a SQL Server and identifying performance problems.

SQL Profiler allows you to create and monitor one or more traces on a local or remote SQL Server. Trace output can be sent directly to the screen, to a database table, or to a file.

SQL Server Query Analyzer

When you wanted to execute an ad hoc query against the database in version 6.5, you had a choice between ISQL/w and the query window in Enterprise Manager. Both of those options have been removed and consolidated into the Query Analyzer application in SQL 7 (see Figure 11.2).

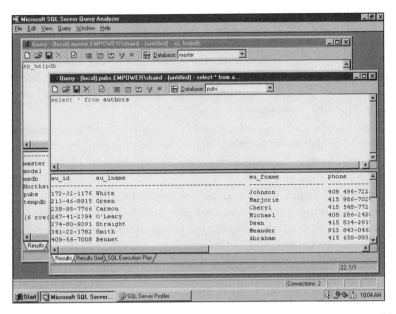

Figure 11.2   The SQL Server Query Analyzer provides a convenient way to issue ad hoc queries and identify performance problems in queries.

The Query Analyzer is similar in form to the older query applications, with a few notable enhancements:

- *Multiple query windows.* Different queries now show up in different child windows, using the Windows Multiple Document Interface (MDI) standard.

- *Color-coded query text.* SQL Script text is now color-coded, in much the same way source code is colored in most programming environments. Keywords, operators, and comments are shown in different colors for easier reading.

- *Four execution options.* Query Analyzer now allows you to output the results of the query in the standard format or in a grid. You may also produce a graphical representation of the query plan by clicking on the Display Execution Plan button. Finally, clicking on the Run Query Analysis button runs the Query Analyzer, which will execute your query and make suggestions on indexes that need to be added or changed.

Using the Query Analyzer is easy. You type your SQL query into the query window (or load it from a text file) and then click on the appropriate execution button to get the results you want. The keyboard shortcuts Alt+X and Ctrl+E still operate as they did in the SQL 6.5 tools: They execute the query and show the results in the standard format (respectively).

Performance Monitor

Performance Monitor is an application that ships with Windows NT that provides several monitoring features. The two most important from a tuning standpoint are the chart feature and the logging feature. Both allow you to monitor one or more *counters*. A counter is the fundamental unit of monitoring in Performance Monitor and is defined by three basic components:

- *Object.* Each major component of an NT Server is defined as an object in Performance Monitor. Notable examples are the processor, disk, network, and memory. In addition, SQL Server defines several additional objects for monitoring.

- *Counter.* Each object defines counters, or specific information that can be monitored for that object. For instance, the processor object defines counters such as %Processor Time, which shows the percentage of time the processor spends performing nonidle work, and %Privileged Time, which shows the percentage of time the processor spends working on system-related tasks (such as handling I/O or network requests).

- *Instance.* When applicable, a counter can provide specific instances for monitoring. In a multiple-processor system, the %Processor Time counter can be examined for each processor.

The chart view displays one or more counters in real-time. The specified counters are sampled at a user-definable interval and displayed on a graph. Changing the interval is useful because a shorter interval can show you immediate changes as they take place, whereas longer intervals are useful for showing trends.

The logging feature periodically samples all counters for a set of specified objects and then saves the information to a file for later analysis. The saved file can be used as the source of data for a chart. Logging server activity over the course of a day or several days is useful in analyzing trends.

Tracking Down a Performance Problem

Finding where the performance problem is in an application can often be a difficult task in and of itself. Usually, the best steps to follow are these:

1. First, verify that the problem is actually with the client/server application. Rule out workstation-specific problems by trying the application on another workstation. Rule out network problems by verifying good connectivity, examining a

---

Highlight a Performance Monitor Chart Line for Easy Identification

While in chart view, you can press Ctrl+H to highlight the current counter in white. This highlighting helps you focus on a single counter when you're looking at a cluttered chart.

network trace, or even running the application on the server itself (if practicable).

2. Verify that the database design is appropriate to the type of application. Read the sections "The Three Types of Database Applications," "Application Design," and "Database and Index Design" for more information.

3. Attempt to trace the problem to one or more queries that are performing poorly. See the next section, "Isolating Slow Queries," for information on how to find bad queries. Then use the tips in the section "Query Design and Optimization" to tune the query or queries.

4. If the performance of the application is still poor after you work on suspect queries, perhaps the issue lies with the server hardware or software configuration. Read the section "Diagnosing Server Bottlenecks" for help identifying these issues. Then read the appropriate subsections within the section "Server Optimization Strategies" for help resolving the bottlenecks.

5. Have the software developers attempt to diagnose the problem. Keep in mind that poor application performance could also be a result of poor client application design, as discussed briefly in the section "What Are the Goals of Performance Tuning?"

If, after following the preceding steps, you are unable to locate the cause of the performance problem, consider using an outside source, such as Microsoft Technical Support, for help diagnosing the problem.

Isolating Slow Queries

Even with a good database and application design, slow queries still happen. Although the SQL Server query optimizer attempts to use the best possible query plan, it can become confused when queries are complicated.

If you are diagnosing a problem with an application that was written in-house, finding the problem query or queries should not be too difficult. Simply have a developer supply the queries for analysis. Alternatively, you can use the SQL Profiler utility (described earlier in this chapter in the section "SQL Server Profiler") to look for slow-running queries while the application is running. SQL Profiler is also useful for tracking down slow-running queries in a third-party application.

After you find the problem query, start the SQL Query Analyzer application so you can execute the query independently of the application. Run the query from the Query Analyzer to ensure that the query is actually at fault and not the application.

If the query is running acceptably from the Query Analyzer, the problem is probably in the application program. Although this is usually not the case, problems with ODBC, DB-Lib, OLEDB, or the application itself can cause performance problems. For example, the ODBC SQL Server driver gives you the option of transparently wrapping each query in a stored procedure. Although this can marginally improve performance for queries executed multiple times, the profusion of ODBC stored procedures (stored in TempDB) can consume extra server resources and bog down a server.

If the query runs slowly even from the Query Analyzer, try to isolate the problem further. If the query is in a view or stored procedure, remove it to determine whether the problem is in how the optimizer handles the view or stored procedure. Remove any triggers from the table to ensure that the performance problem is actually in the query, not the trigger. The key is to determine where the problem actually lies. (Again, the problem is usually in the query, but you want to eliminate other variables to make sure that is the case.)

Having isolated the problem (be it the query, view, stored procedure, or trigger), you can further diagnose the problem with the Query Analyzer. See the section "Query Design and Optimization" for tips.

Diagnosing Server Bottlenecks

After you determine that slow queries are using the best possible query plans, you're ready to take a look at how the server resources are affecting application performance. Even the best-formed queries can be slowed down by a server bottleneck.

Recall that the four basic server resources are processor (CPU), memory, disk, and network. The most likely bottlenecks for a database application are CPU, memory, and disk. Network bottlenecks seldom occur unless there is a lot of network traffic, or unless the server on which the database resides is providing services other than SQL Server (if it's file serving, for example).

When diagnosing server bottlenecks, remember that it is best to gather data over an extended period of time. If possible, log the performance counters you are interested in over the course of one or more days.

CPU bottlenecks often occur if a query performs many joins or if aggregate or other functions are used. In addition, inefficient queries that perform a lot of physical I/O can bog down the processor with I/O requests. To determine whether a CPU bottleneck exists, follow these steps:

1. Using Performance Monitor, examine the Processor: % Processor Time counter for each processor on the system. Values consistently over 80% may indicate a bottleneck.

2. If it seems that a bottleneck exists, examine the Process: % Processor Time counter for the SQL Server Process. Also, examine the Process: % Privileged Time and Process: % User Time counters.

3. If SQL Server is generating the processing activity and the % Privileged Time counter is above 20%, the CPU is servicing many I/O requests from SQL Server. This condition usually means that either one or more queries are running inefficiently or SQL Server does not have enough memory to adequately fill its cache. Heavy nonprivileged SQL Server processor usage can usually be traced back to a query or queries that heavily use aggregation or that perform inefficient joins.

4. If SQL Server is not generating the processing activity, other processes on the server may be generating the activity. Examine the other Process: % Processor Time counters to determine whether other processes on the server are consuming CPU time.

5. When you have located the likely cause of the processor usage, consult the section "Server Optimization Strategies" for tuning tips.

Disk bottlenecks can occur because of problems in the database or index design, a shortage of memory, or a problem with the disk controller or disk drives.

To determine whether a disk bottleneck exists, follow these steps:

1. Examine the Processor: % Processor Time counter for each processor on the system. Examine the Logical Disk: % Disk Time counter for each drive defined on the system that is used by SQL Server. If processor time is consistently low to medium (say, 0–50%) and disk time is high (say, 80–100%), a disk bottleneck is likely.

2. If it seems that a bottleneck exists, check the Logical Disk: Current Disk Queue Length counter for each logical drive used by SQL Server. Values over 2 usually indicate that the disks cannot service I/O requests quickly enough and that the disk subsystem is a bottleneck.

3. If the disk system appears to be a bottleneck, be sure to check the memory counters (see the next paragraph) to ensure that NT and SQL Server have enough memory to run. A memory bottleneck can cause excessive paging and/or excessive physical reads from SQL Server, both of which will impact disk performance.

4. See the section "Server Optimization Strategies" for tips on improving disk performance.

You can generally diagnose memory bottlenecks by following these steps:

1. Examine the SQL Server: Cache Hit Ratio counter. If it is consistently below 80 percent, SQL Server is starved for memory and cannot maintain an adequate cache size.

2. Examine the Memory: Pages/Sec. counter. If this counter stays high over an extended period of time, one or more applications (or NT itself) are starved for memory.

Disk Counters Must Be Enabled

To use the LogicalDisk and PhysicalDisk counters in Performance Monitor, you need to turn on NT disk performance monitoring. From a command prompt, execute the command `diskperf -y`, and then reboot the server.

If you want to monitor individual physical disks in a stripe set, you need to execute the command `diskperf -ye` and reboot the server.

3. If the SQL Server: I/O-Page Reads/Sec. counter remains at a high value for extended periods of time (spikes are normal), SQL Server might need more operating memory.

Application Optimization Strategies

Assuming the server hardware is sufficient to run your database, your best chance for significant performance improvements comes from correcting deficiencies in your application and database design. The next few sections give detailed optimization strategies for each of these areas.

Database and Index Design

Starting with a good database design is like making sure the foundation of a house is sound before building the house. If your database design is poor, anything you build on it (namely, your applications) will probably perform poorly. So what constitutes a good database design? Really, the answer is twofold: A good database has both good *structure* and good *indexing*. Let's start with structure.

Normalizing for Performance

For most OLTP and general-purpose databases, the database should be normalized to third-normal form. The biggest reason for normalizing is to maintain data consistency by eliminating redundant data. Normalizing also has the side effect of "slimming down" tables—that is, reducing the number of columns in each table. Also, the number of tables usually increases after normalization. These side effects enable you to reap performance improvements.

Numerous narrow tables are good for a variety of reasons. Consider these facts:

- Narrow tables have smaller row sizes, which means more rows fit on a page, which means SQL Server can read more rows from disk faster.

- Narrower tables tend to have fewer composite (multicolumn) indexes than wider tables do. SQL Server can use narrower indexes more efficiently.

- Narrower tables tend to have fewer indexes than wider tables. Reducing the number of indexes on a table improves the performance of data modifications because SQL Server uses less overhead maintaining the indexes.

- More tables mean more opportunities for indexing. With a limit of one clustered index per table, this especially means more opportunities for clustered indexes.

Database Design Is a Developer Topic

A full discussion on database design (for both OLTP and OLAP) is outside the scope of this book.

■ Adding more tables can improve concurrency because multiple users may be less likely to interfere with one another.

One negative effect of normalization is the need to perform joins between tables that contain related data. However, SQL Server has always been reasonably good at processing joins, and several features new in the 7.0 query processor improve the performance of joins. Even with the improved join processing, excessively normalizing a database can still cause performance problems due to table joins and lower concurrency due to multiple tables being locked in a transaction. A good rule of thumb is to normalize to third-normal form and then denormalize specific trouble spots.

Designing a database for analytical (OLAP) applications is a different matter. The needs of OLAP applications differ from the needs of OLTP applications (see the section "The Three Types of Database Applications," earlier in this chapter). Therefore, OLAP databases may break some of the traditional database design rules in these ways:

■ Denormalizing certain tables to reduce joins and improve performance, especially for large result sets.

■ Storing preaggregated data or derived data in the database.

■ Storing data in a star or snowflake schema for use by a data warehousing tool.

Indexing for Performance

A good database design alone does not ensure good performance. The other component of a good database design is a database's indexes. Unlike the table design for a database, indexes can be easily changed without affecting the database's structure or data. For this reason, it pays to experiment with different indexes.

One question often arises in this discussion: "Why not index every column?" Well, SQL Server will use an index only if the *cost* of using that index (in terms of I/O) is less than the cost of scanning through the table to find a record or records. Hence, SQL Server may never use some indexes. Indexes also consume space in a database and slow data modifications. For these reasons, it pays not to over-index.

Fortunately, initially choosing what to index is not difficult. Here are some rules of thumb for choosing which columns to index:

■ Index primary keys and foreign keys. Because these fields are typically used for joins, indexing them can often improve the performance of queries that join tables.

■ Index columns that are often used in the WHERE clause of queries. The query optimizer will use these indexes as appropriate to limit the size of the result set pulled from a table, which improves query performance.

■ Indexes with fewer columns are generally better than indexes with many columns. This is because SQL Server can fit more index rows on a page for a narrow index, which improves I/O performance. Generally, you should create only composite indexes when one or more columns are searched together as a unit or when a composite index can be used for a *covered* query.

- In a covered query, all columns returned by the query are contained in the index. In this situation, SQL Server does not actually need to touch the data page containing the row; all the information returned resides on the index pages. These types of queries, when used properly, can yield terrific performance. Just be sure to empirically test the performance of the covered query and make sure that the space consumed by the index is worth the extra performance.

- Index columns that are used to sort or group data in the table. Because an index logically orders (or physically orders, in the case of a clustered index) the rows in a table, such an index can dramatically improve the performance of a sort, grouping, or aggregation.

When creating an index, you have the choice between creating a clustered and a nonclustered index. Clustered indexes work best for retrieving rows based on a range of values in the index and for sorting and grouping on the index columns. This is because the data rows are physically ordered by the index key, which results in very fast I/O anytime a contiguous range of rows must be retrieved. Remember, too, that you are limited to one clustered index per table. So choose carefully based on how you think data in the table will be accessed.

Indexes work best when data in the key is selective. For example, if you were to index a table containing a listing of Kansas City residents, indexing on last name would probably be a good idea. Even for a common name like "Jones," the number of rows returned (say 25,000) would be small in comparison to the total number of rows in the table (say, 1.3 million). The selectivity in this example is around 2%: Finding all people with the surname "Jones" returns only about 2% of the table rows.

On the other hand, indexing on a column that is not very unique (such as gender) is useless to SQL Server. If you assume that Kansas City's distribution of women and men is roughly equal, about half the table's rows would be returned if SQL Server tried to narrow its search with the index on gender. In this case, SQL Server will ignore the index, and space in the database will be wasted.

Choosing a Good Clustered Primary Key

By default, a clustered index is created on a primary key defined with the PRIMARY KEY constraint. When the primary key monotonically increases (as it does when an IDENTITY column is used), a clustered index is better used elsewhere. In this case, you can specify that the primary key should use a nonclustered index with the PRIMARY KEY NONCLUSTERED syntax for the constraint.

Another consideration for choosing a clustered primary key is that it should be as small as possible. The reason for this is an architectural change that was introduced in SQL Server 7.0. If a clustered primary key exists on a table, SQL Server uses this index as the row pointer in other nonclustered indexes on the table. In effect, SQL Server searches through the nonclustered index pages first and then searches through the clustered index pages to find rows. Having a very wide clustered primary key on a table can slow index searches with the nonclustered indexes as well.

After you've built indexes on a database, you can use the new Index Tuning Wizard to fine-tune those indexes. The Tuning Wizard uses the SQL Profiler to collect performance information on queries run against a database. Based on the information it collects, the wizard then suggests changes to the current indexing scheme for the database. Hopefully, if you've followed the guidelines presented here, the Index Tuning Wizard won't have much to suggest.

Now that you've looked at how your database design can affect performance, you can move on to the topic of application design and how it affects performance.

Application Design

Application design, next to database design, is the biggest contributor to the performance of a client/server application. Why? In the case of a database application, the client has much more control over the server than the server has over the client. Clients, for the most part, are free to submit any sort of queries they want, control how long transactions stay open, and dictate how many query results are returned. The queries processed by the database server then dictate how the server will perform.

The trick, then, is to design applications so they do not "misbehave" and place an undue load on the server. OLTP, OLAP, and batch applications often have different needs and goals, so each application type has different guidelines for what constitutes a good application design. Let's begin with OLTP applications.

Because OLTP applications must support a large number of concurrent users with fast response times, it's important to keep application interaction with the database to a minimum:

- *Pool user connections when possible.* A single-user connection in SQL 7.0 requires about 40KB of server overhead memory. Add 1,000 users, and that quickly becomes 40 megabytes of memory required to maintain those connections! OLTP users rarely need all the "bandwidth" supplied by a connection; in a well-designed OLTP application, connection utilization is fairly low. For this reason, using a single connection for multiple users is both practical and desirable.

  Connection pooling can be implemented in a variety of ways. ODBC 3.x supports connection pooling, so applications using ODBC for data access can take advantage of this feature. Internet Information Server (IIS) also supports connection pooling, as does Microsoft Transaction Server (MTS).

- *Keep result sets small.* OLTP applications rarely need to pull back thousands of rows of data. For that matter, these types of applications rarely need to use all the columns in a table. Queries built with SELECT * and poorly selective WHERE clauses consume unnecessary server processing time and network bandwidth. A much better choice is to use syntax like SELECT column1, column2, column3. The key here is to think like you're eating at a buffet: "Take only what you will eat, and eat all you take."

- *Keep transactions short.* Transactions lock other users out of modifying the database, so you want to keep transactions as short as possible to maintain the best possible concurrency. User interaction should almost never be required to complete or roll back a transaction. What would happen if a user left a transaction open over his or her lunch break?

- *Use stored procedures.* Using stored procedures to encapsulate an application's query processing is a good application design practice. From a performance standpoint, stored procedures are good for two reasons. First, because they are precompiled, you get a small performance boost because you save SQL Server the time and effort required to compile the query. Second, you save some network bandwidth; instead of sending large query strings over the network, you send a single execute statement. Encapsulating business logic on the server—by way of stored procedures or their close cousin, triggers—can also reduce network usage.

- *Gracefully handle timeouts.* To prevent runaway queries, keep the query timeout short for each client, or use a systemwide query timeout with SQL Server's query governor cost limit option. Because a query could time out before it's complete, the application must be able to detect this condition and retry if needed.

- *Gracefully handle deadlocks.* Deadlocks can occur if two connections are holding resources that the other needs. SQL Server contains deadlock detection and resolution routines, and it will terminate a client query to eliminate a deadlock. In this situation, the client must not only handle the query termination but should retry the query after a random interval. The random interval should prevent recurring deadlocks.

- *Do not mix OLTP and OLAP queries.* OLTP and OLAP queries are fundamentally different in nature. Because OLAP queries often require more indexing, additional indexes can slow any data modifications made by OLTP queries. In addition, the additional resources required by OLAP queries can bog down a server that is processing transactions.

  In cases where OLTP and OLAP queries must be performed against the same database, it can be beneficial to schedule OLAP queries for periods of lower activity and then create and drop OLAP indexes on an as-needed basis.

For OLAP applications, a smaller number of users are often supported, and slower response times are allowable. There are fewer rules of thumb for designing a good OLAP application, but they do exist:

- *Minimize ad hoc queries.* If possible, tune the database indexes to support a number of predefined reports. This ensures that the server can most efficiently process those queries, which leaves processing power for others.

■ *Denormalize for performance.* Because OLAP databases often have few to no updates, normalization for data integrity is often not needed to the extent it is in OLTP databases. Normalized databases require more joins, and because joins can cause performance problems, especially with OLAP queries, denormalizing an OLAP database can improve performance without causing the usual negative side effects of denormalization.

■ *Use preaggregation.* Data warehousing tools, like the Microsoft OLAP Services that ships with SQL Server 7.0, can intelligently preprocess OLAP data to minimize query processing time.

■ *Use read-only databases.* Prevent users from making modifications to the database, and use the no-lock optimizer hint in queries to prevent SQL Server from holding locks when processing the query. Preventing SQL Server from locking the database can significantly reduce the overhead needed to process the query.

■ *Enforce query timeouts.* As with OLTP applications, enforce a per-client query timeout or a systemwide timeout with the query governor cost limit option. These settings will prevent runaway queries from overburdening the server.

■ *Do not mix OLTP and OLAP queries.* For the same reasons listed previously in the OLTP section, mixing OLTP and OLAP queries is rarely a good idea.

Recall that batch processing typically imports or exports large amounts of data, or creates and modifies large amounts of data, or both. For these reasons, batch applications have a few guidelines of their own:

■ *Use bulk-copy instead of row-by-row transfers.* SQL Server provides a number of ways for you to quickly load large amounts of data into a database. Often, bulkloading data is thousands of times more efficient than inserting it row-by-row into a database. For more information on loading data, see Chapter 8.

■ *Use set processing rather than iterative processing.* SQL Server is optimized for processing large sets of data quickly. For this reason, you should strive to do as much data processing with queries instead of cursors (both client-side and server-side). Finding a set processing solution to an iterative problem can often improve performance by an order of magnitude.

■ *Isolate batch processing in a separate database when appropriate.* If a batch process (such as a data load from a mainframe) involves heavy data scrubbing, isolating that process in a separate database allows you to maintain good concurrency in the production database. In addition, isolating the process allows you to keep the production transaction log from filling up.

■ *Isolate batch processing from other applications.* Batch processes may run queries to update data that bog down the server and lock large portions of the affected database. If this is the case, consider running the batch process during off-peak hours or scheduled downtime.

Now that you know application optimization in a general sense, turn your focus to how to write efficient queries, which are the backbone of any database application.

Query Design & Optimization

If you are following the general guidelines for optimizing your applications, the next thing to optimize are individual queries used by an application. Even the best applications usually have a few queries that run slowly. This section offers a few rules of thumb for writing efficient queries:

- *Minimize the size of result sets.*

  Large result sets require more I/O from the server, which can degrade performance. In addition, certain resource-intensive portions of a query (such as sorts, groups, and aggregates) work faster if you minimize the size of the data set.

- *Avoid using variables in the WHERE clause.*

  Using a WHERE clause such as "WHERE Column = 5" instead of "WHERE Column = @MyValue" allows SQL Server to use any indexes on that column more efficiently, because it knows the value it is searching for during query compilation instead of during the query execution.

- *Avoid using expressions in the WHERE clause.*

  Using string processing or other functions in the WHERE clause has basically the same effect as using a variable: SQL Server cannot evaluate the expression at compilation time. This causes SQL Server to perform additional processing and may result in a good index being ignored by the query processor.

- *Break complex queries into multiple queries and store intermediate results in temporary tables.*

The other important skill to master is the art of query optimization. The main tool you can use to optimize queries is the SHOWPLAN output provided by SQL Server on request. SHOWPLAN basically translates SQL Server's query plan into a human-readable text or graphical output. You can use SHOWPLAN output to identify bottlenecks in a query plan. Based on the results of the query analysis, you can restructure the query or add and change indexes to improve performance. Books Online has good coverage of how to read SHOWPLAN output.

At this point, you've learned about the three biggest contributors to a client/server application's performance: database design, application design, and query design. The discussion continues with a look at system-level configuration and how it affects performance.

Server Optimization Strategies

The remainder of the chapter focuses on optimization strategies for the server, including the hardware, operating system, and SQL Server itself. Remember that the strategies presented here will work best after you have applied the application and database optimization strategies presented in the previous sections. Most performance improvements gained by server optimization are modest compared to improvements gained from good application design.

Choosing the Right Hardware for Your Server

Adding or upgrading hardware can have mixed results; if your database application is optimized to the point where hardware is the bottleneck, upgrading your server often will improve the performance of the system significantly. On the other hand, throwing hardware at a problem with your fundamental database design probably will not work.

When choosing hardware for your server, you want to keep two goals in mind. First, the server should use the most efficient hardware you can afford. (For example, if you can afford a server that uses SCSI drives, don't buy a server with older IDE technology because the SCSI drives have better throughput.) Second, choose a server that has room to expand—especially a server that allows you to add additional processors and memory. Choosing an expandable server allows your server to grow along with your growing computing needs.

The following are a few guidelines for choosing server hardware:

- *Processor.* Buy the fastest processor you can, and then upgrade to multiple processors if necessary. (Again, you will need to choose a server that leaves room to add more processors.) Adding additional processors does cause NT and other SMP applications to incur additional processing overhead. Also, be sure to choose a processor that supports a second-level cache; a faster processor without a cache will suffer performance problems because it will have to wait on data from RAM.

- *Memory.* Buy a moderate amount of memory to begin with, and then add additional memory if the system requires it (see "Diagnosing Server Bottlenecks" earlier in this chapter). If possible, purchase a server that supports the more efficient EDO (extended data out) RAM or synchronous DRAM. Again, be sure to leave yourself room to expand by purchasing high-density memory and leaving memory slots open.

- *Disk.* SCSI technology is generally better than IDE for several reasons. First, most SCSI disk systems support faster data transfer rates. SCSI technology also provides better support for multiple drives. Also, look for disks with faster seek times and rotational speeds, which improve throughput.

- *Network.* Choose a bus-mastering network card, if possible. This type of card reduces the number of network interrupts that must be handled by the CPU.

Of course, these are just general guidelines. It isn't always possible to choose the perfect server. However, the two areas where you should not skimp are the disk subsystem and memory.

NT Server Configuration

There isn't much you can do to directly improve a SQL Server's performance by tuning the NT Server itself, but here are a few tips on improving performance, especially for larger databases:

- In the Network Control Panel applet, under the properties for the Server service, you can optimize the service for network applications (as opposed to file sharing). This tunes the NT network subsystem to better work with the network access used by SQL Server.

- Disable unneeded services on the SQL Server and ensure that the server is not a domain controller (primary or backup).

- Offload other services, such as file and print sharing, to other servers. These services consume system resources that could be used by SQL Server.

SQL Server Configuration

SQL Server 7.0, unlike prior versions of this product, was designed to be largely self-tuning. In other words, it will adjust its resource usage based on the current load placed on the server. In this release, the following resources are self-tuned by SQL Server:

- *Disk space.* Database files now automatically grow and shrink depending on the amount of data in the database. For more information, see Chapter 4.

- *Memory.* SQL Server will adjust its memory usage based on its current load and the amount of available memory on the system. SQL Server will attempt to maintain a minimum of 5MB of free physical memory on the server.

- *Locks.* SQL Server now allocates a pool of available locks based on roughly 2 percent of the memory allocated to SQL Server at startup. The pool of available locks grows and shrinks depending on the demand for locks in the databases on the server.

Be Cautious with Write-Back Caching Controllers

Write-back caching stores data to be written to disk in a cache, and data is written in larger chunks, which improves performance. However, write caching can pose problems for SQL Server. For the transaction log to function properly, SQL Server must be guaranteed that a transaction is written to disk. If a write cache is not flushed (say, due to a power outage), a database could become inconsistent.

All good controller cards that have write caching will have a battery backup that maintains the cache in the event of an unexpected shutdown. When the system returns, the cache is flushed to disk, and the write is guaranteed. Avoid write caching cards that do not have a backup, or disable the write-caching feature.

- ■ *User connections.* Connection objects are now allocated and deallocated as users connect to and disconnect from the server. The only upper limit to the number of open connections is the system-defined limit of 32,767 connections per server.

- ■ *Open objects.* SQL Server now allocates object handles (used anytime a table, stored procedure, or other database object is referenced) on an as-needed basis.

You may still manually set the configuration values for these settings, although Microsoft does not recommend that you do so. The great benefit of this auto-tuning is that SQL Server conserves system resources during periods of low activity. In prior versions of SQL Server, you would need to tune these settings to support the maximum workload the server experienced during the day. Now, you can let SQL Server manage its own resources.

In addition to the "big five" configuration settings listed previously, SQL Server now automatically tunes many other configuration settings. As a matter of fact, SQL Server 7.0 has about 20 fewer settings that you can adjust. Lock escalation and read-ahead behavior are two examples of configuration settings for which Microsoft has eliminated the need for fine-tuning. For a complete and detailed list of configuration settings, see the "Setting Configuration Options" topic in SQL Server Books Online.

One tuning option that remains in SQL Server 7.0 that you must use cautiously is the "Priority Boost" setting. Turning on this option increases the priority of the SQL Server process in the NT scheduler. While this setting can improve performance in some cases, it can also starve other processes of processor time. Consider using only Priority Boost with a dedicated SQL Server, and then monitor it closely to ensure that the operating system processes are not starved for CPU time.

Another tunable parameter that may be worth investigating is the "max asynch io" setting. This setting controls how many I/O operations may be outstanding on a particular file. If you have a specialized disk controller, especially one that supports striping, you may see some improved throughput by increasing this setting. About the only way to tune this parameter is by running a benchmarking tool (such as the TPC-B benchmark kit) and empirically testing your server with different settings. Start with 32 (the default) and note the benchmark result. Increase the value of this parameter (be sure to restart the SQL Server Service after each change) until the benchmark results no longer improve. At that point, you have found the optimum setting for this parameter.

Choosing the Right Flavor of SQL Server

As did SQL Server 6.5, SQL Server 7.0 will ship in both "Standard" and "Enterprise" editions. The Enterprise edition of SQL Server supports more than four processors per server, very large amounts of memory, and clusters. (For more information on clustering, see Chapter 10.) Enterprise SQL Servers are designed to meet the needs of very large and heavily used databases.

Also like SQL 6.5, SQL 7.0 will ship in a "Small Business" edition. This edition imposes a 50-connection limit and a database size of 10GB and will not support the specialized OLAP tools that ship with SQL 7.0.

Finally, the most intriguing addition to the SQL Server family is the "Desktop" version of SQL Server. This version runs on the Windows 9x and NT Workstation operating systems and is included with both the Standard and Enterprise editions. Unlike other desktop versions of some RDBMSs (such as Desktop Oracle), the desktop and server versions of SQL Server are the same product, so there are virtually no differences between running a SQL Server on Windows 9x and NTS. Of course, there are some limitations: Trusted security mode is not supported in Windows 9x; the OLAP, full text query, and English query features are not supported; and the workstation will be unable to handle the high volume of user connections allowed on an NTS installation.

The goal in offering these different "flavors" of SQL Server is to support the widest range of applications running on the widest range of servers. Based on your expected needs, choose the version that will work best for you.

Conclusions

Performance tuning and optimization is unfortunately not a cut-and-dried administrative task. Because client/server database application performance can be affected by many factors, troubleshooting and correcting performance problems can be frustrating and time-consuming. The strategies presented in this chapter should be effective in most situations; however, sometimes even the best optimization strategies fail.

If all else fails, consult outside resources, such as Microsoft TechNet, Microsoft Developer Network Library, or Microsoft Technical Support for additional help. Also, getting a second opinion from another database administrator in your organization or an outside consultant may be helpful; two sets of eyes are often better than one.

Finally, remember that no matter how much you optimize your application, another performance bottleneck will exist somewhere. Typically, bottlenecks get more expensive to correct as you continue optimizing. You will need to decide when the cost outweighs the benefit of a particular optimization.

Index

C

D

R

Books for Networking Professionals

New Riders

Windows NT Titles

Windows NT TCP/IP
By Karanjit Siyan
1st Edition Summer 1998
500 pages, $29.99
ISBN: 1-56205-887-8

If you're still looking for good documentation on Microsoft TCP/IP, then look no further—this is your book. *Windows NT TCP/IP* cuts through the complexities and provides the most informative and complete reference book on Windows-based TCP/IP. Concepts essential to TCP/IP administration are explained thoroughly, then related to the practical use of Microsoft TCP/IP in a real-world networking environment. The book begins by covering TCP/IP architecture, advanced installation and configuration issues, then moves on to routing with TCP/IP, DHCP Management, and WINS/DNS Name Resolution.

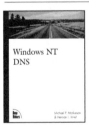

Windows NT DNS
By Michael Masterson, Herman L. Knief, Scott Vinick, and Eric Roul
1st Edition Summer 1998
325 pages, $29.99
ISBN: 1-56205-943-2

Have you ever opened a Windows NT book looking for detailed information about DNS only to discover that it doesn't even begin to scratch the surface? DNS is probably one of the most complicated subjects for NT administrators, and there are few books on the market that really address it in detail. This book answers your most complex DNS questions, focusing on the implementation of the Domain Name Service within Windows NT, treating it thoroughly from the viewpoint of an experienced Windows NT professional. Many detailed, real-world examples illustrate further the understanding of the material throughout. The book covers the details of how DNS functions within NT, then explores specific interactions with critical network components. Finally, proven procedures to design and set up DNS are demonstrated. You'll also find coverage of related topics, such as maintenance, security, and troubleshooting.

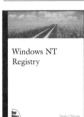

Windows NT Registry
By Sandra Osborne
1st Edition Summer 1998
500 pages, $29.99
ISBN: 1-56205-941-6

The NT Registry can be a very powerful tool for those capable of using it wisely. Unfortunately, there is very little information regarding the NT Registry, due to Microsoft's insistence that its source code be kept secret. If you're looking to optimize your use of the Registry, you're usually forced to search the Web for bits of information. This book is your resource. It covers critical issues and settings used for configuring network protocols, including NWLink, PTP, TCP/IP, and DHCP. This book approaches the material from a unique point of view, discussing the problems related to a particular component, and then discussing settings, which are the actual changes necessary for implementing robust solutions. There is also a comprehensive reference of Registry settings and commands, making this the perfect addition to your technical bookshelf.

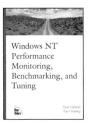

Windows NT Performance Monitoring, Benchmarking, and Tuning

By Mark Edmead and Paul Hinsberg

1st Edition Fall 1998

400 pages, $29.99

ISBN: 1-56205-942-4

Performance monitoring is a little like preventative medicine for the administrator: No one enjoys a checkup, but it's a good thing to do on a regular basis. This book helps you focus on the critical aspects of improving the performance of your NT system, showing you how to monitor the system, implement benchmarking, and tune your network. The book is organized by resource components, which makes it easy to use as a reference tool.

Windows NT Terminal Server and Citrix MetaFrame

By Ted Harwood

1st Edition Winter 1998

500 pages, $29.99

ISBN: 1-56205-944-0

It's no surprise that most administration headaches revolve around integration with other networks and clients. This book addresses these types of real-world issues on a case-by-case basis, giving tools and advice on solving each problem. The author also offers the real nuts and bolts of thin client administration on multiple systems, covering such relevant issues as installation, configuration, network connection, management, and application distribution.

Windows NT Security

By Richard Puckett

1st Edition Winter 1998

600 pages, $29.99

ISBN: 1-56205-945-9

Swiss cheese. That's what some people say Windows NT security is like. And they may be right, because they only know what the NT documentation says about implementing security. Who has the time to research alternatives; play around with the features, service packs, hot fixes, and add-on tools, and figure out what makes NT rock solid? Well, Richard Puckett does. He's been researching Windows NT Security for the University of Virginia for a while now, and he's got pretty good news. He's going to show you how to make NT secure in your environment, and we mean really secure.

Windows NT Administration Handbook

By Eric Svetcov

1st Edition Winter 1998

400 pages, $29.99

ISBN: 1-56205-946-7

Administering a Windows NT network is kind of like trying to herd cats—an impossible task characterized by constant motion, exhausting labor, and lots of hairballs. Author Eric Svetcov knows all about it—he's administered NT networks for some of the fastest growing companies around Silicon Valley. So we asked Eric to put together a concise manual of best practices, a book of tools and ideas that other administrators can turn to again and again in administering their own NT networks. Eric's experience shines through as he shares his secrets for administering users, for getting domain and groups set up quickly and for troubleshooting the thorniest NT problems. Daily, weekly, and monthly task lists help organize routine tasks and preventative maintenance.

Planning for Windows NT 5

By David Lafferty and Eric K. Cone
1st Edition Spring 1999
400 pages, $29.99
ISBN: 0-73570-048-6

Windows NT 5 is poised to be one of the largest and most important software releases of the next decade, and you are charged with planning, testing, and deploying it in your enterprise. Are you ready? With this book, you will be. *Planning for Windows NT 5* lets you know what the upgrade hurdles will be, informs you how to clear them, guides you through effective Active Directory design, and presents you with detailed rollout procedures. MCSEs David Lafferty and Eric K. Cone give you the benefit of their extensive experiences as Windows NT 5 Rapid Deployment Program members, sharing problems and solutions they've encountered on the job.

MCSE Core Essential Reference

By Matthew Shepker
1st Edition Fall 1998
500 pages, $19.99
ISBN: 0-7357-0006-0

You're sitting in the first session of your Networking Essentials class and the instructor starts talking about RAS and you have no idea what that means. You think about raising your hand to ask about RAS, but you reconsider—you'd feel pretty foolish asking a question in front of all these people. You turn to your handy *MCSE Core Essential Reference* and find a quick summary on Remote Access Services. Question answered. It's a couple months later and you're taking your Networking Essentials exam the next day. You're reviewing practice tests and you keep forgetting the maximum lengths for the various commonly used cable types. Once again, you turn to the *MCSE Core Essential Reference* and find a table on cables, including all of the characteristics you need to memorize in order to pass the test.

BackOffice Titles

Implementing Exchange Server

By Doug Hauger, Marywynne Leon, and William C. Wade III
1st Edition Fall 1998
450 pages, $29.99
ISBN: 1-56205-931-9

If you're interested in connectivity and maintenance issues for Exchange Server, then this book is for you. Exchange's power lies in its ability to be connected to multiple email subsystems to create a "universal email backbone." It's not unusual to have several different and complex systems all connected via email gateways, including Lotus Notes or cc:Mail, Microsoft Mail, legacy mainframe systems, and Internet mail. This book covers all of the problems and issues associated with getting an integrated system running smoothly and addresses troubleshooting and diagnosis of email problems with an eye toward prevention and best practices.

SQL Server System Administration

By Sean Baird, Chris Miller, et al.

1st Edition Fall 1998

400 pages, $29.99

ISBN: 1-56205-955-6

How often does your SQL Server go down during the day when everyone wants to access the data? Do you spend most of your time being a "report monkey" for your co-workers and bosses? *SQL Server System Administration* helps you keep data consistently available to your users. This book omits the introductory information. The authors don't spend time explaining queries and how they work. Instead they focus on the information that you can't get anywhere else, like how to choose the correct replication topology and achieve high availability of information.

Internet Information Server Administration

By Kelli Adam, et. al.

1st Edition Winter 1998

300 pages, $29.99

ISBN: 0-73570-022-2

Are the new Internet technologies in Internet Information Server 4.0 giving you headaches? Does protecting security on the Web take up all of your time? Then this is the book for you. With hands-on configuration training, advanced study of the new protocols in IIS 4, and detailed instructions on authenticating users with the new Certificate Server and implementing and managing the new e-commerce features, *Internet Information Server Administration* gives you the real-life solutions you need. This definitive resource also prepares you for the release of Windows NT 5 by giving you detailed advice on working with Microsoft Management Console, which was first used by IIS 4.

UNIX/Linux Titles

Solaris Essential Reference

By John Mulligan

1st Edition Winter 1998

350 pages, $19.99

ISBN: 0-7357-0230-7

Looking for the fastest, easiest way to find the Solaris command you need? Need a few pointers on shell scripting? How about advanced administration tips and sound, practical expertise on security issues? Are you looking for trustworthy information about available third-party software packages that will enhance your operating system? Author John Mulligan—creator of the popular Unofficial Guide to Solaris Web site (sun.icsnet.com)—delivers all that and more in one attractive, easy-to-use reference book. With clear and concise instructions on how to perform important administration and management tasks and key information on powerful commands and advanced topics, *Solaris Essential Reference* is the reference you need when you know what you want to do and you just need to know how.

Linux System Administration

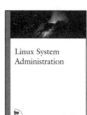

By James T. Dennis

1st Edition Winter 1998

450 pages, $29.99

ISBN: 1-56205-934-3

As an administrator, you probably feel that most of your time and energy is spent in endless firefighting. If your network has become a fragile quilt of temporary patches and workarounds, then this book is for you. For example, have you had trouble sending or receiving your email lately? Are you looking for a way to keep your network running smoothly with enhanced performance? Are your users always hankering for more storage, more services, and more speed? *Linux System Administration* advises you on the many intricacies of maintaining a secure, stable system. In this definitive work, the author addresses all the issues related to system administration, from adding users and managing files permission to internet services and Web hosting to recovery planning and security. This book fulfills the need for expert advice that will ensure a trouble-free Linux environment.

Linux Security

By John S. Flowers
1st Edition Spring 1999
400 pages, $29.99
ISBN: 0-7357-0035-4

New Riders is proud to offer the first book aimed specifically at Linux security issues. While there are a host of general UNIX security books, we thought it was time to address the practical needs of the Linux network. In this definitive work, author John Flowers takes a balanced approach to system security, from discussing topics like planning a secure environment to firewalls to utilizing security scripts. With comprehensive information on specific system compromises, and advice on how to prevent and repair them, this is one book that every Linux administrator should have on the shelf.

Linux GUI Application Development

By Eric Harlow
1st Edition Spring 1999
400 pages, $34.99
ISBN: 0-7357-0214-7

We all know that Linux is one of the most powerful and solid operating systems in existence. And as the success of Linux grows, there is an increasing interest in developing applications with graphical user interfaces that really take advantage of the power of Linux. In this book, software developer Eric Harlow gives you an indispensable development handbook focusing on the GTK+ toolkit. More than an overview on the elements of application or GUI design, this is a hands-on book that delves deeply into the technology. With in-depth material on the various GUI programming tools, a strong emphasis on CORBA and CGI programming, and loads of examples, this book's unique focus will give you the information you need to design and launch professional-quality applications.

Lotus Notes and Domino Titles

Domino System Administration

By Rob Kirkland
1st Edition Winter 1998
500 pages, $29.99
ISBN: 1-56205-948-3

Your boss has just announced that you will be upgrading to the newest version of Notes and Domino when it ships. As a Premium Lotus Business Partner, Lotus has offered a substantial price break to keep your company away from Microsoft's Exchange Server.

How are you supposed to get this new system installed, configured, and rolled out to all of your end users? You understand how Lotus Notes works—you've been administering it for years. What you need is a concise, practical explanation about the new features, and how to make some of the advanced stuff really work. You need answers and solutions from someone like you, who has worked with the product for years, and understands what it is you need to know. *Domino System Administration* is the answer—the first book on Domino that attacks the technology at the professional level, with practical, hands-on assistance to get Domino running in your organization.

Lotus Notes & Domino Essential Reference

By Dave Hatter and Tim Bankes
1st Edition Winter 1998
500 pages, $19.99
ISBN: 0-7357-0007-9

You're in a bind because you've been asked to design and program a new database in Notes for an important client that will keep track of and itemize a myriad of inventory and shipping data. The client wants a user-friendly interface, without sacrificing speed or functionality. You are experienced (and could develop this app in your sleep), but feel that you need to take your talents to the next level. You need something to facilitate your creative and technical abilities, something to perfect your programming skills. Your answer is waiting for you: *Lotus Notes & Domino Essential Reference.* It's compact and simply designed. It's loaded with information. All of the objects, classes, functions, and methods are listed. It shows you the object hierarchy and the overlaying relationship between each one. It's perfect for you. Problem solved.

Networking Titles

Cisco Router Configuration & Troubleshooting

By Pablo Espinosa and Mark Tripod
1st Edition Winter 1998
300 pages, $34.99
ISBN: 0-7357-0024-9

Want the real story on making your Cisco routers run like a dream? Why not pick up a copy of *Cisco Router Configuration & Troubleshooting* and see what Pablo Espinosa and Mark Tripod have to say? They're the folks responsible for making some of the largest sites on the Net scream, like Amazon.com, Hotmail, USAToday, Geocities, and Sony. In this book, they provide advanced configuration issues, sprinkled with advice and preferred practices. You won't see a general overview on TCP/IP—we talk about more meaty issues like security, monitoring, traffic management, and more. In the troubleshooting section, the authors provide a unique methodology and lots of sample problems to illustrate. By providing real-world insight and examples instead of rehashing Cisco's documentation, Pablo and Mark give network administrators information they can start using today.

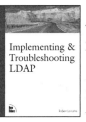

Implementing &
Troubleshooting
LDAP

Implementing & Troubleshooting LDAP

By Robert Lamothe
1st Edition Spring 1999
400 pages, $29.99
ISBN: 1-56205-947-5

While there is some limited information available about LDAP, most of it is RFCs, white papers, and books about programming LDAP into your networking applications. That leaves the people who most need information—administrators—out in the cold. What do you do if you need to know how to make LDAP work in your system? You ask Bob Lamothe. Bob is a UNIX administrator with hands-on experience in setting up a corporate-wide directory service using LDAP. Bob's book is NOT a guide to the protocol; rather, it is designed to be an aid to administrators to help them understand the most efficient way to structure, encrypt, authenticate, administer, and troubleshoot LDAP in a mixed network environment. The book shows you how to work with the major implementations of LDAP and get them to coexist.

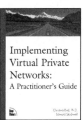

Implementing
Virtual Private
Networks:
A Practitioner's Guide

Implementing Virtual Private Networks: A Practitioner's Guide

By Tina Bird and Ted Stockwell
1st Edition Spring 1999
300 pages, $29.99
ISBN: 0-73570-047-8

Tired of looking for decent, practical, up-to-date information on virtual private networks? *Implementing Virtual Private Networks*, by noted authorities Dr. Tina Bird and Ted Stockwell, finally gives you what you need—an authoritative guide

on the design, implementation, and maintenance of Internet-based access to private networks. This book focuses on real-world solutions, demonstrating how the choice of VPN architecture should align with an organization's business and technological requirements. Tina and Ted give you the information you need to determine whether a VPN is right for your organization, select the VPN that suits your needs, and design and implement the VPN you have chosen.

New Riders \ How to Contact Us

Visit Our Web Site

www.newriders.com

On our Web site you'll find information about our other books, authors, tables of contents, indexes, and book errata. You can also place orders for books through our Web site.

Email Us

Contact us at this address:
newriders@mcp.com

- If you have comments or questions about this book
- To report errors that you have found in this book
- If you have a book proposal to submit or are interested in writing for New Riders
- If you would like to have an author kit sent to you
- If you are an expert in a computer topic or technology and are interested in being a technical editor who reviews manuscripts for technical accuracy

international@mcp.com

- To find a distributor in your area, please contact our international department at the address above.

pr@mcp.com

- For instructors from educational institutions who wish to preview Macmillan Computer Publishing books for classroom use. Email should include your name, title, school, department, address, phone number, office days/hours, text in use, and enrollment in the body of your text along with your request for desk/examination copies and/or additional information.

Write to Us

New Riders Publishing
201 W. 103rd St.
Indianapolis, IN 46290-1097

Call Us

Toll-free (800) 571-5840 + 9 + 4557
If outside U.S. (317) 581-3500. Ask for New Riders.

Fax Us

(317) 581-4663

New Riders

We Want to Know What You Think

To better serve you, we would like your opinion on the content and quality of this book. Please complete this card and mail it to us or fax it to 317-581-4663.

Name_____

Address _____

City _____ State _____ Zip _____

Phone _____

Email Address _____

Occupation _____

Operating System(s) that you use _____

What influenced your purchase of this book?
- ❑ Recommendation
- ❑ Table of Contents
- ❑ Magazine Review
- ❑ New Rider's Reputation
- ❑ Cover Design
- ❑ Index
- ❑ Advertisement
- ❑ Author Name

How would you rate the contents of this book?
- ❑ Excellent
- ❑ Good
- ❑ Below Average
- ❑ Very Good
- ❑ Fair
- ❑ Poor

How do you plan to use this book?
- ❑ Quick reference
- ❑ Classroom
- ❑ Self-training
- ❑ Other

What do you like most about this book?
Check all that apply.
- ❑ Content
- ❑ Accuracy
- ❑ Listings
- ❑ Index
- ❑ Price
- ❑ Writing Style
- ❑ Examples
- ❑ Design
- ❑ Page Count
- ❑ Illustrations

What do you like least about this book?
Check all that apply.
- ❑ Content
- ❑ Accuracy
- ❑ Listings
- ❑ Index
- ❑ Price
- ❑ Writing Style
- ❑ Examples
- ❑ Design
- ❑ Page Count
- ❑ Illustrations

What would be a useful follow-up book to this one for you? _____

Where did you purchase this book? _____

Can you name a similar book that you like better than this one, or one that is as good? Why?

_____

_____

How many New Riders books do you own? _____

What are your favorite computer books? _____

_____

What other titles would you like to see us develop? _____

_____

Any comments for us? _____

_____

_____

_____

Fold here and tape to mail

Place
Stamp
Here

New Riders Publishing
201 W. 103rd St.
Indianapolis, IN 46290